PENGUIN BOOKS

W9-CJQ-839

KNIFE FIGHTS

John A. Nagl is a retired lieutenant colonel of the U.S. Army. A graduate of West Point and a Rhodes Scholar, he received his Ph.D. from St. Anthony's College, Oxford, where he wrote his thesis on counterinsurgency in Malaya and Vietnam. Nagl served as the military assistant to deputy secretaries of defense Paul Wolfowitz and Gordon England, where he coauthored the U.S. Army and Marine Corps counterinsurgency field manual with generals David Petraeus and James M. Mattis. He is the former president of the Center for a New American Security and the ninth headmaster of the Haverford School in Pennsylvania.

★　★　★

Praise for *Knife Fights*

"A provocative and engaging book by a soldier-scholar who played a crucial role in reviving counterinsurgency in the American military at a time (2004–2008) when the Powers That Be did not especially want it revived, despite the nation's deep involvement in two insurgencies it appeared to be losing. Much has been written about this subject—and, indeed, about this author—elsewhere, but Nagl's memoir offers at one and the same time arresting new insights into the saga of counterinsurgency's adaptation in Iraq and Afghanistan, and a very sound, approachable overview of the doctrine's constituent parts." —*The Daily Beast*

"[An] invaluable memoir of service . . . [*Knife Fights*] is also a cautionary tale of how the U.S. Army became an 'un-learning' institution, 'over-learning' the lessons from Vietnam that were most convenient to its bureaucratic interests and 'under-learning' those lessons most central to victory in this type of warfare. . . . Nagl's exceptional memoir chronicles an important period in the wars of insurgency the United States waged following 9/11; it is also a story of how one professional soldier received a brutal education not just in war but in the harsh reality of politics." —Daniel Green, *Foreign Policy*

"Nagl devoted the next twenty years to teaching the Pentagon table manners. 'Eating Soup with a Knife' inspired the title of his dissertation and his intellectual rallying cry. *Knife Fights* is the story of [Nagl's] career and an intellectual genealogy of contemporary counterinsurgency doctrine. . . . A window into how the Pentagon thinks and, crucially, how it—slowly— changes its mind."   —*Harper's Magazine*

"An essential addition to military history collections."   · —*Booklist*

"A lively memoir that combines battlefield experiences with military politics . . . Nagl warns that our lack of patience means that Iraq's and Afghanistan's futures remain uncertain—and readers will note that he wrote this book before the current meltdown in Iraq. A thoughtful, lucid, not-terribly-optimistic autobiography of a scholarly soldier." —*Kirkus Reviews*

"This work is both a memoir and a treatise on American war strategy in the post-9/11 world; Nagl writes evocatively about his wartime experiences, clearly explaining his theories of waging asymmetric warfare. . . . Nagl offers perceptive critiques of the serious mistakes made by Secretary of Defense Donald Rumsfeld and the military's general officer corps."
—*Publishers Weekly*

"An honest and informative glimpse into both the past and the future of the ongoing war on terror. Military buffs, policy wonks, and anyone wishing to learn more about America's role in the world should find Nagl's work an alluring and important read."   —*Library Journal*

"A wonderfully readable and strikingly forthright memoir by a brilliant Army officer turned think tank leader who achieved an exceptional record on the battlefield, in the academic arena, in a high-powered job in the Pentagon, and as one of the so-called insurgents who helped transform the way the U.S. military thought about, prepared for, and conducted the wars of the post–9/11 era."
—General David H. Petraeus, U.S. Army (ret.), commander
of the surge in Iraq

"John Nagl's illuminating journey as a combat soldier-leader-thinker provides a refreshing perspective of the changing character of today's security challenges. To those searching for a relevant and historically grounded understanding of today's erupting realities, his book is uniquely enlightening."
—General Jim Mattis, U.S. Marines (ret.)

"In *Knife Fights*, John Nagl takes the reader from the halls of the Pentagon to the deserts of Iraq and Afghanistan, and illuminates the modern battlefields—both in Washington and overseas—in harsh and vivid light. His work on counterinsurgency is deep and profound, and this book is the essential backstory both of the intellectual process that underpins it and the personal journey that formed it. A powerful and meaningful memoir that will resonate in today's Army and tomorrow's society."

> —Admiral James Stavridis (ret.), supreme allied commander at NATO 2009–2013 and current dean of the Fletcher School at Tufts University

"A magnificent memoir from one of the most brilliant officers of his generation. *Knife Fights* details John Nagl's journey from the halls of West Point and Oxford to the battlefields of Desert Storm and Operation Iraqi Freedom, as well as his struggles and triumphs among Washington's power elite. Highly recommended for those who seek to understand how the Army overcame its initial dysfunction to wage the messy counterinsurgency wars in Iraq and Afghanistan."

> —Peter R. Mansoor, Colonel, U.S. Army (ret.); author of *Surge: My Journey with General David Petraeus and the Remaking of the Iraq War*

"There are many books from veterans of America's costly wars in Iraq and Afghanistan. Few will combine the intellectual heft, emotional power, and exemplary moral courage of John Nagl's *Knife Fights*. It traces the development of the author from his early days as a cadet at West Point to the darkest days of fighting in Al Anbar province in Iraq and beyond. This book will stand on its own special shelf as a personal memoir of a soldier/scholar, a warrior, and a great teacher. Highly recommended for all military students, and anyone interested in the journey of an institutional insurgent and patriot who followed his own path."

> —F. G. Hoffman, National Defense University, Washington, D.C.

"Brimming with poignancy and integrity, John Nagl's book is an instant classic of America's decade of war in the greater Middle East. Its core argument, moreover, is undeniable: that insurgency and counterinsurgency have been part of the history of war since antiquity and thus will be part of its future. May the United States Army and Marine Corps hold close the lessons of this book!"

> —Robert D. Kaplan

"John Nagl's *Knife Fights* is a brave book by a soldier-scholar who has always put himself out there for the right reasons. John's remarkable memoir is a directed telescope into how the U.S. Army changed its doctrinal paradigm for the first time since World War I from 'closing with and destroying the enemy' to 'protecting the population.' Readers will also see that he was a key intellectual force in this shift and how difficult these changes are for the institutions—and for the catalytic advocates like John."

—David E. Johnson, senior researcher at the RAND Corporation; inaugural director of the Chief of Staff of the Army Strategic Studies Group; author of *Fast Tanks and Heavy Bombers: Innovation in the U.S. Army, 1917–1945, Hard Fighting: Israel in Lebanon and Gaza*, and *The 2008 Battle of Sadr City: Reimagining Urban Combat*

"John Nagl has written an exceptional book that shows in words the type of bravery he exhibited on the battlefield. Nagl deftly reveals what worked and didn't work in Washington, Iraq, and Afghanistan after 9/11. His critique of Donald Rumsfeld is uniquely powerful because he writes from the vantage point of an Army officer who waged war in the Sunni Triangle and afterwards served in the defense secretary's office. *Knife Fights* is essential reading—the rare memoir of war that integrates ideas, combat, and politics. It is an invaluable addition to the literature of wars that we are still trying to comprehend."   —Peter Maass, author of *Love Thy Neighbor*

KNIFE FIGHTS

A Memoir of Modern War
in Theory and Practice

JOHN A. NAGL

PENGUIN BOOKS

PENGUIN BOOKS

An imprint of Penguin Random House LLC

375 Hudson Street

New York, New York 10014

penguin.com

First published in the United States of America by Penguin Press,
a member of Penguin Group (USA) LLC, 2014
Published in Penguin Books 2015

THE LIBRARY OF CONGRESS HAS CATALOGED THE HARDCOVER EDITION AS FOLLOWS:

Nagl, John A.

Knife fights : a memoir of modern war in theory and practice / John A. Nagl.

p.   cm.

Includes bibliographical references and index.

ISBN 978-1-59420-498-2 (hc.)

ISBN 978-0-14-312776-5 (pbk.)

1. Counterinsurgency—United States.   2. United States—Military policy—21st century.
3. Military art and science—United States.   4. Nagl, John A., 1966–   I. Title.

U241.N34   2014   2014032905

355.02'180973—dc23

Printed in the United States of America

1   3   5   7   9   10   8   6   4   2

BOOK DESIGN BY AMANDA DEWEY

FRONTMATTER MAPS BY JEFFREY L. WARD

Penguin is committed to publishing works of quality and integrity.
In that spirit, we are proud to offer this book to our readers; however,
the story, the experiences, and the words are the author's alone

In Memoriam

PFC Jeremiah D. Smith

1LT Todd J. Bryant

SPC Joseph Lister

SGT Jarrod Black

SGT Uday Singh

SFC Gregory B. Hicks

SPC William R. Sturges

SPC Jason K. Chappell

SGT Randy S. Rosenberg

CPT Matthew J. August

1SG James T. Hoffman

SGT Daniel M. Shepherd

1LT Neil A. Santoriello

2LT Brian D. Smith

PFC Brandon Davis

PFC Cleston Raney

SPC Michael Karr

SGT Sean Mitchell

1LT Doyle Hufstedler

SPC Roger G. Ling

2LT Jeffrey C. Graham

SSG Sean G. Landrus

SGT Travis A. Moothart

Ghost Stories

I have put them away
kept them inside
the ghosts of the lieutenants
and the Captain
and the First Sergeant
their bodies torn by shrapnel
or a sniper's bullet
or gone
just gone
into hundreds of shards of flesh
the size of my still living hand
but they have been standing watch over my dreams
and now they will not go away.

If you have been to war
if you have held a microphone in your hand
begging for MEDEVAC
with the blood of your friends on your hands
pouring out your soul over the airwaves
to keep your friends from becoming ghosts

from joining the shades in an unholy company

of men who have given

limbs and eyes and hearts—

If you have held that bloody hand mike

then you will never forget that day

that day when time stopped and life stopped

and never really started again

no matter how hard you try

to make the ghosts go away.

Here, bullet.

Here.

Take me.

So that I can join the ghosts

so that my company will again be complete

armless legless eyeless

a company of memories

a company of shades.

Take me again to the land of the Two Rivers

where the Tigris and the Euphrates meet

where the elephant grass grows man-high

in the irrigation canals.

We will return to the warren of Baghdad streets

where the women wail

and the children beg

and Bulldog Six will issue commands and

Apache Red One will take point and

Bulldog White One will grin again

that wonderful grin he had

full of joy

back when he still had a face.

We will join the company of ghosts

who were our enemies

who waited for us in alleys and in canals

who wore sandals and man-dresses

and spoke in a language we could not understand

and fought for reasons we could not understand

but they fought well

these men we turned to ghosts.

They fought us

and we fought them

and now we are all together

what is left of us

in the halflight shadows inside my head

where I see ghosts

ghosts

that will no longer leave me.

Adapted from the author's review
of Brian Turner's Here Bullet*

---

* published in the *Journal of the Royal United Services Institute,* December 2007

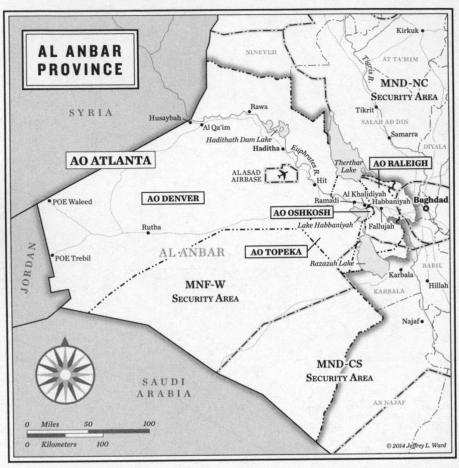

AL ANBAR PROVINCE

SYRIA

NINEVEH

Kirkuk

Tigris R.

AT TA'MIM

MND-NC
SECURITY AREA

Husaybah
Rawa
Tikrit
SALAH AD DIN
Al Qa'im
Samarra
DIYALA

Hadithath Dam Lake
Haditha

AO ATLANTA

Euphrates R.

Therthar Lake

AO RALEIGH

AL ASAD AIRBASE
Hit

POE Waleed

AO DENVER

Al Khalidiyah
Habbaniyah **Baghdad**

Ramadi

AO OSHKOSH

Rutba
Lake Habbaniyah
Fallujah

JORDAN

AL ANBAR

AO TOPEKA

POE Trebil

Razazah Lake

Karbala
BABIL

Hillah

KARBALA

MNF-W
SECURITY AREA

Najaf

MND-CS
SECURITY AREA

SAUDI ARABIA

AN NAJAF

0   Miles   50   100
0   Kilometers   100

© 2014 Jeffrey L. Ward

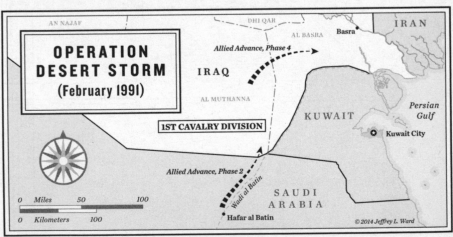

AN NAJAF
DHI QAR
IRAN

OPERATION DESERT STORM
(February 1991)

AL BASRA
Basra

Allied Advance, Phase 4

IRAQ

AL MUTHANNA

Persian Gulf

KUWAIT

1ST CAVALRY DIVISION

Kuwait City

Allied Advance, Phase 2

Wadi al Batin

SAUDI ARABIA

Hafar al Batin

0   Miles   50   100
0   Kilometers   100

© 2014 Jeffrey L. Ward

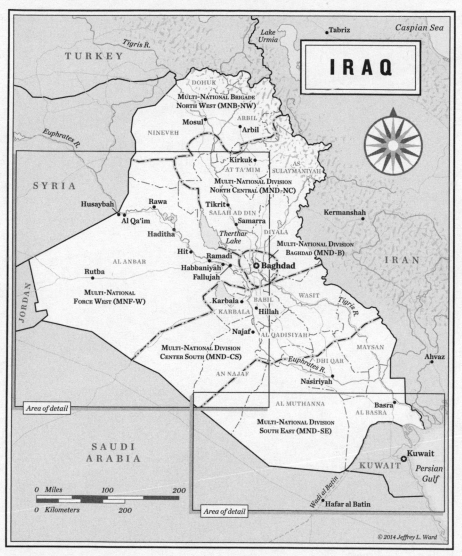

Caspian Sea

IRAQ

TURKEY

Tigris R.

Lake Urmia ·Tabriz

DOHUK

MULTI-NATIONAL BRIGADE NORTH WEST (MNB-NW)

NINEVEH

Mosul·

ARBIL

·Arbil

Euphrates R.

SYRIA

Kirkuk·

AT TA'MIM

AS SULAYMANIYAH

MULTI-NATIONAL DIVISION NORTH CENTRAL (MND-NC)

Husaybah

Rawa·

Tikrit·

Kermanshah·

Al Qa'im·

SALAH AD DIN

Haditha·

Samarra·

Therthar Lake

DIYALA

MULTI-NATIONAL DIVISION BAGHDAD (MND-B)

IRAN

AL ANBAR

Hit·

Ramadi·

⊛ **Baghdad**

Rutba·

Habbaniyah·

Fallujah·

WASIT

Tigris R.

MULTI-NATIONAL FORCE WEST (MNF-W)

Karbala·

BABIL

KARBALA

Hillah·

Najaf·

AL QADISIYAH

MAYSAN

·Ahvaz

JORDAN

MULTI-NATIONAL DIVISION CENTER SOUTH (MND-CS)

AN NAJAF

Euphrates R.

DHI QAR

Nasiriyah·

Area of detail

AL MUTHANNA

Basra·

AL BASRA

MULTI-NATIONAL DIVISION SOUTH EAST (MND-SE)

SAUDI ARABIA

KUWAIT

⊛ ·Kuwait

Persian Gulf

| 0 | Miles | 100 | 200 |

| 0 | Kilometers | 200 |

Area of detail

Wadi al Batin

·Hafar al Batin

© 2014 Jeffrey L. Ward

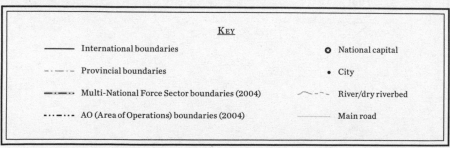

Contents

Preface 1

1. Ghostriders in the Storm 5

2. Learning to Eat Soup with a Knife: *A Counterinsurgent at Oxford and West Point* 29

3. Back to Iraq: *Al Anbar 2003–2004* 55

4. The First Washington Fight: *Iraq* 107

5. Clear, Hold, and Build 129

6. Proof of Concept: *Iraq 2007–2008* 151

7. The Second Washington Fight: *Afghanistan* 185

8. Counterinsurgency Revisited: *Learning from Our Mistakes* 211

Epilogue. Good-bye to All That 243

Acknowledgments 255
Notes 257
Further Reading 259
Index 263

Preface

This is a book about modern wars and how they affect the lives of young men and women. It is a tale of wars that needed to be fought and wars that were not necessary but that happened nonetheless, at enormous cost in blood and treasure. It is also an intellectual coming-of-age story, that of both the author and the institution to which he devoted most of his adult life, the American military. It is a book about counterinsurgency and its journey from the far periphery of U.S. military doctrine to its center, for better and, some would argue, for worse. It is also, then, a book about America's role in the world, and specifically about when and how we use military force abroad in the name of national security.

The book largely takes the form of a memoir, which feels somewhat self-indulgent to me—I was very much more shaped by than shaper of the events this book relates. But my hope is that following the arc of my own learning curve will be the easiest way for a reader to understand the broader story of the American military's radical adaptation to a world of threats very different from those involving nuclear weapons and Soviet tanks massed at the Fulda Gap that I studied at West Point a generation ago. Following that arc will also help to explain why, after decades of responsibility for the lives of American soldiers, I have recently shouldered the responsibility to prepare another generation of young men for a life of service far from the battlefield, in the classrooms and on the playing fields of friendly strife as the ninth headmaster of The Haverford School.

The U.S. military changed quickly after 9/11—not quickly enough from the perspective of those we lost and had injured, but quickly indeed by the standards of very large, hierarchical institutions. Some say the military in fact has changed too quickly, embracing counterinsurgency with a fervor that has had unforeseen negative consequences. I do not take that view. This book is not a pep rally, not a victory lap around counterinsurgency's successes in Iraq, and certainly not in Afghanistan, where they have been thinner on the ground. But as the historian Arthur Schlesinger, Jr., liked to say, the right question is often "Compared to what?" Any intellectually serious reckoning with America's post-9/11 wars has to contend with what the alternatives were once the decision to invade Iraq had been too hastily made and too poorly implemented. In the wake of mistakes there are sometimes no good choices; in both Iraq and Afghanistan, counterinsurgency was the least bad option available.

I had the rare opportunity to be involved in both the theory and the practice of war, helping write doctrine and also living with the consequences of implementing doctrine in the field as an officer responsible for the lives of America's sons and daughters. The bulk of my combat experience was in Iraq, and Iraq is central to the story this book tells. But the shadow of Afghanistan hangs over all of it, even the Iraq story.

The first post-9/11 consequence of the American military's pre-9/11 focus on large, conventional combat operations wasn't the failure to see the Iraq War for what it was. First there was the Afghan campaign of the fall of 2001, a campaign conceived of and initiated by the CIA because the American military had no plan on the shelf that spoke to such a situation. The Afghan campaign's initial success at scattering America's enemies allowed us to make the mistake of immediately pivoting to Iraq, sinking us into the morass of two ground wars in Asia when one would have been more than enough.

Focusing on Iraq meant taking our eye off the ball in Afghanistan and Pakistan, allowing the Taliban and Al Qaeda to regroup and gain strength, blinding us to the true nature of the situation there until it was almost too late.

If Iraq was the midterm, Afghanistan is the final exam. It's a lot harder than the midterm. And while we eked out a passing grade on the midterm, after a horrible start, the final grade remains in doubt, an incomplete. We're unlikely to know the answer for some years to come, but the Afghan end state is important for the future of the region and for America's place in the world—a world that is likely to be roiled by insurgency and counterinsurgency for decades to come.

The story begins in a very different place and time, a time when the Soviet Union had just been tossed into the dustbin of history, its internal contradictions rendered unbearable after its own painful war in Afghanistan. America stood unchallenged as the world's only superpower for the first time in history, but Saddam Hussein had misread American determination to enforce the international security regime it had created in the wake of the Second World War. For the first time since Vietnam, the United States deployed the full weight of American power abroad. It was a heady and unsettling time for a young man who had studied war but never seen it.

1.

Ghostriders in the Storm

When do you want to meet the men, Lieutenant?" The Puerto Rican accent was always thick, but it got thicker when he was mad. We'd goad him on purpose, pretending not to be able to understand him, until Sergeant Claudio got so frustrated that he'd throw his hat onto the hot sand and stomp off spouting unintelligible Puerto Rican expletives. It never got old.

But that came later, after I'd met the men. "Um, now, I guess," was my answer, sounding a bit more like the soft graduate student of international relations I'd recently been and less like the gruff, hardened first lieutenant of armor I hoped to project to my troops.

I'd just left Oxford in the summer of 1990. After allowing me to read books and drink warm English beer for two years, the Army had ordered me to remedial tank training at Fort Knox before an assignment to Fort Hood, Texas, the largest army post in the free world. While in Kentucky, I took the opportunity to invite my British girl-friend on her first trip to the States, but our planned leisurely drive across the country was cut short by Saddam Hussein's invasion of Kuwait. President Hussein clearly didn't realize that the mighty Lieutenant Nagl had earned his master's degree and been assigned to the storied First Cavalry Division; had Saddam possessed better intelligence, none of this might have happened.

Susi ended up spending a week in Fort Hood's appropriately named Poxon House during the annual summer cricket invasion as I prepared for deployment as a combat replacement. She carefully picked up the crickets that came under the door, trying to keep their legs attached as she returned them to their friends outside, but cricket legs are surprisingly poorly connected to their abdomens. Her failures staggered in endless, helpless circles outside our door, wounded veterans of an invasion that didn't have to happen. An alternative strategy was a thick kill zone of Raid sprayed outside the hotel door mantel, designed to deter invasion of the homeland. This chemical warfare only ensured that the survivors who made it through the kill zone into the objective of our hotel room died slowly and noisily during the night.

I hoped that the experience of the crickets was not an omen as I sweated through the bedsheets after a series of predeployment immunizations and packed my own chemical gear for deployment. My job would be to replace the first tank platoon leader in the First Cavalry Division's second "Blackjack" brigade to meet an untimely end.

As it turned out, I didn't have to wait for bullets to start flying to get my chance. A young officer facing severe personal difficulties decided, on the very October day that he led his platoon from the port of Dammam into the Saudi desert as part of Operation Desert Shield, that tanking wasn't going to be his thing. Stuff got real for him when the tank treads first met the sand. I could have kissed the guy, but the Army wasn't amused. It made him the assistant division post exchange officer and then sentenced him to take a boat back to Texas with the tanks after the war. I got four tanks of my own, along with Sergeant Pablo Claudio and fourteen other tankers—the "Red Aces," which I thought was a pretty cool name. The tank company of which we were a part was also well named; for reasons that are lost to history, Alpha Company, First Battalion, 32nd Armor, was known for its radio call sign "Ghostriders."

The soldiers of Ghostriders' Red Platoon were sprawled against and on top of a tank when Claudio and I walked up, and they stayed comfortable when he introduced me. The First Cav was operating under field conditions, dispensing with salutes and other parade-ground niceties. When a soldier did salute an officer in the field, he invariably said "Sniper check, sir!" Smart officers learned to render salutes first so that any snipers in the area would shoot the soldier instead. This passes for humor in a combat zone.

There were no snipers in the area, or at least none who made their presence felt as the sun went down behind Claudio's tank and I introduced myself to the men. All was well until I asked if there were any questions. Every platoon in the Army has one smart-aleck specialist. Mine said that yes, he had a question: had I been told that I was getting the worst platoon in the battalion, or in the entire brigade?

Years of West Point honor code training kicked in, and I answered truthfully, "They said this was the worst platoon in the brigade." I let that sink in for a second, then added with as much hope as conviction, "And that just changed."

Thus ended the welcome session. A little bit of bravado is a good thing for any tank officer to have, but it's especially useful when taking command of a dispirited unit on the verge of combat. We headed off to the Tent, General Purpose–Medium (GP Medium, for short) that would be home for the next few months, Sergeant Claudio and I walking behind the tankers.

They were a motley crew. My wingman was a very large African-American staff sergeant, Sergeant Harrison, known for his rule breaking in garrison and his extraordinary ability in the field. He had been hurt by the battalion commander's quip that he should be stored in a glass case engraved with the phrase "Break glass in case of war." It was hard to imagine a more competent tanker to have on your wing, and I would rely heavily on Sergeant Harrison as I learned my trade over the next six months. He was known by his call sign as "Red Deuce" or simply "Deuce."

Claudio's wingman was Sergeant Jim Kebble, a graduate of the Army's notoriously difficult tank master gunner course. He knew more about the M1 Abrams than anyone in the company, including the mechanics. Sergeant Kebble was pretty gross even among tankers, who regularly appear in coveralls encrusted with grease and hydraulic fluid. Claudio and I would sometimes have to order him to take a tanker shower from a five-gallon water can suspended from his tank's gun tube. Sergeant Kebble was Red Three, Claudio's wingman, and also served as the company's master gunner in charge of gunnery training exercises.

Each tank had a four-man crew: the tank commander, an officer or senior sergeant; the gunner, generally a junior sergeant, who controlled the weapons systems; the loader, who fed the main gun with fifty-pound shells in seconds, over and over again in a firefight; and the driver, isolated in the hull rather than in the turret, who kept the tank running and pointed in the right direction. My own gunner was Sergeant Ted Shoemaker, a thirteen-year Army veteran from West Virginia who had been reduced in rank, or "busted," when his then-wife was found to be dealing drugs from their military quarters in Germany. "Shoe" had been oblivious to her double life but was punished regardless because his battalion commander felt that he should have known what his wife was doing when he wasn't around.

It was a tough break for Shoe but a bonus for me, as he would otherwise have had a tank of his own instead of then being sentenced to teach a new lieutenant the ropes. Sergeant Shoemaker was close to

*Specialist Jud Davis, Sergeant Shoe, me, and Specialist Mac in
Wadi Al Batin during Operation Desert Shield, 1990.*

Specialist Jud Davis, our driver, another good old boy from Kentucky.
John "Mac" McAllister, our loader, was wiry, strong, and not the sharp-
est knife in the drawer. We would become a crew over the next six
months, able to do amazing things with our tank. Just as well—amazing
things would need doing. Shoe inked an ace of spades on my combat
vehicle crewman helmet, which I proudly display in the only remaining
photograph of our crew.

A GP–Medium was just the right size for a tank platoon. Each soldier had a cot, with his two duffel bags stored underneath it. Tank
commanders took the four places closest to the tent's two doors so that
they had humanity close on only one side. Rank has its privileges, even
if it's only a bit of canvas on which to string some cord to hang sweaty

clothes. Stifling in the summer, the tent got cold enough in the winter that we'd sometimes pull up a tank to the flap doors first thing in the morning to warm it up with engine exhaust, as the turbine didn't create carbon monoxide like an ordinary internal combustion engine. It did make everything in the tent smell more like diesel fuel, but that was better than most of the other smells that occupied it.

The days quickly developed a battle rhythm consisting of physical training—calisthenics followed by long runs over the desert sand—hasty wash-ups in the gravity-fed shower enclosures when the water truck had come the day before to fill them up, and then tank maintenance or training exercises. Breakfast and dinner were prepared by the cooks at battalion and trucked out to our company location, with brown bag "Meals, Ready to Eat" (or excrete, depending on the variety) for lunch.

Mealtimes were when the company officers would get together to plan training, discuss personnel issues, or just gossip. Ghostrider Six, the company commander, was a thin, vain, handsome captain with a short temper. His second-in-command, "Five," Executive Officer and First Lieutenant Scott Riggs, was a Texan with a real gift for leadership who had served as a tank platoon leader in Korea before joining the First Cav. Scott—or "Turtle," from the way he looked when wearing his helmet—would become a source of endless wisdom to the other lieutenants in the unit. Other than me, his charges included Buffy, a fraternity boy still locked in college attitudes who led the second "White" platoon, and Pete Johnson, a natural sportsman from California who could hit anything with a rifle or shotgun but couldn't qualify a tank to save his life. Pete, or "Blue One," became my best friend in the unit over dozens of games of chess that he invariably lost. He would later become one of the few Army chaplains to sport a Ranger tab, signifying his graduation from the elite infantryman's school.

We were stationed on a strategic patch of ground just south of the

Saudi Arabian border with Iraq in a dry riverbed, or wadi, that ran from northeast to southwest and was named after the Saudi town of Al Batin. The arrival of the First Cavalry Division's tanks, artillery pieces, and Bradley infantry fighting vehicles here in Wadi al Batin marked the success of Operation Desert Shield. Saddam Hussein's Army stood little chance of breaking through the Cav and continuing his assault into Saudi Arabia unless he used chemical weapons to disable us first, which would have caused some of us to die slowly and agonizingly but mostly would have limited our ability to operate our weapons effectively. That, President George H. W. Bush had promised, would result in the strongest possible reaction from the United States (a clear threat to use nuclear weapons in response to a chem strike), but we spent a lot of time practicing tasks in our chemical suits in case the threat of nuclear retaliation didn't work.

Our gas masks went with us everywhere. I used mine as a pillow when I slept on top of the tank during exercises away from base camp. One night a soldier on radio watch sounded the chemical alarm after hearing a report of "Gas! Gas! Gas!" on the radio. I scrambled inside the tank to my duty position, abandoning my fart sack, or sleeping bag, but putting my mask on before closing my tank commander's hatch with a clang to seal out the invading chemical cloud. I looked down to see Sergeant Shoe sitting in his gunner's seat with the saddest expression I'd ever seen on his generally jolly face, which was unprotected by a mask. He'd left it up top while scrambling into the confines of the gunner's hole. He pointed mournfully at the hatch.

For a long moment I looked into his sad eyes, then steeled myself, reopened the hatch, and exposed myself and my crew to chemical annihilation to fetch Shoe's mask. He'd have done anything for me after that, even if the whole thing had been a false alarm. Shoe never left his mask behind again.

We expected chemical weapons to be delivered by SCUD missiles—

unguided projectiles with sufficient range to hit our positions from their bases inside Iraq, but so inaccurate that a high-explosive warhead was unlikely to do much damage. Late in the war one conventionally armed SCUD would hit a logistics unit in the Saudi port of Dammam, killing more than a dozen soldiers in the most damaging attack of the entire fight for the United States; but the one that came closest to me cost me only a cheeseburger.

In the town of Al Batin, the First Cav had set up a shower point—GP–Mediums with hot water sprayed at pressure, rather than the cold water trickling down from the gravity-fed showers we used on a daily basis (except for Sergeant Kebble) after our morning workouts. My turn to visit the fabled shower point came up one day, and I was lucky enough to share the trip with Lieutenant Gray Cockerham, from our battalion's Charlie Company. An infantryman, Gray was short and powerful, so strongly built that he was unable to fit into the cramped turret of his Bradley fighting vehicle while wearing a heavy Vietnam-era flak jacket. Gray was also very smart—and, unfortunately for him, hungry that day.

When we arrived at the shower point, he headed straight for the grill to grab a cheeseburger, while I decided to eat after I was clean. Having taken more than my share of hot water, I was happily scrubbed and standing in the burger line when a SCUD suddenly landed in the vacant lot across the street, blowing out the lights and power in the burger stand—and cutting off water in the shower just as Gray was about to lather up. Unsure whether the SCUD had included a chemical warhead with the high explosive, we put on our protective masks—even Gray, for whom a mask was the only thing he was wearing. He dressed quickly, just in time to jump into the back of the Humvee as it roared away, taking us back to our tanks and Brads in case the SCUD marked the start of an Iraqi attack on our positions.

It didn't. Instead, the next move was ours. President Bush, who had previously stated firmly that the Iraqi occupation of Kuwait "would not stand," made the critical decision to continue sending U.S. Army units to Saudi Arabia after sufficient forces were already in place to preclude an Iraqi attack. The additional tanks were intended to send Saddam Hussein the message that we would attack to restore Kuwaiti sovereignty if he refused to yield in the biggest American military operation since the Vietnam War.

The move was greeted with great relief by soldiers who were already growing tired of the desert and who could see in front of them an endless future of beerless, yearlong tours defending Saudi Arabia. A cartoon of Bart Simpson wearing a Kevlar helmet appeared in our tent with the inscription "I'm not waiting here for a year without beer, dude." We increased the tempo of our training, switching our focus from practicing the defense of battle positions to the more complicated task of attacking prepared positions, and were delighted that the Army decided to give us a Christmas present prior to kicking off the assault that appeared increasingly likely to be in our future.

The M1 Abrams tank was an aggressive design that incorporated a 1500-horsepower gas turbine engine and room for a 120mm main gun, although the initial version carried a smaller rifled 105. The smoothbore 120, a German weapon, featured greater range and killing power and a combustible shell casing, most of which burned up inside the gun tube, leaving behind only a small stub that was much prized by tankers as an ashtray. This ensured that the tank didn't fill up with two-foot-long brass shells that tended toward the hot side of the temperature spectrum. Tankers wore boots with leather straps instead of bootlaces because the shells had a history of burning through cotton or nylon. The First Cav, for all its history and bold horsehead-on-a-Norman-shield patch, was still equipped with worn-out "slick" M1 tanks with 105mm guns in 1990.

But just before Christmas, we received new M1A1 tanks with the bigger 120mm main gun, then had the chance to fire practice rounds from our new toys at a range that the division master gunner had carved out of the desert. It was hard to imagine a more explicit indication that we were going to war, but just as hard not to feel more confident about the prospect in the new M1A1, which rocked like a bronco when the 120mm main gun fired its load. We were lucky that Mac was as strong as he was skinny. The 120 round was both heavier and harder to maneuver in the tight confines of the tank's crew compartment than the smaller, shorter 105. Mac was able to load them repeatedly within three seconds, even the heavy high-explosive antitank (HEAT) rounds, designed to be used against armored personnel carriers or, as we would soon demonstrate, infantry fighting positions.

The new year featured a series of artillery raids and practice attacks on the border posts that marked the line in the sand between Saudi Arabia and Iraq. Conducted with live rounds and against manned positions, they were designed to convince the Iraqi military that the First Cav would lead the main American attack, "Hey diddle diddle, straight up the middle," along Wadi al Batin into the teeth of the prepared Iraqi defenses. This had, in fact, been the initial war plan, but a new technology of which Saddam was unaware had opened up a different option to the United States and her allies.

Nascent global positioning system receivers drew on satellites in geosynchronous orbits to precisely identify the location of friendly tank units and enabled the famous "left hook" around Saddam's defenses through what otherwise would have been unnavigable empty desert. Meanwhile, even as this attack was being prepared many miles to the west, the Cav blew tank-size holes through the ten-foot sand berms that marked the border just north of our positions and shelled the guard towers that protected the border. We were working to convince the Iraqis of something they already believed—that we were planning to attack them following the established contours of the wadi, the historical invasion route. It is always easier to convince an enemy that you are going to do just what he thinks you're planning to do anyway, and the deception plan worked marvelously on the operational level of war.

There was, however, a price to be paid for making the deception believable. The day after I fired my first tank round in anger, destroying one of the guard towers along the berm so that our engineers could blow attack lanes through the protective barriers, was Valentine's Day 1991. The next day our sister battalion, the Black Knights of 1-5 Cavalry, passed through the lanes we had constructed in the berms and attacked into what we thought was the enemy's soft underbelly in their Bradley infantry fighting vehicles. We couldn't know that it was the other side's turn to draw blood.

The Black Knights ran into an ambush—T-100 antitank guns dug in on the flanks of the wadi. Tanks were invulnerable to fire from T-100s, at least along their heavily armored frontal arc, but Bradleys were not as well protected. Several American soldiers in Bradleys were killed, and 1-5 was forced to withdraw. Our crusty company motor sergeant, Sergeant First Class Cunningham, helped with the recovery of the disabled vehicles and the cleanup of the remains of the fallen soldiers. It was a subdued dinner that night, as for the first time the cost of war impressed itself on a unit composed almost entirely of soldiers who had never seen combat before.

Of the eighty or so soldiers in Ghostrider Company, only our well-worn first sergeant was a Vietnam veteran. When the company came under mortar fire, the rest of us hunkered down and took it, trusting in luck, our armor, and the minimal skills of our enemy to protect us. Having been on the receiving end of mortar rounds before, he headed away from the enemy as fast as his armored personnel carrier would

go. Like the first sergeant, the Ghostriders had now seen a glimpse of
the elephant, in the wonderful Civil War phrase for combat, and we
weren't sure we liked what we had seen.

There is much to be said about going to war for the first time. Life
is heightened, more intense and intensely focused, like having sex, but
with a real death rather than what the French call the little death at the
end. Rhodes scholar Karl Marlantes, who earned the Navy Cross in
Vietnam after departing Oxford early to serve as a Marine infantry officer, has written a marvelous book about the experience, titled *What It
Is Like to Go to War*. In short, if no one close to you gets killed, and if
you don't get too close to those you kill, it is exhilarating and vivid and
intoxicating, every minute an adventure. But when you lose people you
love, when the vengeful war gods consume the young flesh on which
they thrive, it is unspeakably terrible. The ghosts of the departed on
both sides haunt many of those who fight for the rest of their lives.
Though I knew none of the young men killed in Operation Knight
Strike, their loss was close enough to peel back a translucent corner on
the window into the true horror of war, although I would not see
clearly into the depths of hell until another decade had passed.

We paused briefly after the attack, but we didn't have long to lick
our wounds. The deadline Washington had given Saddam Hussein to
get out of Kuwait approached rapidly, and on February 24 we again
attacked through the berm and up Wadi al Batin, covering the opening
swing of VII Corps's "left hook" far to our west with our own assault
straight up the middle. Quickly overwhelming the T-100 fighting positions that had stymied the Black Knights ten days before, the entire
brigade came on line, running headfirst into prepared defensive positions of an Iraqi infantry division. For the first time in my life, I was
shooting at someone who was shooting real bullets back at me.

Honestly, it wasn't much of a fight. The Iraqi soldiers, demoralized
by weeks of U.S. Air Force bombing, fired mortars and machine guns

at us to little effect, not that the first sergeant stuck around to find out. Their defense hinged on trenches filled with oil that they set afire to establish a smoke screen. It was not particularly effective—oil is hard to set on fire unless it is under pressure, and the Iraqi infantry had few weapons that could put a serious dent in an M1A1 Abrams tank. I can clearly remember firing a HEAT round into a mortar position that was the closest thing to a threat we faced. It disappeared in a satisfying explosion that would probably have given me nightmares if I'd seen the results up close.

I didn't get the chance. By this point, other elements of VII Corps had already advanced through lanes in the border berm farther west, cleared by the famed First Infantry Division, the Big Red One. We had accomplished our objective of convincing Iraqi Republican Guard tank divisions that we were the main attack, and we now received orders to pull back and join the left hook, the *real* main attack. Many Republican Guard tanks were still facing south in our direction, ready to meet the phantom First Cav attack, when they were shot in the flank or rear by our friends in VII Corps who were now bearing down on them from the west, traveling through the trackless desert with the aid of global positioning system satellites.

We scrambled to join them, withdrawing south after our feint and then moving fast to the west, passing through the Big Red One's passage lanes and turning north. Over the next three days the First Cavalry Division had a plausible claim to have moved faster through enemy territory than had any division in military history, although we had the great advantage of following in VII Corps's tracks.

After some ninety-six hours of nearly continuous movement, we pulled up into a lager outside of Basra around midnight on February 27. Bleary from exhaustion, I kicked Sergeant Shoe in the head to wake him up. He was well rested. The tank gunner, wedged into his hole like a passenger in coach on a transatlantic flight, generally sleeps during

road marches. I gave Shoe command of the tank while I curled up behind my hatch on top of the turret in my beloved poncho liner, falling
immediately into an exhausted sleep.

I didn't hear the sound of a multiple-launch rocket system (MLRS)
pulling into positions behind our tanks, and I knew nothing of the
Washington negotiations on ending the war after one hundred hours
of ground fighting. The Army interpreted the "cease fire at dawn"
order that emanated from the national security decision-making machine as a good reason to do as much damage as possible to remaining
Iraqi units, and the MLRS rockets had the range and lethality to make
a mark.

They certainly made a mark on me. I was jerked awake by a sound
like jet engines igniting on my chest as the rocket motors lit a dark
night on fire. Convinced that the end of the world had arrived, I made
the completely illogical decision that I wanted to die on the ground,
rolling off the tank turret into a ten-foot drop onto hard sand. With my
arms wrapped inside my poncho liner, I couldn't break my fall and performed an ignominious face plant that brought me fully awake and
conscious. Unrolling myself, I climbed painfully into the turret, shak-
ing uncontrollably for some time, as Shoe laughed and laughed while
the MLRS fire turned the night into a fiery and very intense day.

They eventually ran out of missiles, and actual daylight found all of
us alive and thrilled with the news that the United States had declared a
cease-fire. It was my twenty-fifth birthday, a fact that I made the mistake of mentioning to Shoe. The platoon celebrated by spanking me in
a small celebration of being alive, a ritual softened somewhat by the
charcoal chemical suit that I, like all the rest of us, was wearing in case
of chemical attack. It was very, very good to be young and alive and
combat veterans of a war that had gone far better than any of us had
expected.

Shoe decided that our combat experience together meant that mil-

itary courtesies could now be disregarded, and he began calling me
John when the two of us talked. Much as I loved him, I couldn't let this
pass. I ordered Shoe to come to the position of attention in the sand
next to the tank and then had him write himself a counseling statement in which he agreed that if he committed the offense of calling
me by my first name again, he would be subject to punishment under
the Uniform Code of Military Justice. There were tears in his eyes
when he handed me the scrawled counseling statement, which I
promptly rolled into a ball and told him to eat. He didn't call me John
quite as often after that.

Not everyone who saw dawn break that morning had similar op-
portunities to begin telling war stories, sadly. Small bomblets from
previous MLRS and air strikes littered the battlefield and proved irresistible even to artillerymen who should have known better; several
were killed picking them up from the desert sands.

Despite these losses, the experience of Desert Storm had been
extraordinary. The U.S. military, still struggling to overcome the lingering shadow of Vietnam, had turned the fourth-largest army in the
world into the second-largest army in Iraq in a mere one hundred
hours of ground combat. President George H. W. Bush, thrilled with
the flush of victory, proclaimed, "By God, we've licked the Vietnam
syndrome once and for all!" Officers in the Pentagon, still haunted by
specters of that earlier war, hung a sign that informed the world, "We
only do deserts."

The reaction back at Fort Hood, Texas—now mercifully free of
crickets—was out of all proportion to the fighting we'd experienced.
For weeks after our return, it was difficult to pay for meals in the local
eating establishments, as veterans of earlier wars—especially Vietnam—
picked up the tab, and M1A1 tanks rolled down Pennsylvania Avenue
led by General H. Norman Schwarzkopf. America simultaneously celebrated the end of the Cold War, the defeat of Saddam Hussein, and the

Chaplain Peter Johnson in 2008, at my retirement parade.
He was thinner in Desert Storm. So was I.

exorcism of the ghosts of Vietnam in a unipolar moment that would stretch for a decade.

Pete Johnson and I rented a two-bedroom apartment in Killeen, in a complex on New Bacon Ranch Road that featured a pool and a lot of people our age. A religious man, he engaged in long debates on the Bible and the nature of God with secular Susi, my British girlfriend, when she returned to Killeen for part of the summer after the war. They ultimately agreed to disagree on most things spiritual. Coming from Bedfordshire, familiar with centuries-old designations like *New London Road* and *Kingston Road*, Susi was amused by the name *New Bacon Ranch Road*, wondering about the provenance of Old Bacon Ranch Road. She was hugely impressed by the giant wolf spider we caught in my bedroom and kept in a terrarium in the kitchen. I named it after her and regularly fed crickets to Susi the Spider, releasing her back to the wild only when she became with spiderlets just before the Ghostriders deployed to the National Training Center (NTC) at Fort Irwin, California, for a monthlong exercise in February 1992, almost exactly a year after our fight in Desert Storm.

Turtle became the battalion motor officer, responsible for keeping all the forty-four tanks, fourteen Bradley fighting vehicles, and numerous trucks and armored personnel carriers up and running, and I replaced him as Ghostrider 5, the Alpha Company second in command. Life centered on fixing everything that we'd broken in the Iraqi desert and getting ready for the rotation through the NTC, slated to occur exactly a year after Desert Storm. The NTC simulated fights between visiting American units and an American opposing force (OPFOR), which used Soviet tactics and visually modified American equipment in a high-tech game of "laser tag." NTC rotations were the toughest challenge faced by Army units in the United States. The NTC was the crown jewel of the Army's training revolution of the 1980s, designed by Vietnam veterans who wanted to ensure that the next time their army had to fight, their successors would experience the traumas of their "first battle" against weapons that hurt nothing but their pride. Combat is hard, and those fighting for the first time make many mistakes— crazy things like troops shooting themselves accidentally with their own weapons, and hard things like not maintaining security in 360 degrees all night long, a mistake the Ghostriders would fall prey to at the NTC despite our recent experience of real combat. The NTC intentionally presented more difficult challenges than Army forces could expect to see on a real battlefield.

The three-week NTC deployment in February 1992 was as difficult as promised. The fight was a home game for the OPFOR; they knew the ground like the backs of their hands, which, given the time they spent in the desert every year, themselves resembled high plains desert.

Hundreds of miles away from anything that resembles civilization, the only pleasure the OPFOR gets on a regular basis is beating up on conventional Army units that rotate through fights in the desert sands to learn combat tactics, techniques, and procedures. The OPFOR was particularly grumpy at the time we visited, unimpressed by the jaunty First Cavalry Division combat patches we were sporting to indicate our service in Desert Storm. These soldiers had missed the war, remaining at Fort Irwin to train National Guard units for the fight, and had something of a chip on their combat-patchless shoulders. The OPFOR intended to show the Ghostriders what it was like fighting a well-trained, well-led enemy rather than the ragtag Iraqi army we had sliced through a year before.

As an experienced combat unit, we expected to have a relatively easy time of it but were quickly disabused of that notion. Our rotation was made even more difficult by the addition of an Alaska National Guard infantry company that augmented the OPFOR's understrength infantry units. The Nanooks, as we called them, didn't all speak understandable English—they were particularly hard for Puerto Rican Claudio to comprehend—but they did delight in shouting "Woop! Woop! Woop!" to imitate the sounds the laser-tag Military Integrated Laser Engagement System on our tanks made when hit with a simulated anti-tank guided missile. Twenty years later I still sometimes wake up from NTC nightmares with cheerful Nanook shouts of "Woop! Woop! Woop!" echoing in my ears. This is not as crazy as it sounds. An old friend of mine, a graduate of the Army's incredibly challenging Ranger school as well as two tours in Vietnam, used to wake up in Southeast Asia in a cold sweat, calming himself down by repeating the mantra "It's only Vietnam, not Ranger School."

The memory of one simulated fight in particular still stings. We dug our tanks into fighting positions—an arduous exercise involving bulldozers preparing ten-foot-deep holes with parapets to enable the tanks to pop up and down like the fuzzy little creatures in the Whac-A-Mole arcade game. Digging a single fighting position is a matter of six or even eight hours, almost always done at night when tank crews would rather be sleeping, but it's worth the hard work and lost sleep. Tanks in well-prepared fighting positions are all but invulnerable to enemy tank fire. In Iraq, the enemy tanks had been hidden behind sand berms that didn't stop bullets but did indicate their locations to marauding airplanes. Pushing up berms is easy; digging tanks in is harder but far more effective. This night we managed to get all fourteen tanks dug in, with good fields of fire over the expected enemy approach route the next morning—and, almost unbelievably, got them dug in while a few hours of shut-eye were still available.

Or so we thought. The Nanooks had crept up on us from behind, infiltrating through the mountains that protected our flanks and rear from enemy armored vehicles but not from Eskimos. Methodically, one by one, the Nanooks defeated a dug-in tank company in detail, using man-portable (albeit heavy) missiles, precisely targeted artillery shells, and sheer dogged determination. The world's most advanced ground combat systems—M1A1 tanks that only a year earlier had defeated the world's fourth-largest army on its home turf with ease—were perversely vulnerable to small bands of determined human enemies whose language we could barely understand but who knew our vulnerabilities and had the right weapons to take advantage of them.

The experience was, frankly, infuriating, although I didn't have much time to process it as I watched the OPFOR tanks roll untouched past our tank company the next morning, our laser-tag lights flashing and sirens sounding "Woop! Woop! Woop!" We had another battle to prepare to "fight." Its details are lost to my memory, but I'm pretty sure the Nanooks were again featured and again got the better part of the bargain.

I kept returning to that fight in my mind for months afterward—having defeated an enemy tank army in Iraq, how was it that we had been rolled up by light infantry, and by Eskimo light infantry at that? Soldiers we couldn't see and were unprepared to fight had struck us in our vulnerable flanks and rear, defeating millions of dollars in modern technology with simple weapons and stealth. Sitting at Susi's kitchen table in Oxford a month after the fight, cleaned and caught up on sleep, I described the two fights to her and decided at her urging to work out the lessons on paper.

The result, "A Tale of Two Battles," was published as the cover story in *Armor* magazine a few months later—fortunately for my Army career, with a painting of my unit in combat in Iraq, rather than of us being defeated by an Eskimo infantry at the NTC, on the cover of the magazine. By then I had left Fort Hood and arrived at Fort Knox, Kentucky, for the Armor Officer Advanced Course, a school designed to prepare captains to command tank companies and cavalry troops. The nation keeps its tanks and its gold at Fort Knox; we joked that the tanks were there to protect the bullion, and every year some lieutenant got in trouble for intentionally hitting his golf ball onto the grounds of the bullion depository, which was right next to the golf course.

"A Tale of Two Battles" analyzed our "Woop Woop Woop" defeat at the hands of the sneaky Nanooks. It concluded that, in the wake of the Cold War and the defeat of the Iraqi Army in Desert Storm, the United States was far more likely to face unconventional challenges, like ghostly infantry light fighters conducting night raids, than the tank-on-tank conflict that we had engaged in so convincingly in Iraq. The article, which urged the Army's armored forces to spend more time preparing to fight light infantry and decrease its focus on defeating enemy tank armies, was the talk of Fort Knox for a few weeks, until other issues intervened. The lessons of that fight, however, continued to bounce around in my head for years to come. You learn more from a defeat than from a win, and both the Army and I had a lot to learn from that fight at the National Training Center.

The advanced course was full of twenty-six-year-old captains, a majority of them veterans of Operations Desert Shield and Storm, confident in themselves and in the organization of which they were a part. In those days, Army men married early, usually to high school or college girlfriends, and the maternity ward was busy celebrating postdeployment arrivals. Those officers who had somehow missed the memo and had not married a girl from back home or the general's daughter from their first duty station were strongly encouraged to do so. In fact, the major who instructed my small group pulled me aside and chided me for living in sin with Susi, who spent much of the summer at Fort Knox with me. Knox was a big step up from Fort Hood two years before, as the Kentucky crickets remained largely outside our bedroom. The second-floor apartment made their invasion plan much more difficult.

Filled with the joy of being young and alive and with orders to Germany, and without properly considering the difficulties inherent in combining an agnostic only child from England with a recovering Catholic and oldest of six from Omaha, Susi and I eloped to St. Louis over Columbus Day weekend. Hints of the challenges inherent to the relationship should have been clear when my mother, visiting Oxford a few months before Desert Storm on her first overseas trip, had innocently asked Susi about her religious beliefs. Judy was relieved when Susi said she was a Druid, patting her on the hand and replying, "At least you're not a Protestant."

We married without the required wedding permit in St. Louis's Botanical Gardens on a splendid autumn day, my best man a West Point classmate, her maiden of honor another American Rhodes scholar

who happened to be driving cross country on the fateful weekend. The
minister, Rev. Cedric Booker, wears a lapel pin that proclaims "Love"
and is grinning from ear to ear in the only surviving photo of the entire
wedding party, taken by the Botanical Gardens' wedding police. Attempting to enforce the marriage tax, the wedding police failed to
break up the brief ceremony before the bride was kissed. They good-
naturedly took a wedding photo and posed for one themselves before
driving off in their golf cart to check other wedding parties for permits.
There was something in the air that weekend. The best man and best
woman subsequently fell in love with each other, got engaged, and
then married other people after my West Point classmate fell for his
French tutor while his fiancée was in Russia. We remain friends with
both couples today, although we're careful not to invite them both to
the same events.

Now freed of the social opprobrium that emanated from the Army
toward officers who chose to live in sin with their girlfriends, I bade
Susi farewell as she returned to Oxford to finish up her master's thesis.
We would reunite in Germany early in the new year, in a splendid town
named Büdingen—"Swingin' Büdingen" to the troops. The cavalry
squadron headquarters and the officers' club still featured swastikas left

over from the Nazi army in the iron stair railings, but the focus of the unit was on another war.

The conflict in Bosnia raged even as the American public attempted to ignore it, but the prospect of our involvement there focused the attention of the First Squadron, First U.S. Cavalry. The Army was so uncomfortable with low-intensity conflict and stability operations that it called this kind of fight Military Operations Other Than War, or MOOTW for short (pronounced "moooh-twa"). We spent many weeks at the old German army training center of Grafenwöhr conducting crowd control operations, hunting insurgents (although that was a word we never used), and otherwise working through tactical solutions for ethnic conflict situations. Despite the fact that the fight we were preparing for had numerous similarities to the war in Vietnam, we were writing the book as if for the first time. I continued to write for *Armor* magazine, penning a piece with another officer from the squadron about the lessons we had learned during our training in an attempt to disseminate them more widely through the Army.

Ultimately 1-1 Cavalry didn't intervene in former Yugoslavia until late 1995, by which time I had completed both a year as the squadron supply officer and taken and then given up command of Apache Troop, a unit with nine tanks, thirteen Bradleys, and two mortar tracks. One of the high points of my command was the gunnery exercise in which my tank crew earned a perfect thousand-point score on the culminating test of individual tank proficiency, Tank Table VIII. Although the range at Grafenwöhr is relatively narrow and the M1A1 quite a tank, shooting a grand is still a rare event and was good enough to earn us recognition as the top tank crew in the U.S. Army in Europe that summer.

The massacre of some eight thousand Bosnian men and boys at Srebrenica finally led the United States to overcome the lingering ghosts of Vietnam and intervene in force to put an end to the bloodshed. It was one of my tanks that led the American convoy across a bridge over the Sava River into Bosnia, red and white cavalry guidon snapping in the breeze.

But I wasn't in it; by the time Apache Troop finally was sent into this fight, Susi and I had returned to Oxford, against the advice of the Army. It wanted me to command another cavalry troop or, even better, accept Major General Montgomery Meigs's offer to serve as his aide-de-camp as he assumed command of the famed First Infantry Division. Either job would increase my chances for a coveted early promotion to major and pave the way for a career that might include general officer rank. I ignored the good advice of my assignment officer and chose a different path, returning to one of the oldest universities in the world to study an ancient form of warfare. The battle against the Nanooks continued to work inside my head, and I was determined to learn about a kind of warfare that I was increasingly convinced the United States would have to fight again, whether it wanted to or not. Insurgency, I was convinced, was coming back, and the Army needed people who understood it.

2.

Learning to Eat
Soup with a Knife

A Counterinsurgent at Oxford
and West Point

Returning to Oxford was a gift; in fact, Susi gave me a copy of an old book titled *A Time of Gifts* to commemorate the adventure we were facing. Few Army officers get one chance to attend graduate school, and almost none get two. I was fully aware of my good fortune in earning an assignment to teach at West Point and deeply gratified by the assessment of the Military Academy's faculty that I probably needed a refresher course in intellectual pursuits after five years of tanking in Iraq, Texas, California, and Germany.

It was an odd time to choose to study counterinsurgency. The newspapers were full of the conflict in Bosnia, and the thinkers who mattered in defense policy circles were studying peacekeeping or a nascent revolution in military affairs (RMA) that promised to apply the lessons of the information revolution to the future of warfare. According to the dictates of the RMA, what could be seen would be hit, and what could be hit would be killed—all painlessly (for our side, anyway) and from a great distance. These ideas, and the difficulty the Army faced in rapidly deploying units to Bosnia, were the wellsprings behind the Future Combat System, a proposed series of Army combat vehicles that would rely for protection not on heavy armor but on situational awareness. The idea was that we would see our enemies and shoot them long before they could shoot us. Moreover, future battles would be fought in deserts, like the last one, and the population would be just as irrelevant as it had been when the First Cavalry Division bypassed nomadic Bedouin tribes en route to Basra during Operation Desert Storm.

I was convinced that these conclusions were incorrect, that in fights to come we were far more likely to fight insurgents and guerrillas in cities than tanks in open deserts. The rest of the world had seen the ease with which America's conventional military forces cut through the Iraqi military. They would have to be crazy to fight us that way again. I therefore resolved to write my doctoral dissertation on counterinsurgency, the kind of war that I thought was the most likely emerging challenge for American troops. The more I learned, the more I realized that it was also in many ways the most dangerous kind of war that the U.S. military could face.

It was certainly the most likely. Throughout the history of warfare, guerrilla conflict has been more prevalent than conflict between nations represented by armies on a "conventional" field of battle. It is an ancient form of war. In the latter stages of Alexander the Great's invasion of Persia in 329 B.C., after a decisive conventional campaign, Alexander confronted a problem that would frustrate the U.S. Army (and me personally) in Iraq more than two thousand years later. British General and military strategist J. F. C. Fuller captured well the dilemmas faced by any army fighting an insurgency:

In this theatre the whole mode of fighting was to differ from what it had been. No great battles awaited Alexander; he was to be faced by a people's war, a war of mounted guerrillas who, when he advanced would suddenly appear in his rear, who entrenched themselves on inaccessible crags, and when pursued vanished into the Turkoman steppes. To overrun such a theatre of war and subdue such an enemy demanded generalship of the highest order, much higher than needed against an organized army on the plains.[1]

I read voraciously into the long history of guerrilla warfare, from ancient to modern times. An important moment of insight came while reading T. E. Lawrence's classic book *Seven Pillars of Wisdom: A Triumph*, Lawrence's memoir of his leadership of a guerrilla Arab rebellion against the Ottoman Empire's conventional forces during the First World War. I was reading Lawrence in the bathtub of our apartment, having returned from a run through Port Meadow with a friend who was studying the foreign policy of Pope John Paul II, when I discovered Lawrence's malaria-infused musing on the problems that his band of insurgents posed to the conventional army that opposed them. "War upon rebellion was messy and slow," he wrote, "like eating soup with a knife." It was a eureka moment; I immediately knew that I had found the title of my dissertation. I couldn't wait to give Susi the good news, but she was rather less excited about it and encouraged me to get dressed lest the neighbors complain.

Seven words down, ninety-nine thousand, nine hundred, and ninety-three to go. To meet the hundred-thousand-word requirement, I had decided to compare the British Army's experience fighting insurgency in Malaya from 1948 to 1960 with that of the U.S. Army in Vietnam. In both cases, armies that had been prepared to fight other conventional armies had had to adapt to a very different kind of war, changing their doctrine, organization, and to a certain extent even their concept of themselves if they wanted to win.

The British fought their campaign in the multiethnic colony of Malaya, which is today independent of Britain and known as Malaysia. Their opponents were Communist insurgents, mostly ethnic Chinese, many of whom had fought against the Japanese occupiers of Malaya during the Second World War. In the aftermath of that war, the insurgents wanted independence from Britain and resorted to terror and assassination in an attempt to get it. (The Brits, like most empires, had a continuing problem with rebellious colonists.)

The British Army fumbled its initial response badly, as conventional armies tend to do when facing an unfamiliar enemy. Fresh from their victory against the armies of Japan and Germany, British battalion and brigade commanders at first focused their attention on sweeps of hundreds of troops through the jungle aimed at the insurgent forces. Although the British Army had gained substantial experience in fighting small-unit jungle actions against the Japanese during the Second World War, the rapid demobilization of the Far Eastern Forces afterward combined with the dominance of the Western European experience in the careers of most regular soldiers to promote a "conventional" attitude to the war against the Malayan insurgents. Susi and I visited a number of somewhat aged veterans of these conflicts in day trips from Oxford that generally included pitchers of gin and tonic and, as a result, indecipherable notes from the meetings. One of them was the charming Richard Clutterbuck, whose description of the British tactics from those early years of the war, which the troops called "jungle bashing," is astoundingly similar to accounts of U.S. units in Vietnam:

> The predilection of some army officers for major operations seems incurable. Even in the late 1950s, new brigade commanders would arrive from England, nostalgic for World War II, or fresh from large-scale maneuvers in Germany. On arrival in Malaya, they would ad-

dress themselves with chinagraphs [grease pencils] to a map almost wholly green except for one red pin. "Easy," they would say. "Battalion on the left, battalion on the right, battalion blocking the end, and then a fourth battalion to drive through. Can't miss, old boy." Because it took the better part of a day, with more than a thousand soldiers, to get an effective cordon even a half-mile square around a jungle camp, the guerrillas, hearing the soldiers crashing through the jungle into position, had no difficulty getting clear before the net was closed. Except for a rare brush with a straggler, all the soldiers ever found was an empty camp, but this enabled the officers to claim they had "cleared the area of enemy." This would be duly marked on the maps, and the commanders would go to bed with a glow of satisfaction over a job well done. The soldiers, nursing their blisters, had other words for it.[2]

Over time innovative younger officers developed more effective techniques to defeat the guerrillas at their own game by gaining the support of the local people. Flexible senior officers emphasized the interrelationship of political and military goals and encouraged the creation, testing, and implementation of more effective counterinsurgency doctrine. The new tactics brought results, reinforcing the learning process by providing the innovative junior leaders with tangible proof of the importance of their efforts. The British public's patience and acceptance of the traditional role of the British Army in policing the empire—limited wars to achieve limited objectives—provided support for the long effort, which ended when the freely elected government of Malaya finally declared the Emergency over in 1960. The British Army had successfully adapted to overcome the challenges of a Communist insurgent war and an obsolete doctrine in what became seen as the classic case of successful Western counterinsurgency in the twentieth century.

The lessons of Malaya are many; I often joke that they include fighting insurgents on an island or peninsula with borders that can be

easily defended against infiltration, choosing enemies who are easily
visibly distinguishable from the majority of the population, and fighting insurgents before CNN is invented to turn an unblinking eye on
tactics and procedures that may sap domestic and international support for the effort. Malaya is famous as the shining example of the
"hearts and minds" school of counterinsurgency, the idea that the population must be protected in order to allow them to reveal the identity
and location of the insurgents. The phrase was popularized by British
General Sir Gerald Templer, "The Tiger of Malaya," who was the
source of much of the counterinsurgency learning that marked the
campaign. Templer later said that he regretted the phrase, and in fact
he oversaw the use of techniques that would be seen today as relying
upon excessive force, including resettling entire communities in con-
centration camps and limiting food distribution to civilians to prevent
its donation to insurgents. Still, the Malayan campaign demonstrated
that armies could adapt to defeat insurgencies, although the process
was just as messy and slow as Lawrence described. The Brits took
twelve years to figure it out and finish the war on favorable terms.

I found the comparison with the Americans in Vietnam instructive.
Taking over a war against Vietnamese guerrillas who had been fighting the French for independence for the better part of a decade, the U.S.
Army struggled to understand the enemy it was facing and the tactics
it should use against them. Dwight Eisenhower had wisely refused to
bail out the French when a large force was trapped and forced to surrender at Dien Bien Phu, ending the French colonial experience in Asia
but leaving behind a power vacuum. Ike had deployed just under a
thousand advisers to the country by the time his presidency was over. It
was John F. Kennedy who was determined to fight against Communist
insurgency wherever it presented itself, noting in his inaugural address
America's determination to "pay any price, bear any burden, meet
any hardship, support any friend, oppose any foe, in order to assure the

survival and the success of liberty." And eighteen months later, in his speech at the graduation of the West Point Class of 1962, Kennedy warned the young officers of the difficulty of the task ahead:

> Where there is a visible enemy to fight in open combat, the answer is not so difficult. Many serve, all applaud, and the tide of patriotism runs high. But when there is a long, slow struggle, with no immediately visible foe, your choice will seem hard indeed.

The choices were harder than President Kennedy ever could have imagined, both for policy makers in Washington and for the army in the field. In a war that was far more complex than the Malayan Emergency, American arms did what they knew how to do, a strategy that was titled "search and destroy" but could just as well have been called "jungle bashing." William Westmoreland, the Army general who commanded American troops during the critical years of the war, wrote in his memoirs:

> Base camps established all units were constantly on the offensive, seeking any enemy that might be encountered: guerrillas, local force, or main force. This is not to say that the men were constantly under fire, as they might have been in a prolonged conventional campaign. As often as not, the enemy was not to be found.[3]

There were many who argued for a different strategy when fighting ghostlike enemies in Vietnam, more akin to the one that the British had eventually adopted and proven successful in Malaya. The U.S. Marine Corps implemented a concept it called the Combined Action Platoon, which stationed small units of Marines with Vietnamese forces inside villages to protect the population; despite its initial success, General Westmoreland prohibited it for not being offensive-minded and violent enough. Unhappy with the results he was seeing, Army Chief of Staff Harold K. Johnson commissioned a high-level study of

the conduct of the war in mid-1965. Under the leadership of General
Creighton Abrams, the Program for the Pacification and Long-Term
Development of South Vietnam (PROVN) group was tasked with "developing new courses of action to be taken in South Vietnam by the
United States and its allies, which will, in conjunction with current actions, modified as necessary, lead in due time to successful accomplish-
ment of U.S. aims and objectives."[4] The results were striking: a
repudiation of the Army's current emphasis on search and destroy operations and a move toward pacification through winning the population over to the government's cause. The final report of the PROVN
study, submitted to Johnson in March 1966, stated:

> The situation in South Vietnam has seriously deteriorated. 1966 may
> well be the last chance to ensure eventual success. "Victory" can only
> be achieved through bringing the individual Vietnamese, typically a
> rural peasant, to support willingly the GVN. The critical actions are
> those that occur at the village, district, and provincial levels. This is
> where the war must be fought; this is where that war and the object
> which lies beyond it must be won.[5]

But General Westmoreland was unable to change his spots, and
the Army continued his search and destroy strategy until Creighton
Abrams replaced him in July 1968, after the Tet Offensive in February
of that year had shaken American support for the war to its core. Great
powers do not lose small wars because they run out of tanks, soldiers,
or money. If a great power like the United States loses a relatively small
war like Vietnam, it does so because of a lack of public support at
home. After Tet, the American people lost faith in their Army's ability
to win the war in Vietnam at a reasonable cost, and it is hard to blame
them for their dismay and doubt. The killing of American college students at Kent State by National Guard soldiers symbolized a country at
war with itself.

In Malaya, the British military had learned quickly enough to keep the British population "on side," a task that was easier in an earlier day without the focused eye of the global media watching every move. In Vietnam, the American military had also learned from the bottom up, but the high command did not absorb the lessons until disaster on the battlefield shook national confidence in the war effort. Learning in a large organization, I concluded, is a process in which subordinates close to the point of the spear identify problems and suggest solutions—a common trait of all successful businesses. The key variable in determining whether organizations adapt or die is not at the lower levels but at the top: key leaders have to determine that real change is required. If they make that decision, it is comparatively easy to transmit instructions on how to respond to changes in the environment; in the military, such instructions are called "doctrine," and they are codified in field manuals, leader development courses, and training scenarios.

My thinking was heavily influenced by Richard Downie, an Army colonel who had written his own doctoral dissertation on how armies learn after conflicts and published it under the title *Learning from Conflict: The U.S. Military in Vietnam, El Salvador, and the Drug War.* His dissertation had been titled *The U.S. Army as Learning Organization;* it was clear that he did not view the title as an oxymoron.

Sir Michael Howard, whose theatrical Oxford lectures I had had the good fortune to attend, once wrote that "in structuring and preparing an army for war, you can be clear that you will not get it precisely right, but the important thing to ensure is that it is not too far wrong, so that you can put it right quickly." The reason innovation is so hard in military organizations is that they face real enemies very seldom—generally once in a generation. As a result, doctrine can go very far wrong—even to the point of completely ignoring doctrine for an entire, and ancient, kind of warfare that presents enormously difficult challenges for con-

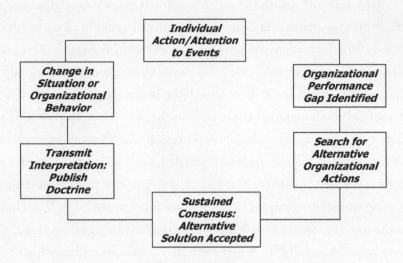

Organizational Learning Chart.

ventional military forces. And that, of course, is what the U.S. Army did when it turned its back on Vietnam and other "small wars."

Michael Howard had been the Chichele Professor of the History of War at All Souls' College before becoming the Regius Professor of History. (Oxford offers great job titles and splendid office space, although the salaries are not commensurate with the prestige.) His successor in the Chichele Chair was Robert O'Neill, an Australian military academy graduate and Rhodes scholar. Bob was a veteran of Vietnam as well as of my two theses; which experience marked him more deeply is an open question. My master's dissertation, on American and Japanese economic and military relations after the Second World War, had been heavily influenced by an American spending her junior year abroad who studied those subjects, but specialized in pubs, during my first year at Oxford. I knew nothing about Japan and little about economics, as my master's marks showed, but I learned a lot about JYAs and British drinking culture during that first year. Despite my questionable priorities while earning my master's, Bob signed up to supervise my doctoral dissertation as well, although he was more careful about providing oversight of my research topic than he had been the first time.

Bob was also the senior member of the Oxford University Strategic Studies Group (OUSSG), a club for those interested in geopolitics and strategy for which I served as vice president while earning my master's degree and later as president during my D.Phil. studies, gaining invaluable ex-

Bob O'Neill in Vietnam.

perience in chairing meetings, asking hard questions of senior people, and managing a budget. Bob and his wife, Sally, were the best of mentors and friends, an oasis of unpretentious competence and compassion in what can be a very hard place for Americans to understand. The experience of working with Bob again, the joy of spending time visiting various historic sites in England with Susi and her mother, who lived nearby, and the wonder of hearing firsthand stories of the Malayan Emergency and the broader British retreat from empire at the knees of veterans of those campaigns (always with a gin and tonic in hand) were some of the greatest of the gifts we shared in that time of gifts. I headed to West Point in the summer of 1997 clutching my freshly minted doctorate with hopes of a bestselling counterinsurgency book dancing through my head.

From Bob's able hands, I was passed to those of another Vietnam veteran and student of international affairs: Colonel Daniel Kaufman, who had been my sponsor when I was a West Point cadet and was now

Dan and Kathryn Kaufman in Atlanta in 2013, still feeding me thirty
years after I arrived on their doorstep as a West Point plebe in 1984.

professor and head of the department of Social Sciences at West Point,
which I was joining as an assistant professor. Dan had played an important role in sending me back to graduate school on the banks of the
Thames to earn my Ph.D. and in ensuring that I got it done well within
the required two years by threatening me with bodily harm if I failed
to do so. I soon found myself on Dan's front porch, Sam Adams in
hand, overlooking the Hudson River and comparing my stories of Desert Storm and Oxford with his rather more significant tales of Vietnam
and Cambridge, Massachusetts, where he had earned his master's and
doctorate. Colonel Kaufman was in a mood for reminiscing, remembering a visit I had paid to his office after Christmas of my freshman
year at West Point, first semester grades in hand. After examining them
with an experienced eye, Colonel Kaufman had told me to pay atten-

tion, then said: "This is what you're going to do, son. You're going to major in international relations, become an armor officer, get a Rhodes scholarship, study international relations at Oxford, and then come back to teach for me here in the Sosh Department. What are your questions?"

I had none. Sitting on the porch, Dan asked me if I remembered that visit (as if I could forget it), then told me that a decade later he was finally going to be in a position to officially appraise my performance as what the Army called my "senior rater," and that he had boiled it down to a single sentence of only three words. Confident in my role as straight man, I asked him what that sentence would be. Dan replied, "Officer follows instructions."

The department of Social Sciences teaches economics, political science, and international relations to West Point cadets, some of whom in their turn become Sosh professors, or "p's," themselves, in an endless cycle of service in foreign conflicts, good graduate schools, and self-replication. This is one of the great strengths of West Point, which sees its mission as "to educate, train, and inspire the Corps of Cadets." Army captains fresh from the battlefields of Korea, Vietnam, or Iraq— or even the simulated battlefields of the National Training Center— may not be the best of all possible educators, but they could certainly train and inspire malleable cadets like me. My own role models as a cadet included Steve Daffron, a cavalryman who taught economics and became a very senior banker at J. P. Morgan after leaving the Army; Jay Parker, the least likely infantryman the Army had ever seen who was famous for his "Politics and Film" class, erudition, and disorganization; and an Army captain named David Petraeus, who had stood out even in that band of hard-charging soldier-scholars. No slouch in spotting talent, I confidently picked Petraeus to make full-bird colonel for sure and ended up spending the summer before my final year at West Point with him on an internship at the Supreme Headquarters of the Allied Powers Europe (SHAPE).

Major Petraeus was, by then, a speechwriter for General Jack Galvin, the grandly named Supreme Allied Commander Europe, for whom he had worked twice earlier in his career. I literally shared a corner of Petraeus's small speechwriting desk, drafting a paper on co-operation developing armaments among the countries of NATO and attempting to sample every one of the several hundred beers produced in the small country of Belgium. Demonstrating a reasonable degree of success in both endeavors, I made it into Petraeus's little black book of officers he might choose to call upon should he get the chance, although I didn't recognize that he was keeping track of my progress at the time. Major Petraeus was more interested in running than in drinking beer, but two Air Force Academy cadets and, especially, the lone Naval Academy midshipman on the same SHAPE internship filled the drinking buddy gap nicely. SHAPE billeting, which had seen a generation of service academy interns, had thoughtfully provided us with bachelor officer quarters a short 134 steps from the officers' club. We checked a number of times that summer to make sure neither the club nor the BOQ had moved, and neither ever did.

That summer internship was the cherry on the cake of a fantastic experience at West Point. I'd fallen in love with the place the first time I saw its granite walls appearing to grow out of the hard rock on which George Washington had sited a fort controlling the Hudson River during the Revolutionary War, statues of Douglas MacArthur and Dwight Eisenhower and George Patton standing as tall among the buildings as their namesakes did in my imagination. Although I'd intended to follow in my father's footsteps and become an electrical engineer, being assigned to Dan Kaufman's mentorship as an impressionable freshman coincided with a crushing defeat in plebe calculus. By the time I had to choose a major, it was international relations and national security that I signed up for, a program perhaps not coincidentally then under the stewardship of Lieutenant Colonel Kaufman.

A full decade later I was back in the Social Sciences department, attempting to provide the same education, mentoring, and role modeling to a new generation of cadets that Petraeus and his cohort had provided to mine under Kaufman's leadership. Susi and I were living on West Point's campus in a small apartment with a tiny balcony. We could just squeeze two deck chairs onto it and hold a cutting board on our knees as a sort of dinner table, but the view of the Hudson River from the balcony made the gymnastics worth it. The old, deep river had cut deeply into the granite hills over millennia, creating a point on the western side that forced sailing ships, whichever way the wind was blowing, to slow down to negotiate a ninety-degree turn. West Point's commanding position over that critical point in the Hudson had led George Washington to fortify the post during the Revolutionary War. He had a great chain strung across the great river, guarded by cannons and colonial insurgents who were determined not to let the British Army practice the classic counterinsurgency technique of slicing the rebellion into smaller, more digestible pieces. West Point held despite Benedict Arnold's decision (inspired by love of an Englishwoman, always a dangerous choice) to traitorously hand over the plans to its defenses to the British, and today the cannons and a piece of the Great Chain preserved on Trophy Point recall an important episode in the birth of a rebellious nation.

It is a privilege granted to few to return to a beloved alma mater to become part of the fabric of the institution. My cadet dreams of walking in the shoes of Captains Daffron, Parker, and Petraeus came true, and I now stood where giants in my own development had trod. The cohort of officers with whom I taught had its own giants, at least two

Paul Yingling, bloodied but unbowed, brawling.

of whom have already earned their general officer stars, and a large number of whom served with valor in the wars of the decade that would follow our teaching assignment.

My closest intellectual comrade in this field was Paul Yingling. Paul had grown up over a bar outside Pittsburgh, enlisted in the Army to better himself, gone to college at Duquesne on an ROTC scholarship, and earned a commission as an artillery officer before fighting in both Desert Storm and Bosnia. At that point the long arm of the Sosh Department found Paul and sent him to the University of Chicago. Paul was razor sharp, and over chess games and debates about international relations theory, we managed to forge a friendship that endures. Paul's most notable characteristics, other than his intellect, are his stubbornness, his deeply felt sense of integrity, and his love of a good fight; all would be on display on a national stage in the decade to come.

Teaching was a joy; it was easy to see that we Sosh professors, or "p's," stood in front of classrooms filled with those who would in their turn become our replacements a decade hence. In those years at the end of a decade of peace, I taught international relations and national security studies and American foreign policy to future heroes Walt Cooper and Jim Golby and Liz Young. Out of the classroom, I helped them compete for Rhodes scholarships so that they too could imbibe warm beer and learn the lessons of empire.

One of the more interesting and certainly the most driven of this group was Craig Mullaney, a working-class kid from Rhode Island with an intense desire to excel. I met Craig during my first year of teaching when he was just a sophomore, a "yearling" in West Point parlance (because juniors had once been sent away from the academy for summer visits to military posts aboard cattle cars and hence were called "cows"). Craig majored in history, and Susi took a seat on his thesis committee and taught him and some of his classmates to cook in our apartment. Craig remembers making a hash of peeling pears because he was using the blunt edge of the knife, a good analogy for the brute-force approach he took to winning a Rhodes himself.

I continued to work on turning my dissertation into a book when not teaching cadets or mentoring those seeking scholarships, learning more about the organizational culture of the U.S. military, and watching the way it affected decisions on the use of force that marked the Clinton presidency. It became increasingly clear that the loss in Vietnam had shaken the confidence of the U.S. military for a generation. Stung by the defeat, the Army decided to turn away from counterinsurgency campaigns to focus on the kinds of war it liked best: conventional campaigns against conventional enemies. A generation of officers, including Colin Powell and Jack Galvin, turned the Army that had known

bitter defeat in Vietnam into the military force that triumphed in Desert Storm, but the apparent revitalization of American arms had a hidden underbelly: it intentionally turned away from an entire category of
war, with no guarantee that a future enemy would not exploit the gap-
ing hole in America's military preparedness. It was as if a football team
had devoted itself exclusively to defending against the forward pass,
tearing up the playbook on run defense, and even deciding not to practice against a "three yards and a cloud of dust" offense.

The overwhelming desire of the Army to avoid future iterations of
Vietnam was enshrined in the Powell-Weinberger Doctrine, named
after the chairman of the Joint Chiefs of Staff and secretary of defense
who in separate speeches promulgated a very restrictive series of rules
governing the employment of American military force. The U.S. military would be employed only in wars in which there were clear military
targets, strong public support, and a well-defined exit strategy. Lacking those three things, America should not deploy her armed forces.

These restrictions meant not only that the American military was
all but unemployable in the messy conflicts that marked the post–Cold
War era but also that it was unprepared to fight, if called upon to do so,
in wars more politically complicated than Desert Storm. The military
got very good at winning battles through training at places like the
National Training Center (where most units performed better than
mine had when we faced defeat at the hands of the Nanooks, or at least
claimed they did in officers' club discussions afterward). Although the
military knew how to win battles, it had no sense of how to use American power to achieve political objectives—to win wars. More than a
decade later, retired Army General Jack Keane would tell Jim Lehrer
that in Iraq:

> We put an Army on the battlefield [in Iraq] that I had been a part of
> for 37 years. It doesn't have any doctrine, nor was it educated and

trained, to deal with an insurgency. . . . After the Vietnam War, we purged ourselves of everything that had to do with irregular warfare or insurgency, because it had to do with how we lost that war. In hindsight, that was a bad decision.[6]

That hindsight was yet to arrive while I was teaching at West Point, but the gap in understanding of the relevance of insurgency and counterinsurgency had more immediate implications for my publishing prospects. No one was interested in a book on how armies learn to succeed in counterinsurgency, and both Princeton and Cornell University Presses, leaders in the field of international security, were uninterested in the book that I had titled *Learning to Eat Soup with a Knife* after Lawrence of Arabia's eureka-inspiring phrase. I did manage to get a chapter of the dissertation published in the little-read Princeton journal *World Affairs*. Although I couldn't get the book published, I presented in that article some of the conclusions—that counterinsurgency was not going away, that the U.S. military had better (re)learn how to do it well, and that it was important to build the ability to learn into modern military organizations—at a political science convention. The ideas were politely received by an audience that had next to no ability to influence actual policy. I also had the chance to coauthor a monograph, with retired Army Colonel Don Snider and fellow Major Tony Pfaff, on the challenges of limited wars to military professionalism. It argued, "If the Army continues to resist organizing training and equipping itself to fight and win the wars it is currently being asked to fight, it may no longer have a sufficiently professional officer corps when the next big war occurs."

Captains assigned to West Point arrive during one summer and are brought up to speed in a teaching boot camp before the start of the fall semester; then during their second summer, they serve as drill sergeants themselves, mentoring cadets assigned to their own summer

In our little West Point apartment in 1999.

training. I was sent to Camp Buckner, a post some fifteen miles from West Point that is known as "the greatest summer of your life" when endured as a yearling and by other aphorisms when assigned there as a captain.

The most memorable part of my second summer at Buckner came during my tour as camp staff duty officer. Susi was visiting her mother in England, and I had brought George the Dog, our pit bull rescue mutt, with me to staff duty. George got away from me and found himself a skunk; although the skunk fared poorly in the encounter, earning a broken neck, it would be hard to argue that George, his eyes swollen shut from the spray, had won the campaign. I made the command decision to abandon my post as staff duty officer to transport George home for a thorough scrubbing, then returned to duty a bit the worse for wear myself. The next morning I reported to the camp commander that I had abandoned my post; he asked me what had led me to make that choice, then before I could answer asked, "What's that smell?" As a result of my transgression, dogs were prohibited at Camp Buckner— my most important contribution to national security that summer.

My contributions the next summer were more substantial, or at least fought on more complicated battlefields. I worked in the office of the deputy assistant secretary of defense for requirements, plans, and counterproliferation policy, Dr. Jim Miller, whom I had met during my second Oxford tour while he was enjoying a Marshall Fellowship in honor of the fiftieth anniversary of the Marshall Plan. Jim was a six-foot-four Iowa boy who had played tennis at Stanford and then earned his doctorate at Harvard's Kennedy School, studying the impact of very deep cuts in nuclear weapons.

During his Marshall Fellowship, Jim had spent two solid hours physically walking me through the University Park while intellectually walking me through my doctoral dissertation in stunningly Socratic fashion. That walk is for me a constant reminder of the value of the right question asked at the right time. Although I was ostensibly writing a paper on the future of arms control for another mentor, former Air Force officer Jim Smith, my real education in Miller's office was a glimpse into the role played by senior civilian officials in the Pentagon, people who called general officers by their first name. I decided that my future should include service as a Pentagon political appointee with the opportunity to influence national policy on issues of capabilities for waging war and preserving peace.

Officers assigned to West Point as professors generally arrive as captains and are promoted to major during their tenure. Some few are selected for promotion before their year group is promoted in "due course"; these fortunate officers are instead promoted "below the zone," gaining a head start in the race for general officer stars. I was disappointed not to earn that distinction, but I shouldn't have been surprised. My decision to spend four of my first ten years in the Army at Oxford studying international security issues and counterinsurgency was made against the express advice of my Army career managers, and if I had been seeking a conventional Army career, their advice would have been exactly right.

My decision to attend West Point more than a decade earlier had been heavily influenced by my father, an Iowan who was part of the first generation of his family to go to college, in his case Marquette, on a Naval Reserve Officer Training Corps scholarship. Dad became a small part of Admiral Hyman Rickover's famous nuclear Navy, enormously proud of being asked to solve a nuclear equation on a blackboard during his brief interview with the great man. Many others were not so lucky, finding themselves locked in closets if their answers failed to satisfy Admiral Rickover, who almost single-handedly created the U.S. Navy's nuclear propulsion program and its exacting focus on safety.

Dad's career was far less distinguished than Rickover's, however, consisting in its entirety of a tour teaching nuclear engineering at Mare Island Naval Base in Vallejo, California, where first I and then my sister Emily were born. Dad left the Navy as soon as he was able, and after brief tours in Pennsylvania and Wisconsin tending nuclear reactors, he ended up in Omaha, Nebraska, which boasted a power plant at Fort Calhoun that became his second home for more than twenty years. It was not being around nuclear power but smoking a pack a day for thirty years that killed him as my final year teaching at West Point came to a close. I flew to Kansas City, where the family had recently moved, and was there at home with him when he died in his own bed, his wife of thirty-five years next to him, all six of his children under the roof. I delivered the eulogy, focussing on the responsibility he had felt to provide for his family physically, leaving out the emotional distance that his own upbringing had instilled in him and that my mother had attempted to bridge on her own.

He left behind a big Cadillac, an inheritance from a friend that Mom had never driven and didn't want to start driving now. I sat down with her to talk about alternatives, intending to suggest an immensely practical Subaru, when she brightly said that she knew just what she wanted to trade the Caddy for: a new Volkswagen Beetle. I knew immediately that she was going to be just fine on her own, and more than a decade later that little beetle-green Beetle is just touching fifty thousand miles, evidence of many trips to choir practice and occasional visits to her own family in Iowa.

Dad's illness had prevented me from applying for a White House Fellowship, which would have provided a year working in the executive branch of the U.S. government in Washington. Although Sosh p's often competed for White House Fellowships at the conclusion of their teaching tours, I couldn't in good conscience ask to be assigned to Washington at that point. The alternative assignment, to the U.S. Army Command and General Staff College at Fort Leavenworth, Kansas, would put me less than an hour from my dying father. As it turned out, cancer took him before we moved to Leavenworth, but being close to Mom in her first year of widowhood was another gift the Army gave me, as was including Paul Yingling in my Leavenworth cohort.

Command and General Staff College (CGSC) was a yearlong course that at that time was reserved for those judged to be in the top half of their year's group of officers, the cohort who began service during a certain calendar year. The joke among students was that CGSC consisted of the Army's top half being taught by its bottom half, since service as an instructor was not highly valued by the Army, but I thought highly of the officers who taught me and enjoyed the classroom exchanges that they led. I was less impressed by the curriculum, which was designed for an army that was fighting replicas of Desert

Storm rather than repeatedly engaged in messy fights like Somalia and Bosnia.

CGSC did provide me with time to focus on turning my doctoral thesis into a book, a task still undone three years after completion, now accompanied by those rejection letters from the university presses at Princeton and Cornell. I swallowed my pride and contacted Praeger Press, a trade publisher that I later discovered was rumored to have been funded by the CIA. Many of the books on Vietnam that I cited had been published under Praeger's imprint, so there was historical continuity, even if Praeger didn't have the cachet of an academic press that I desired. It was finally accepted for publication, although I spent many more night and weekend hours getting the manuscript into accordance with Praeger's guidelines for footnotes and bibliography format. The process took longer than I'd ever imagined it could, and it didn't bear fruit until 2002, when counterinsurgency was about to be in vogue as it had not been since Praeger's heyday forty years before. I engaged in a bitter struggle with Praeger about the book title, wanting to use Lawrence's simile. My editors at Praeger refused, insisting on the prosaic *Counterinsurgency Lessons from Malaya and Vietnam* on the cover of the book, with *Learning to Eat Soup with a Knife* relegated to subtitle status.

Always a glutton for punishment, I took the opportunity to write a master's thesis at Leavenworth and chose the topic *Asymmetric Threats to the Security of the United States through 2010,* earning a master of the military arts and sciences degree for arguing in June 2001 that enemies of the United States would use irregular ways and means to accomplish their objective of harming us. Al Qaeda's attack on the USS Cole occurred during the writing process, underlining the relevance of my work. At the end of each of the first two trimesters, I wrote a memo to the head of the school suggesting changes to the curriculum, never receiving a reply, but either despite or because of my grousing, I was selected as the George C. Marshall Award winner as the top member of our class. Captain Petraeus had previously earned this distinction, known as the White Briefcase despite the fact that the actual award is a demilitarized .45 pistol behind glass. When writing about the award in the Oxford alumni journal, I joked that this was the perfect metaphor for the U.S. Army of 2001 as constrained by the Powell-Weinberger Doctrine: a nonfunctional antique, kept behind glass to prevent access.

In truth, I was thrilled to join the long list of Army officers who had received the honor and even more pleased that the Army had seen fit to assign Susanne and me to the First Infantry Division at Fort Riley, Kansas, just two hours down the road from Kansas City. Mom drove her new beetle-green Beetle to the graduation ceremony at Fort Leavenworth, and it was there that I told her that Susi, visiting her mom in England to convey good news, was with child. Life looked peaceful and bright.

3.

Back to Iraq

Al Anbar 2003–2004

fter graduation, Susi and I moved down Interstate 70 from Leavenworth to Fort Riley, Kansas. This was the historic home of the
famed First Infantry Division that had blown the holes in the berm
through which my tank had passed from Saudi Arabia into Iraq during
Desert Storm and that had earlier distinguished itself in World Wars I
and II and in Vietnam.

Like most new majors, I was assigned to the division staff for a year
as I waited for a position in one of the four tank battalions that called
Fort Riley home. Division headquarters was a short walk from the
brick apartment that the Army had provided for us in historic Old Post,
and as we awaited the arrival of our son, we got acquainted with a new
Army installation and a new community, and I spent nights checking
footnotes on my doctoral dissertation.

On the beautiful morning of September 11, I was walking into
work after an early PT test when the sergeant major told me that he'd
heard about an attack on New York while driving in. We rushed to the
division conference room, which was showing live news coverage of

the World Trade Center, and we watched the towers fall. Like other
U.S. military installations all over the world, Fort Riley immediately increased security at its gates and prepared for combat.

The nation was in shock, and even Fort Riley, safe from any conceivable terrorist predations in the middle of Kansas wheatfields, was
affected. In the whirl of more rigorous guard procedures and heightened efforts to prepare our equipment for war, the arrival of Jack
Frederick on October 13, 2001, was a wonderful reminder that life
nonetheless would go on. He was born at the base hospital just a mile
from our quarters, and Susi, with her high pain threshold, didn't ask for
an epidural until it was too late; her version of "natural childbirth" included not even an aspirin. Jack was small but healthy, and we took him
home the next day, when the joys of fatherhood began competing with
the pain inherent in completing the index of a doctoral dissertation
that was still in the process of becoming a book. I don't think I'd fully
realized what love was until Jack's arrival, and he grew and smiled and
soon began to talk, long bursts of nonsensical syllables that sometimes
reminded me of my own writings.

Although the initial attacks on the Taliban regime in Afghanistan
didn't include any tank units, they did include the innovative use of
special forces calling in air strikes against the Taliban, a story that made
its way into the version of *Counterinsurgency Lessons from Malaya and
Vietnam: Learning to Eat Soup with a Knife* that finally saw print late in
2002. Given the raw emotional appeal of the title on which my publishers insisted, it was no surprise that it took months after publication for
the book to crack the one millionth bestselling title on Amazon, a fact
often pointed out to me by a soldier on the staff of the First Battalion,
34th Armor Regiment, who took immense joy in tracking my minus-
cule sales ranking by the day. He did a lot of push-ups as a result.

By then I was the executive officer, or XO, of 1-34, having escaped
from division headquarters after working for a year in what young offi-

cers considered a kind of purgatory. The XO is second in command of a tactical Army unit, responsible for logistics, maintenance, and oversight of the staff. While 1-34 Armor, the Centurions, was a good unit, XO wasn't my first choice; the fun major's job in a tank battalion is S3, or operations officer. That job comes with a tank of one's own, while the XO is stuck in the rear with the gear, as the saying goes, proud owner of a Humvee that draws enormous scorn if it goes down for maintenance issues. I'd originally been slated to be the S3 of 1-34 but got bumped for a late-arriving officer from Korea, Marty Leners, a West Point graduate a year younger than I who had earned a Silver Star for Valor in Desert Storm. The brigade commander called me at division headquarters to give me the bad news, asking what I would say if he told me that he needed me to serve as XO instead of Centurion 3. I promptly told him that I would cry but would try not to do so until after he hung up the phone. He told me to deal with it.

As it turned out, over the course of the next year the XO had more to do than did the "three." The fun began when one of our tankers discovered that the nuclear, biological, and chemical (NBC) protective system on his M1A1 was inoperative in a big way. The system is essentially an air conditioner built into a box on the side of the tank. Not well designed for the rigors of tanking, it had a habit of ingesting sand and dirt and hence not performing its assigned task of providing filtered air inside the tank, allowing the crew to breathe easily without wearing a cumbersome protective mask like the one that Sergeant Shoe had forgotten outside our tank back in Desert Storm. The system was supposed to be checked monthly, but somehow these checks had been missed. When I saw the system that had failed—it literally had a solid chunk of sand and mud covering delicate air control components—I ordered that every one of the tanks in the battalion be inspected. All were broken, rendering the battalion's tanks being declared non-mission-capable for deployment to combat operations. That was a big deal in a tank battalion that was then on call for a number of contingency missions around the world, with a priority toward the "fight tonight" mission to defend South Korea against a North Korean attack.

It turned out that pretty much every tank in the U.S. Army had the same problem. We were just the first to discover (or perhaps more likely, report fully) the systemic failure. The battalion's crews and mechanics went to work tearing the systems down to bare metal, sandblasting them to remove rust, body-coating the clean metal, and then rebuilding the systems. The NBC system rebuild quickly became the most important thing happening at Fort Riley that hot summer-into-fall of 2002, and Brigadier General Frank Helmick, the assistant division commander for support, spent a fair amount of time in the 1-34 motor pool overseeing the process. Helmick was a career paratrooper who was on his first assignment to a heavy tank unit, a thin, intense, deeply dedicated Army officer who would remember the time we spent together in the motor pool in days to come when he needed an action officer in the Pentagon. He also remembered a PT test we'd run together, when I failed to beat him in the two-mile run but won "trying points" for throwing up as I crossed the finish line—the second-best possible outcome in General Helmick's eyes. At Fort Riley, while 1-34 was the first tank battalion in the Army to fall to having zero fully mission-capable (FMC) tanks—a fact that was reported all the way up to the Pentagon—we were also the first battalion to come back up to 100 percent FMC, and we passed word of our repair procedures around the Army.

"Big Army" had not been heavily involved in the liberation of Afghanistan from the Taliban; that had largely been a Special Operations Forces and CIA endeavor. But it was going to play a role in the pending invasion of Iraq, and we knew it. I was deeply unconvinced of the need for the invasion, despite the fact that I accepted the intelligence picture that Saddam Hussein was in possession of weapons of mass destruction. (I was in good company; Colin Powell, by now secretary of state, believed it too, a big factor in my own mistaken faith in the assessment.) As a student of the Cold War, I knew that the United States had lived for more than forty years with a Soviet Union that had been dedicated to the destruction of the West and possessed a huge nuclear stockpile; the doctrine of mutually assured destruction prevented those weapons from ever being used to attack us. I believed that Saddam Hussein's Iraq, with a far smaller arsenal even according to the worst-case projections, could be easily deterred with America's far larger arsenal. Not many people were interested in what an Army major at Fort Riley thought about the decision to invade Iraq, but I did what I could to ward off the invasion. Among other things, I told my friend Jim Miller, who was no longer serving in the Pentagon but still well connected in Washington, that I thought the invasion of Iraq was unnecessary—even if Saddam did have weapons of mass destruction, Iraq had a return address and could be deterred, unlike a terrorist group—and likely to be a costly disaster.

This attitude was shared by a number of other people whose concerns would not have much impact on a Washington that was convinced of the need for war. One of them was a retired lieutenant colonel with whom I'd taught at West Point while he was still wearing the uniform. Conrad Crane had earned a history Ph.D. from Stanford and taken a position at the Army War College in Carlisle Barracks, Pennsylvania, after his retirement from the Army. Con and fellow War College professor W. Andrew Terrill argued in a prescient War College publication dated February 1, 2003:

> If this nation and its coalition partners decide to undertake the mission to remove Saddam Hussein, they will also have to be prepared to dedicate considerable time, manpower, and money to the effort to reconstruct Iraq after the fighting is over. Otherwise, the success of mil-

itary operations will be ephemeral, and the problems they were designed to eliminate could return or be replaced by new and more virulent difficulties.[1]

Concerns raised by many officers about the need for the invasion and the likely cost, including the need for a postwar occupation of Iraq, were not widely heeded, however, and the war commenced in March 2003. The call largely bypassed Fort Riley. The only unit that was tagged to go was 2-70 Armor, a sister tank battalion commanded by a tall former college defensive end named Jeff Ingram. During the invasion, Ingram's tank battalion was assigned to support the famed 101st Airborne Division commanded by Major General David Petraeus, who had zipped right past the full-bird colonel rank I'd predicted he would someday wear when I was a cadet sharing the major's desk at SHAPE. Petraeus relied heavily on 2-70's tanks, and Lieutenant Colonel Ingram earned a Silver Star for Valor during the fight, as did a number of his soldiers. He was also wounded by a mortar fragment that hit his back during one firefight, but battled through, reporting for medical treatment only after the shooting had died down. The doctor pulled a tiny piece of metal out and sewed Jeff up with just two stitches, one fewer than required by battalion guidelines that Jeff himself had instituted for a Purple Heart award. Jeff joked with the doc, asking him if he could squeeze in one more very small stitch, but the doctor held firm and Jeff went without the medal initially established by General George Washington. He was a great Army officer, and Fort Riley was proud of him, but the closest the rest of us came to the war was watching Jeff on television.

Major General Petraeus had Rick Atkinson, a Pulitzer Prize–winning reporter and historian who had authored a great book on Vietnam and West Point under the title *The Long Gray Line*, embedded with him throughout the invasion. Atkinson's resulting book, *In the Company of Soldiers*, should really have been titled *In the Company of* a

Soldier. He reported that several times during the invasion, Petraeus asked himself, "Tell me how this ends." That quote would later become the title of a book by Linda Robinson about Petraeus's role in altering the answer to that question for the better, but for the time being it hung in the air as a well-informed concern from a man who had written his doctoral dissertation at Princeton on the lessons taken from the Vietnam War and their influence in its aftermath.

Petraeus and Crane were right to be concerned about the subsequent phases of this war, although they were not joined in that concern by the civilian officials responsible for the outcome. Secretary of Defense Donald Rumsfeld was not enamored of postconflict stability operations and had repeatedly insisted on a smaller invasion force than the uniformed military recommended. Marine Lieutenant General Greg Newbold, the director of operations on the Joint Staff, finally rebelled when Rumsfeld demanded cuts in troop strength below those he thought acceptable. Newbold resigned from the corps in protest but did not make public his concerns about what he saw as unacceptable risk to the mission and to the troops until years later, in a *Time* magazine piece titled "Why Iraq Was a Mistake."

Rumsfeld won the argument with General Newbold, and the initial invasion force was—just barely—big enough to topple Saddam Hussein but nowhere near large enough to meet the obligation of an occupying force to provide security for the Iraqi people in the wake of the war. Army Chief of Staff General Ric Shinseki, who had been wounded in Vietnam and commanded U.S. forces in Bosnia, had told House Armed Services Committee chairman Ike Skelton that "several hundred thousand" troops would be required to hold Iraq together in the wake of the invasion, a number that Deputy Secretary of Defense Paul Wolfowitz scoffed at the next day in congressional testimony. Wolfowitz described Shinseki's estimate as "wildly off the mark" and said "the notion that it would take several hundred thousand American troops just seems outlandish."

In fact, it was not even prescient; it was simply an extrapolation based on previous successful postconflict military occupations, including the one that Shinseki had led in Bosnia. Mark Twain famously said that "history doesn't repeat itself, but it rhymes," and military doctrine itself is merely distilled history, lessons drawn from the long history of warfare. The insufficiency of troops to secure Iraq's cities, much less lock down the many supposed weapons of mass destruction storage sites that were the presumptive purpose for invading in the first place, was just one of many shortfalls in one of the least successful military operations in American history.

Another was the complete absence of plans or planning for the postconflict phase of operations, called Phase IV in military parlance, following the major combat operations of Phase III. In its official after-action review, the Third Infantry Division, which had conducted the Thunder Run into Baghdad and captured Saddam International Airport. Fardus Square, says that it requested from its higher headquarters, the Army's V Corps, instructions once Baghdad had fallen to American tanks, but that "none were found." It is a seditious line, intended to insulate the Third ID against guilt for the failures that followed, and a scathing indictment of the civilian leadership of the Pentagon that oversaw the preparations for a war of choice that we began on our own schedule. Because we knew that we were chasing a bus, we should have had a plan for what we were going to do once we caught it.

Throughout the first term of George W. Bush, the Department of Defense under Secretary Rumsfeld had been in a state of something approaching undeclared war with Colin Powell's State Department, and the disaster that was the postwar occupation of Iraq was one of the casualties. Rumsfeld fought and won a battle over which department of the U.S. government would be responsible for postwar Iraq and then did very little to fulfill the task he had asked to be given. He selected retired Army Lieutenant General Jay Garner, who had been in charge of securing Kurdish areas of Iraq after Operation Desert Storm, to run the Office for Reconstruction and Humanitarian Assistance (ORHA) to secure Iraq after this invasion. However, he gave Garner only a few weeks to prepare ORHA for these responsibilities before the invasion began. (Planning for the postwar occupation of Germany and Japan began in 1942, three years before the end of the war.) Although ORHA failed horribly, it is hard to blame Garner for the disasters of the occupation, and he deserves credit for calling his team, composed largely of retirees, the "space cowboys," after the film of that name describing the rescue of Earth from a meteor by a team of similarly experienced renegades.

Garner was quickly replaced by former ambassador Paul Bremer, who arrived in May 2003 with instructions to head what was now called the Coalition Provisional Authority (CPA), still under the Pentagon's control. Bremer quickly promulgated orders to disband the Iraqi Army, outlaw local elections, and prevent any members of the Ba'ath Party, which had previously ruled Iraq, from holding positions of authority in the new government structure, throwing those in the top four Ba'ath Party levels out of their jobs and taking away their pensions and other benefits. These three decisions were disastrous, playing a huge role in incubating the chaos that erupted not long after Bremer's arrival.

Perhaps the most grievous was the decision to completely disband the Iraqi Army without telling its members how they would be looked after or what the plans were to construct a new army (other than seven infantry battalions, a total force of some 5,000 troops). In fact, at the time many American officers were working with Iraqi Army veterans to negotiate their help in maintaining security. There weren't nearly enough Americans to police the streets, and there certainly weren't enough Arabic translators to handle the degree of interaction with the population that would be required. Jeff Ingram, whose tanks had made it to Baghdad and who was now responsible for securing a sector of the city that far exceeded his grasp, was meeting daily with an Iraqi major general who told Jeff that he had an entire Iraqi division of some 10,000 troops standing by to provide security on the streets. All Jeff had to do was pay them. General Petraeus was also meeting with senior Iraqi officers in northern Iraq to try to garner their support for the new Iraq and had already run a caucus election to select an interim provincial council and governor in Sunni-dominated Nineveh Province.

An order came down from Bremer that the Iraqi Army would be disbanded. General Petraeus traveled to Baghdad to protest the decision when he heard of it, able to predict the results, but there was no chance of overturning this decision, made somewhere between the Pentagon office of Undersecretary of Defense for Policy Doug Feith and Ambassador Bremer. (Each blames the other in his memoirs.) When Jeff informed the Iraqi general of this decision, the astonished Iraqi general informed him, "This means that I will be fighting you tomorrow." Jeff acknowledged the possibility, then the two officers gravely saluted each other. Although his sector had been quiet to that point, attacks on Jeff's troops began the next morning.

The story was repeated on a broader scale everywhere in Iraq. An insurgency developed, composed largely of Sunnis, Saddam Hussein's favorites who had held most of the government positions in prewar Iraq despite being a minority of the Iraqi population. They were also a majority of the senior military, rendered unemployed by the CPA's decision. A large group of organized, angry men who knew how to use weapons that were literally lying loose in the unsecured ammunitions bunkers of what had fairly recently been the world's fourth-largest army now had no job and no prospects for one, and they took their anger out on the people they believed responsible for this disaster.

The three Pentagon mistakes—not providing enough American troops to secure all the conventional weapons that littered postwar Iraq, preventing the use of Iraqi troops to assist in that effort and secure the population, and putting all the people who knew where the weapons were and how to use them in a permanently subordinate and unemployed status—were a perfect recipe for an insurgency. Counterinsurgency literature suggests that the insurgent begins with nothing but a cause. If the Department of Defense had been trying to set the conditions for irregular war, it could hardly have done better than giving every Sunni in Iraq a reason to fight against the new regime and free access to the weapons required for that fight.

While we watched these events with interest from Fort Riley, 1-34 Armor was focused on another kind of war, and I was learning a new job as (finally!) the operations officer, or S3, of 1-34 Armor. The three was responsible for planning and tracking the execution of operations, leading a staff section that generally included a captain and a few lieutenants as well as a sergeant major, an operations sergeant, and a dozen or so soldiers. The S3 was the senior staff officer; staff captains were in charge of personnel (S1), intelligence (S2), logistics (S4), and maintenance (the battalion motor officer). Although I'd been offered the job of executive officer at the brigade level, I really wanted more time in a battalion and a tank of my own, and I was also attracted by the chance to continue to work closely with the Centurions' operations sergeant major, a crusty and very capable tanker named Sheldon Parks who knew how to swing a hammer. Sergeant Major Parks and his senior noncommissioned officer brothers and sisters across the Army are a national treasure with their decades of experience in making things happen. Sheldon called me "Little Brother" and became my best friend in the battalion.

Even as the insurgency caught fire in Iraq, we were preparing for a repeat of Operation Desert Storm—an NTC rotation against the

dreaded OPFOR, perhaps again augmented by the Nanooks who continued to haunt my dreams at that point. (They've since been replaced
by even more menacing opponents who punish my mistakes more permanently.) We were, in fact, conducting a simulated brigade meeting
engagement against another tank unit on NTC terrain in August 2003
when, just before 1-34 was committed to strike the fictional enemy
in the flank (what enemy in their right mind would attack U.S. tank
units in 2003?), the radio call of "ENDEX" (end of exercise) came
across the net.

This was highly unusual. It was early in our NTC train-up; our
units were being simulated in a computer; and only the battalion commander, Lieutenant Colonel Jeff Swisher, and I were aboard our actual
tanks. The exercise represented millions of dollars of training resources
that were being jerked to a halt just before the climax of the event. Battalion commanders were ordered to report to a classified briefing room
inside the simulation center. Jeff, a West Point graduate three years senior to me and a veteran of the NTC's opposing forces, a physically
small but incredibly tactically proficient armor officer, departed without saying much, as was his wont. Jeff was the very best of the Army
of the 1990s, intensely focused on conventional combat proficiency.

I was pretty sure I knew what was going on. We were going to be
sent to help pacify an Iraq that was beginning to blaze with insurgency.
When Jeff returned, he tersely confirmed that that was, in fact, the
case. Our brigade, some 3,000 soldiers organized into two tank battalions, a mechanized infantry battalion, an engineer battalion, an artillery battalion, and a support battalion, was being sent to reinforce Al
Anbar Province, Iraq's Wild West. Overwhelmingly Sunni, overwhelmingly angry at the turn of events that had Iraq's Shiite majority suddenly holding political power, and completely dedicated to overturning
this outcome, Anbar was the hottest part of Iraq both literally and fig-

uratively. Imagine America's Mountain West reacting to a French occupation of the United States. All of Al Anbar at this point, an area roughly the size of North Carolina, was currently occupied by the Third Armored Cavalry Regiment (ACR), a reinforced but nonetheless overstretched brigade-size unit that was already absorbing heavy casualties. The Third ACR would be replaced by elements of the 82nd Airborne Division, which was grumpy about being largely passed over for a role in the initial invasion of Iraq. A planned airborne operation to seize Baghdad Airport was canceled, and a single brigade of the 82nd followed the Third Infantry Division and the 101st Airborne Division on the road to Baghdad, a bitter pill for a unit used to being first. Our First Brigade of the First Infantry Division would provide the paratroopers with some heavy metal support.

But we would not be able to provide as much as we would have liked to give them. Still operating under Secretary of Defense Rumsfeld's order to cut deployments to the bone, the Pentagon was trying to present the lightest footprint possible, so that only one of our three tank companies would deploy with tanks. The other two would be Humvee-mounted "dragoons," and Jeff Swisher and I would leave our tanks at Fort Riley as well. Picking which of our three tank companies would deploy with all its heavy metal was pretty easy. Apache Company, led by Captain Ben Miller, was the best of the three, and Ben was a natural leader with easy competence and, it would turn out, enormous courage under fire. But Bandit and Cobra were not happy about the decision, and both would deeply miss their beloved tanks over the year to come.

Plans firmed up quickly. The rest of the brigade would station itself in Ramadi, provincial capital of Al Anbar and the seat of government, while 1-34 would be detached, an independent task force responsible for the troubled town of Khalidiyah, midway between

Ramadi and Fallujah, which would be occupied by a brigade of the 82nd Airborne Division. Khalidiyah was a very tough town of 30,000. All we could find out about it on the Internet was that it had been the location of an attack on the Third ACR units that were stretched thinly across Al Anbar, and that the Khalidiyah police chief had been killed by insurgents. The new police chief of Khalidiyah would become an important person in the lives of all of us, although he would not be the replacement chief who was serving there as we were deploying. That second chief would also be killed, horribly, his body left in the town square riddled with bullets on our first day in the town. Being a police chief in Al Anbar was not a good long-term career choice in 2003.

Having our battalion detached from the brigade had its advantages and disadvantages. The brigade commander clearly thought highly of Jeff in choosing him for this independent mission, and he gave Task Force 1-34 an engineer company, an artillery section with its own radar and two 155mm cannons, and a light infantry company that had been detached from the First Cavalry Division, the unit with which I'd fought in Desert Storm, to provide more soldiers for our mission. We also received some intelligence assets from the First Cav, a psychological operations team with the ability to print leaflets and broadcast messages to the Iraqi population in Arabic and, on and off, a special forces team. We were loaded for bear.

However, there were disadvantages to being detached from the brigade as well. Khalidiyah was a particularly violent town, even in a province that was full of tough towns. Starkly provincial, it resisted control from Ramadi even in the best of times, and these were not the best of times. We also had to handle all aspects of base camp operations, from manning guard posts to protect against enemy infiltration of our lines to conducting our own intelligence synthesis and analysis, with the limited assets of a battalion staff that would already be stretched. The experience would challenge all of us, but especially Jeff, who could bear enormous weight but was uncomfortable sharing the emotional stresses of command with anyone else. We were in for what would prove to be a very long year.

The situation wasn't helped by the fact that we were completely unprepared for the war we were about to fight. Our soldiers were tankers, trained and equipped to close with and destroy other enemy armored units. We had to learn to wage war against an insurgency rather than against the enemy tank units we had been designed to confront in open warfare. We had had no training in developing an intelligence portfolio on individual insurgents, conducting security patrols to derive local intelligence, developing local governing councils, training and equipping local police forces, conducting raids to capture or kill high-value targets . . . the list could go on for days.

Marty Leners, now the brigade operations officer, and his assistant Captain Nick Ayers developed a hasty counterinsurgency lane training event that confronted our platoon leaders with many of the challenges we expected they would face on the ground west of Baghdad. (Nick, captain of the West Point debate team as a cadet, would himself return to West Point as a Sosh p a few years later.) We rotated our tank platoons through the training lanes on the few scout Humvees we had available, to give them a taste of the bitter fruit they would be eating—but there was no time available for higher-level staff training on the defeat of an insurgency, and no one to conduct it even if there had been time available. The Army hadn't updated its counterinsurgency field manual since the Vietnam War, and I had had no official Army training on counterinsurgency during my four years at West Point and twelve years in the active Army. My Oxford studies had been academic, in every sense of that word; I knew what we would have to do in theory but had never done it in practice, not even in an exercise. Neither had anyone else in the unit. We would have to learn as we went, making many mistakes along the way.

Although the S3 is responsible for maneuvers within a unit's area of operations, getting the tanks and trucks to the fight is the job of the executive officer, a job I had gratefully turned over to Dave Indermuehle, a big armor officer who was completely imperturbable. Dave honchoed the process of loading our equipment onto railroad cars for the trip to the port of Houston, where they would be driven aboard ships for the transatlantic voyage. Our vehicles now included fourteen up-armored Humvees, given to us as a replacement for Cobra Company's tanks, and fourteen slick Humvees without armor, serving in place of Bandit's tanks.

The Army didn't have enough up-armored Humvees to go around, the legacy of a long-standing internal fight within the Army's Armor force, which believed strongly that only tracked vehicles, like tanks and Bradley fighting vehicles, should be armored. The few armored Humvees the Army did have had been acquired by the military police branch. They were not really designed as fighting vehicles; although a .50 machine gun or a Mark 19 automatic grenade launcher was mounted on top of the truck, it could be fired only by almost completely exposing the gunner to hostile fire. The vehicles themselves were also not ideal for the kind of fight we were joining, as they had flat bottoms that absorbed the impact of explosions underneath the vehicle rather than V-shaped hulls that would direct shock waves around it.

It would take many long years before these shortcomings were remedied—and it took explicit direction from Secretary of Defense Gates to get the services to do what should have been done much earlier. Eventually the Army would procure the right vehicles for the war we were fighting, rather than the war we had planned to fight, but in the meantime we were forced to rely on homemade hillbilly armor welded onto many of the trucks, including mine, Jeff's, and Dave's, and stand in line for bolt-on factory-built armor packages. The command group received theirs last, in August 2004, after eleven months of operating in Al Anbar without any armor save the makeshift systems our welder had managed to fabricate from scrap metal, with sandbags on the floor to absorb some of the impact of mine strikes or improvised explosive device (IED) detonations. It was something you tried not to think about when rolling out on a mission.

We hadn't even had time to install hillbilly armor on our three before our vehicles were due to be tied down on the trains to the port. Tankers are good at loading their vehicles aboard railcars, even though (and perhaps precisely because) the tank treads actually hang off either side of the railcar because the tank is so wide. Loading Humvees, by comparison, is a piece of cake, and almost before we knew it, we were saying good-bye to our families and getting on airplanes out of Topeka.

Good-byes are hard. Jack, of course, at not quite age two, didn't know what was happening, but it was difficult to say good-bye to Susi. We hadn't been married during Desert Storm even though I'd renewed my standing marriage proposal before she'd left cricket-infested Fort Hood, hoping that a potential life insurance payout would sweeten the deal; to her credit, she'd been offended by the suggestion. Like that deployment, this one was for an indeterminate period of time; unlike the last one, this time I would look forward to Susi's e-mails rather than her letters. E-mails at least arrived in good order and in the right order, although they didn't allow her to make the little sketches with which she'd illustrated her letters in the last war we'd done together. We would also get weekly phone calls this time, which were a godsend.

The tankers of the Centurions landed in Kuwait a few days before the ship carrying our equipment arrived—the Army is really, really good at moving big things around the globe—and spent the time getting acclimated to the heat and the time zone. Getting the stuff off the boat was still XO business, so Dave handled that while I worked with Marty Leners to plan the convoys that would take us across the Kuwaiti border into Iraq (again, in the case of Jeff and me and a number of our senior noncommissioned officers, including Sheldon Parks, who wore the combat patches of Desert Storm divisions on our right shoulders). The mess hall had novelty chocolate-dipped ice cream cones that I found irresistible, and some of the guys ended up calling my convoy the Ice Cream Cone Convoy after I gave them firm instructions to eat their ice cream cones while they were still available in Kuwait, as I correctly guessed that they would be harder to come by once we arrived in Iraq.

The Ice Cream Cone Convoy was a bear, with dozens of vehicles and two overnight stops along the way before we finally came over a hill and saw Khalidiyah for the first time. After several days on a road that had eventually become little more than a dirt path, it literally looked like an oasis. The town was built along the Euphrates River, with lush palm trees and elephant grass along the banks and with irrigation ditches bringing water to the desert. It may have had 30,000 souls, with another 30,000 scattered across the farmlands between Ramadi, the provincial capital, to the west and Fallujah to the east.

We would set up camp in a former British Royal Air Force base named Habbaniyah just to the east of Khalidiyah. The palm-tree-lined avenues, roundabouts, and even a theater and an outdoor movie screen provided a great picture of what the British occupation of Iraq must have looked like in the 1930s. The hedgerows of oleanders planted by our predecessors remained to shield the avenues of our base camp like British briars. (*Habbaniyah* means "oleander" in Arabic.)

Habbaniyah's airfield, now in disrepair like the rest of the post, had been designed for propeller planes and could not handle jet aircraft, so the Iraqi Air Force had built a larger air base on a hill south of the post that they called Taqquadam Airfield, or TQ. It had been one of the most important Iraqi Air Force bases before the war and became a major U.S. logistics and air base for all of Al Anbar province. TQ featured MiG fighters that the Iraqis had buried in sand so that they wouldn't be targeted by U.S. planes. Of course, they also would never fly again because of the sand in the electronics and hydraulics. Between TQ and Habbaniyah was a huge ammunition dump with dozens and dozens of bunkers full of weaponry, all unguarded and free for the taking—an insurgent's Walmart with no check-out lanes.

As interesting as Camp Habbaniyah was from an archaeological standpoint, we didn't have a lot of time to admire the oleanders. It had been occupied by an engineer company and a tank company from the Third Armored Cavalry Regiment, which was stretched across all of Al Anbar as a result of the low troop numbers Secretary Rumsfeld had insisted upon while planning the initial invasion. The area was a security vacuum due to the lack of forces, a refuge for what we were then calling "former regime loyalists" (the word *insurgent* was forbidden in official traffic) and foreign fighters. The local economy had catered to the Habbaniyah and TQ airfields, and the surrounding communities had a large population of military and ex-military personnel. The cities also sit along the major roads from Jordan and Syria into Baghdad and had been known for smuggling activities for more than one hundred years. Lots of weapons, lots of former military personnel, and an entire Sunni population known for lawlessness and furious about yielding power to Iraq's Shia majority—welcome to Al Anbar!

The guys from Third ACR were ready to hand over this mess as quickly as possible. Having been shot up repeatedly in Khalidiyah, they essentially didn't go there anymore but did sporadically patrol the ammo dump. There were too few of them and too much of Iraq, with too many insurgents to go around. We brought a lieutenant colonel, two majors, and two sergeants major to the initial brief by Chris Kennedy, the Third ACR major in charge of the *ad hoc* miniature battalion. His bosses were in other parts of Anbar conducting similar hand-offs as the U.S. Army adapted to the fact that it needed more forces in Iraq than it had originally planned. The insurgents may have heard about the briefing schedule, but more likely they were just thrilled to have many more targets to shoot at, as they mortared the initial transition brief Chris provided to us. Welcome to Habbaniyah!

After a couple of days on the ground conducting "right seat rides" with the Third ACR troops to learn as much as we could about our area of operations while they were still sitting next to us and close enough to ask questions, we took responsibility for the sector on September 25, 2003. Our initial notification that we were going to deploy to Iraq during the middle of a simulated tank fight had come exactly two months earlier, on July 25. It's hard to imagine shifting direction more rapidly than we had, moving faster or farther, or being much more poorly prepared for the intensive counterinsurgency fight that was waiting for us.

We immediately began patrolling to get to know the area for which we were responsible. It was huge—thirty-five kilometers north to south and fifty kilometers east to west. The Euphrates River was in the middle of the sector, with only one bridge that would support armored vehicles and another pontoon bridge that could take Humvees in a pinch. The enemy quickly demonstrated that he was willing to fight us for freedom of maneuver, and almost every patrol received enemy contact. One of our First Cavalry Division mech infantry lieutenants was a bullet magnet, getting scratches from RPG fragments or bullets pretty much daily. We stopped putting him in for Purple Hearts after a couple of hits, as it wasn't worth the paperwork and he, amazingly, never got badly hurt. We told him that he'd have to bleed a lot more than he had to that point to get another medal, remembering the two-stitch rule that had kept Jeff Ingram from getting one in the initial invasion.

Unfortunately, other guys were getting hurt a lot worse. Our first casualty in sector came on September 29, when a soldier from the Brigade Reconnaissance Troop, Staff Sergeant Christopher Cutchall, was killed in an IED attack in our sector. Delta Troop of the Fourth Cavalry Regiment was a Humvee-mounted brigade unit riding in vehicles with flat bottoms that absorbed the full impact of explosions. The IED was perfectly buried under the road, three daisy-chained 152mm rounds wired together and command detonated via a wire link. The IED initiated an ambush that then included someone firing a rocket-propelled grenade, or RPG, at the Humvees. I happened to be sharing a ride around the big unguarded Taquaddum Airfield ammunition dump with Captain Ben Miller on his tank at the time of the attack, and we drove to the scene, Ben in the loader's hatch. A long firefight with insurgents ensued that made the front page of *The New York Times* the next morning. It almost included killing the members of a television crew who were filming from the roof of a building—from a distance, a television camera can look an awful lot like a shoulder-fired RPG. The nonevent was a chilling lesson in how this battlefield would differ from the one I remembered in Desert Storm, which had been essentially free of civilians. In this fight, they were everywhere.

As were IEDs. I'd had my first up-close and personal interaction with one the previous day, when the task force was conducting Operation Netscape, designed to saturate the sector with all available forces and challenge the insurgents for control of the countryside. I pulled into a position in my Humvee, not yet equipped with even hillbilly armor, and saw a telltale wire next to the road. I cut it with my Leatherman, a pocket tool beloved of tankers, then followed the wire trail to a 152mm artillery shell partially buried beside the road. We didn't have an explosive ordnance detachment (EOD) team assigned to the task force, so I had one of Ben's tanks detonate the round with a burst from a coaxial machine gun. Unlike the weapons aboard Humvees or even Bradley fighting vehicles, the coaxial machine gun on an M1 is stabilized with gyroscopes and aimed with assistance from a laser rangefinder, making it a very accurate weapon. The fact that the machine gun and crew firing it are protected behind heavy armor is also a plus. Machine guns would become our default method of detonating surface-laid IEDs during the many times we found them without EOD teams in the neighborhood—another technique we hadn't been taught back home. We were making it up as we went along, largely on our own.

We also got better at counterbattery fires, targeting the mad mortarman who occasionally dropped mortar rounds on Camp Habbaniyah as he had during our turnover brief with the Third ACR, generally with little effect. It was a big post and we were spread out pretty widely, and his firing technique was not the best. We worked to further disrupt his aim by regularly firing 155mm artillery shells back at him, when he chose not to fire from positions in close proximity to civilian Iraqi homes. We followed each counterbattery fire with a visit to the firing location, and on one occasion were able to learn from civilians in the neighborhood the identity and home of the mortarman. We visited, finding a weapons cache in the house and the mortarman at home, and sent him off to detention, first at Camp Ramadi, where the brigade was based, and eventually on to the bigger prison at Abu Ghraib. Life was a little better when the mad mortarman was gone, although his ecological niche was later filled by a rocket man we never could catch. He fired from farther away, using rockets with a longer range and from behind the cover provided by the Euphrates River. Although we never took significant casualties from indirect fire on Camp Habbaniyah, our brigade counterparts in Ramadi were more closely packed together and less fortunate. A number were killed by rocket and mortar fire over the course of the year.

The capture of the mad mortarman illustrated a classic principle of counterinsurgency that I recognized from my studies of the subject: to defeat an insurgency, the counterinsurgent must be able to identify the enemy. As any beat cop in a tough neighborhood in Washington, D.C., will tell you, that's tough to do. Even the people who don't support the insurgency are likely to be more afraid of reprisals for "snitching" to the authorities than they are of the effects of insurgent-initiated violence in their neighborhood. Police use saturation patrolling and anonymous tip lines to gather the information they need to get the gang leaders off the streets, but even when they speak the same language as the enemy, the process takes a long time and a lot of work—and the gangs rarely target the police directly, knowing how much hell that would bring down on their heads. How much more difficult, then, to gather the intelligence when the authorities speak a different language and are unfamiliar with local customs and patterns of life, and when the insurgents intentionally target the counterinsurgents—often with the active support of the local people, as was the case in Al Anbar in 2003, still simmering over hatred of the Shia regime that was in the process of being installed in Baghdad.

Counterinsurgency theory suggests that to overcome these challenges, the key is the creation of local forces that have the support of the population—local army and police forces. This eminently sensible plan of action had been supported by Colonel Jeff Ingram, who had been working to put together just such a local security force from a former Iraqi Army unit in his sector of Baghdad when Ambassador Paul Bremer issued the instruction that disbanded the Iraqi Army forever. Understanding the strategic implications of the disastrous decision, General Petraeus had raised concerns to Bremer to try to get him to overturn the ruling, but to no avail, until some five weeks after the army was disbanded, when he told Bremer's key assistant in Baghdad that "CPA's policies are killing our troopers."

Bremer had not, however, banned the creation of Iraqi police units, and there were skeleton police organizations throughout much of Iraq, including in Khalidiyah. Predictably, they became a prime target for insurgents. The Khalidiyah police chief at the time of the invasion in March 2003 had been killed not long afterward, and his replacement was also killed just as Task Force 1-34 was taking over sector from the Third ACR, his bullet-riddled body left in the town square next to the police station. It took a brave man to openly serve as a policeman in Khalidiyah in the fall of 2003, but all the counterinsurgency literature I'd read focused on the importance of police as the closest force to the population, the key to gathering intelligence on insurgent identities and locations and protecting the people from insurgent reprisals.

So it was very early on in our tenure that I gave Ben Miller the task to visit the police station and conduct a joint patrol with the Iraqi Police. Just before staff call that evening, Ben walked up to me wearing his fireproof Nomex tanker's garb, bathed in sweat, and reported, "Sir, I failed."

"Excuse me, Ben?"

"Sir, you told me to go on a joint patrol with the Iraqi Police. We tried, but the clowns were too fast for us. We couldn't catch them."

I had clearly sent a boy to do a man's job. I told Ben that I would join him for a joint patrol with our local police the next day; after eight years of reading the books, I was ready to perform the basic counterinsurgency task of establishing a good relationship with the local security force. How hard could it be?

Pretty hard, as it turned out. In fact, this would become a theme. All the things I'd read about that were required to succeed in counterinsurgency were a lot harder than they'd seemed in the books, including the one I'd written. In this case, as soon as we pulled up next to the police station, the police started to skedaddle in all directions, exactly like—there's no way to avoid the simile—cockroaches when you flip the light on in the middle of the night. But Ben Miller, no fool despite the grief I'd given him for being one the night before at staff call, was ready for them. He'd told two of his fastest soldiers to strip off their body armor and, carrying only their rifles, pin down a couple of the Iraqi Police, or IPs. They succeeded, and Ben led me to a dingy corner of the police station, where the two oldest IPs on the planet, freshly awakened from their midafternoon nap, were clearly less than thrilled about the rare opportunity to go on patrol with U.S. forces. A dialogue ensued, conducted via interpreter.

"Good afternoon. I'm Major Nagl, the operations officer of Task Force 1-34 Armor, responsible for security in this sector. We'd like you to go on patrol with us today and teach us something about Khalidiyah."

I didn't really need the translator to understand their response. Clearly, it was impossible for them to go on patrol with us. Their feet hurt, they needed permission from their boss, who was sadly unavailable at present (having run away faster than they had been able to), this was all highly unusual, their weapons weren't clean . . .

"I'm sorry, guys, you're coming."

"No."

I was starting to get angry. This was their town, and conducting patrols of it was clearly police business. I picked up an AK-47 that was leaning in the corner and pressed it into the hands of the slightly less ancient policeman. "You're going."

"No."

My M4 was suddenly pointed at his chest. "You're going, buddy." There had been nothing about this in any of the books I'd read at Oxford, but adrenaline took over, and the two IPs ended up walking along with us at gunpoint every step of the way through a town that was clearly curious to see so many Americans on their streets in the company of two visibly frightened Iraqi cops. It wasn't until that night, as I tried to understand what had happened, that I finally figured out what the IPs had been so scared of. After our joint foot patrol, we continued to patrol the main drag of Khalidiyah with tanks and Bradleys, but the back streets were again insurgent territory. We'd controlled the streets as long as we stood on them, but after we left, it was as if we'd never been there. It was like pulling your hand out of a bucket of water and hoping that you'd made a lasting impression. The insurgents owned the night, and there was every chance that the IPs who'd been frog-marched in front of our patrol were going to be visited by the insurgents after dark. Our rifles in their backs were a life insurance policy for those guys. They could tell the masked insurgents who would appear in their concrete-block homes later that night that they were cooperating with the Americans only because we'd promised to kill them if they didn't.

In fact, despite all our tanks and artillery and helicopters, the insur-

Visiting a police station on the bridge over the Euphrates in 2004.

gents had an advantage: the people were far more scared of them than they were of us, and for good reason. We wouldn't kill them, certainly not on purpose, but the insurgents would, and regularly did, often slowly, and sometimes in front of their families. It was a challenge understood by everyone who had faced guerrilla enemies at least since Napoleon's opponents coined the word for "little war" two hundred years earlier: the counterinsurgent has to defend everywhere, all the time, while the insurgent can choose his target and his time, always slipping away to fight another day if the conditions aren't exactly right. And because the counterinsurgent is a visitor, working against the clock of declining local and domestic willingness to put up with the costs of the campaign, time is his enemy. An old counterinsurgency aphorism teaches that the insurgent is winning if he isn't losing, but the counterinsurgent is losing if he isn't winning, and this was another bitter lesson that was starting to make a lot more sense than it had when I'd first read it in the hallowed halls of Oxford's Codrington Library.

The strategic offensive for the counterinsurgent is building local security forces like the IPs who in time will take over most of the responsibility for security themselves, but the tactical offensive is conducting targeted kill/capture missions against identified insurgents. And the strategic offensive (building local forces) isn't possible until sufficient progress has been made in the tactical offensive (improving security by going after the insurgents). Counterinsurgents used to practice a different technique. When the Romans confronted a rebellious province, they would first build a road to it, then methodically slaughter the men and boys in sector, sell the women and children into slavery, and salt the fields so that nothing would grow. It was an effective counterinsurgency technique—the Romans rarely had to pacify a given province more than once in a century, and pacifying one province in this manner had a significant demonstration effect on the neighboring ones; but

this technique was obviously not a viable option in an era ruled by
CNN and the Geneva Convention. The Romans bypassed the requirement for gaining intelligence on specific insurgents by assuming everyone was an insurgent. We, on the other hand, worked hard to target
the specific insurgent fish swimming in the sea of the people.

Intelligence came in a number of ways—from local sources who
walked up to the front gate, from people whose homes we visited in
the company of an interpreter, and increasingly over time, from a
police force that grew more confident that we were staying around to
push back against the insurgent control of Khalidiyah and the surrounding villages. We were not permitted to use our Commander's
Emergency Response Program (CERP) monies to pay for information;
that funding was intended to be put to use cleaning streets and otherwise providing employment for the Iraqi population. I always kept a
napkin in my pocket in case someone was willing to provide information; if I dropped it and they picked it up, they could be paid for trash
removal. Regulations are supposed to help win the war, not keep you
from winning it.

However legally or illegally information was obtained, correlating
the products of these disparate sources was enormously difficult, and it
was all but impossible to determine which sources were pursuing their
own agenda, perhaps because of a land dispute or family feud, and
which were genuine. It was also hard, even when we believed we knew
the name of the individual who was planting IEDs along the main road
in Khalidiyah, to figure out where he lived. Houses didn't have numbers, and even well-intentioned Iraqi people struggled to understand
the photographic maps we used in an attempt to pick the insurgent's
home.

This led to some significant frustration. After many days of work
correlating intelligence sources and attempting to identify the right
house, we'd pull together a raid, almost always early in the morning.

Preraid preparations had the aspect of preparing for playing in a football game, working out plays, rehearsing contingencies, then finally suiting up in helmet and pads to conduct a strike that was rarely met with violence but just as rarely turned out to be the right house. More than once the rudely awakened man of the house led us down the street himself a few doors to point out the one that belonged to the person we were looking for. Of course, by this point, with tanks idling on the street and long minutes having elapsed, our target was long gone. The good news was that we now did know where he lived, we hoped, and could return to visit later—but insurgents rarely returned for months to a house they knew we were keeping an eye on, if they ever did.

When we did succeed in a raid, we'd bring the detainees back to Habbaniyah for interrogations conducted by our First Cavalry Division intelligence detachment. Our best asset in this part of the fight was John McCary, a young specialist with very good Arabic skills. A musician and linguist, he'd majored in French at Vassar but then enlisted in the Army after September 11 and volunteered for Arabic training at the Defense Language Institute in Monterey, California. His instructor there nicknamed McCary "the Sponge" for his incredible absorptive capacity, and John put those skills to good use, helping us understand the local power structure, relationships among the local people, and the shape of the insurgent networks we were fighting. McCary and I spent significant time together as I worked to draw out what he'd learned and let him know what gaps we were trying to fill in our intelligence picture of the battlefield.

John's Arabic continued to improve in no small part because of the relationship he developed with our best interpreter, a Jordanian American named Frank Nasrawi. Frank ran a liquor store in Houston before the invasion of Iraq but volunteered for service as a cleared interpreter—one with a security clearance, like McCary, but in Frank's

John McCary (center) with another counterintelligence officer in Iraq.

case with the enormous advantage of being a native Arabic speaker. Frank, known as "Abu Edward" (the father of Edward), gave me my nickname of "Abu Jack" and was easily able to determine when an Iraqi was lying and when he was telling the truth, who knew more than they were saying, and whom we could trust. He could and often did take over negotiations with local Iraqi politicians or IP leaders, a trait I bemusedly permitted but that on at least one occasion perturbed Jeff Swisher mightily, leading to words that I would not have used with a strategic asset like Frank. He was in many ways the face of the task force to the people who mattered in Khalidiyah, and he became an enormously popular interlocutor from whom I learned a great deal. I took great pride when locals began publicly calling me Abu Jack—at Abu Edward's instigation, no doubt, but still a worthwhile step in humanizing our occupation in my eyes.

It was a complicated war, infinitely more difficult than Desert Storm had been, when we simply shot the tanks and troops who weren't wearing the same uniforms that we were wearing. Now we struggled mightily to find our enemy, who killed us from the shadows even as we struggled to build political and military entities that could earn the trust and support of the Iraqi people. As part of this effort, we tried to encourage economic development and the provision of social services through the allocation of Commander's Emergency Response Program (CERP) funds for rebuilding schools and medical clinics. Integrating and prioritizing all these tasks was far and away the most difficult thing I'd ever done, leading me to conclude that while Desert Storm had provided an undergraduate education in warfare, this was graduate school, and I was failing.

We also waged an information operations campaign to attempt to persuade the people to side with us against the insurgents, even though the insurgents could slip into their homes and kill them and the worst we would do was take them away for weeks or months of detention. This was just another verse of the perpetual song that gives the more ruthless insurgents many advantages against a force that supports the rule of law. This imbalance is most pronounced early in a counterinsurgency campaign, before the occupying force has built many local forces, learned the intricacies of local language, culture, and power structures, and adapted its organization, training, and equipment for the demands of the fight it faces, which is only rarely the fight it was preparing for when the call came. We were a classic case of this story, paralleling the British Army in Malaya and the U.S. Army in Vietnam. All of us had much to learn about a kind of war that was as new to them as it was to Task Force 1-34 Armor when we received notice to deploy to a war that was completely unlike the one we were ready to fight and win.

Unfortunately, when an army is unprepared to fight a war, much of the price of learning is paid by young soldiers and officers. In our task force, the platoon leaders paid a disproportionately high price. I had been taught at West Point that lieutenants, who lead patrols from the front, had suffered the heaviest losses in Vietnam, and it was mostly lieutenants and young soldiers that we lost in Al Anbar as well.

Early on, it was the lieutenants of Cobra Company who paid in blood. Their tanks had been replaced with up-armored Humvees, so Cobra was given missions across the Euphrates River, a task that required crossing one of two bridges in sector—almost always the German-constructed reinforced-concrete bridge in the center of town. One way in, one way out, all easily watched by hundreds of pairs of eyes from dozens upon dozens of vantage points. It was Lieutenant Matt Homa who paid the price first, a Cobra platoon leader who just missed being killed by an IED that tore open his chest but missed his heart by an inch. We were extremely fortunate that our battalion surgeon happened to be an honest-to-God open-heart cutter who knew exactly what to do to stabilize Matt and keep him alive.

We weren't as lucky the next time. Todd Bryant was an irrepressible member of the West Point Class of 2002, the class that had heard President George W. Bush telegraph the invasion of Iraq at its graduation ceremony in Michie Stadium with the words "You came to West Point in a time of peace, but you graduate in a time of war." I had liked Todd immediately upon his arrival at the battalion, and one Friday night at Fort Riley, while I was still serving as the battalion executive officer and he had been tagged as staff duty officer for the weekend, I gave him an unusual mission. I had just returned from a route reconnaissance examining the highway from Fort Riley to Topeka's airfield, from which we were on call to be prepared to fly out tanks in case of a post–September 11 emergency. (Yes, you can fly tanks on Air Force C-5 cargo planes, but only one at a time.) I'd been struck on my recon by the number of drinking establishments along the route from Riley to

Topeka, and I was now struck by Todd's downcast demeanor; responding to my inquiry, he told me that he was missing Jen, his new bride,
who was away for a few weeks. Inspired, I saw a chance to kill two
birds with one stone.

"Todd, I have a dangerous and important mission for you. I need
you to personally conduct a route reconnaissance between here and
the Topeka airfield, with particular attention to establishments that
may dispense alcohol and serve as tempting emergency rest stop locations for troops traveling the route. I want your assessment of which
establishments represent the most serious threat to the morals and dis-
cipline of the units of this task force. This is a dangerous mission; you
will be accompanied by a wingman at all times when conducting this
reconnaissance. Do you accept this mission, understanding the risks
involved?"

Todd brightened immediately, drawing himself up to attention and
rendering a crisp salute. "Sir, I will perform this mission to the best of
my ability, knowing full well the dangers that confront me."

"Roger, lieutenant. Execute." It was about a week later that Todd
and Matt Homa reported to my office with a PowerPoint presentation
that far exceeded my expectations, rating each establishment along the
route (I seem to recall more than a dozen) that might present a moral
hazard to task force troops. The presentation was lost during the deployment, fighting, and redeployment, but the criteria Todd and Matt
chose by which to rank the relative advantages and dangers of each
establishment were very inventive, truly a credit to the long history of
the U.S. Cavalry. Although I didn't know it at the time, the task became
semilegendary among the lieutenants of the battalion, several others
of whom conducted their own research to test Todd and Matt's data
and conclusions in what was likely a significant boost to the register
receipts of some of the entertainment institutions I'd noticed along the
road to Topeka.

Todd was killed early on the morning of October 31, 2003, the first member of his West Point class to fall in combat: an IED detonated directly under his seat while he was conducting a patrol along the northern side of the Euphrates River. His loss was jarring to the whole unit and to all those who loved him, including me. Todd had been a very popular officer who came to the Task Force Tactical Operations Center just to seek me out for political discussions. A Reagan Republican, he was a strong defender of the George W. Bush administration, which made for stimulating arguments.

Bill Murphy, Jr., later wrote a wonderful book about Todd and some of his classmates, titled *In a Time of War,* which featured Todd as the main character. Reading the book years later, I found it hard to believe that Todd was killed less than halfway through the book, even though I'd heard the explosion that killed him. Many scholars of British literature speculate that William Shakespeare killed Mercutio off early in *Romeo and Juliet* because Mercutio was far more interesting than the drip Romeo and was taking over the story. In many ways, Todd was our battalion's Mercutio, quick with a sword and a quip, young and strong and full of promise. His loss was hard for us, for his family, and for his young widow as well, but it would not be our last.

An important part of any counterinsurgency fight—arguably the most important—is conducting information operations in support of the friendly government and against the insurgents, directed at audiences both in country and back home. Although Jeff Swisher had handled the press during the fight in which Staff Sergeant Cutchall was killed, after that appearance he generally delegated working with the U.S. press to me. I became used to the routine of spending an hour talking with American reporters at our front gate, earning lots of props from my friends for using the word *nefarious* in one interview to describe the enemy we were fighting. I thought little, then, of the request in December from brigade to talk with Peter Maass of *The New*

York Times Magazine until Maass showed up not only with a photographer but also with a sleeping bag and a backpack. I told him that he traveled pretty heavy for a one-hour interview, and Peter replied that he was planning to spend a few weeks with us. That required a call to brigade for instructions. They confirmed that *The New York Times* would be embedding in our unit, and shadowing me, for some time to come.

Peter had discovered *Counterinsurgency Lessons from Malaya and Vietnam,* still languishing on the Amazon.com rankings at around a million, and thought it would be interesting to talk with the author, especially when he discovered that the author was currently deployed in Al Anbar fighting his first counterinsurgency campaign. To Peter's greeting that it was an honor to meet an expert on counterinsurgency, I replied that I thought I'd known something about COIN until I started trying to do it myself.

Peter was with the task force for an interesting few weeks, including the Sunday morning when Saddam Hussein was captured by the Fourth Infantry Division. Important as that day was for soldiers throughout Iraq, for Task Force 1-34, that Sunday was the day Al Qaeda in Iraq car-bombed the police station downtown. The bomb killed thirty-four policemen during the morning shift change and two little girls who were innocent bystanders. After the debacle of our joint patrol at the point of my M4, the IPs had gradually begun working with us more freely, happily going on joint patrols without the encouragement of an M4 barrel in their back and occasionally even providing useful information. Although the evidence of a car bombing was incontrovertible—the car bomb's engine block was thrown fifty feet inside the police station—the angry crowd that quickly gathered at the site of the attack became convinced that the explosion was the result of an American attack helicopter that had coincidentally overflown the area at about the time of the attack.

Iraqis bury their dead quickly, given the country's heat and lack of electricity for refrigeration and the Muslim instruction to return the fallen to the earth within twenty-four hours, and the funeral procession that afternoon at the graveyard next to the police station quickly turned into a near-riot. I was still conducting postincident cleanup at the police station, taking pictures and quite literally picking up pieces of Iraqi policemen, when Ben Miller suggested that it might be a good time to go someplace safer. With our route back to Camp Habbaniyah blocked by the crowd, I retreated to Forward Operating Base Killeen, a site we'd set up to have a permanent presence downtown with oversight of the bridge and some views across the river to the spot where Todd had been killed. The platoon manning Killeen let us in and then drew concertina wire back across the gate, separating the Americans from the angry crowd of Iraqis who glared at us but eventually spilled away. It was something of a metaphor for the American occupation—two groups of people who wanted the same thing, the Americans to leave and the Iraqis to take over their own country, but who were separated by a cultural chasm that couldn't be bridged at that time.

We'd suspected an Al Qaeda in Iraq (AQI) presence in our sector for a long time, but the car bomb attack was incontrovertible evidence that someone far more capable than the local Sunni insurgents was fighting against us. The local insurgents topped out at the technological limit of burying South African 152mm artillery rounds under the roads and had no capability to train or employ suicide car bombers. The police station bombing targeted a strategic objective and was designed to drive a wedge between us and the Iraqi Police, whose growing cooperation promised to make it harder and perhaps impossible for AQI to operate in our sector. Worse, there would be more AQI attacks coming, like this one, likely filmed for their propaganda value. A filmed attack could be used to recruit more suicide bombers not just in Iraq but throughout the Middle East. Welcome to the war against AQI.

Peter Maass got a good picture of the confusion inherent in a counterinsurgency campaign. I took him along when I attended a memorial service for one of our soldiers, held in Ramadi the day after the car bomb on the police station and the capture of Saddam Hussein. On the trip from Ramadi back to Habbaniyah, we ran into an angry crowd of Iraqis, the largest I had ever seen, protesting Saddam's capture. Jeff Swisher's Humvee got hung up on the median as we attempted to maneuver around the disturbance, and we were not in a good place. I asked Peter if he had seen the movie *Black Hawk Down*, in which a small group of Americans gets ambushed by a crowd in Somalia. Jeff's driver managed to free the Humvee, and we made it back to base camp safely, although the trail .50 gunner in our convoy opened up on the way out of the area when he saw an Iraqi aim an AK-47 in our direction.

Peter's editors in New York must have liked the story, because in early January *The New York Times* got back in touch requesting a photo shoot. They sent a photographer out to Habbaniyah from Baghdad expressly to get a shot of me—a ridiculous risk/reward calculation in my eyes—and I paid for the decision. Jeff just shook his head when he saw me posing in front of my Humvee, but Ben Miller walked by singing "I Feel Pretty." The shot they ended up using on the cover of the magazine had me in front of a map of sector, with my face half in shadow. Peter titled his article "Professor Nagl's War." The reaction from my friends was immediate and powerful—if it was my war, I needed to turn this thing around, and fast. I also caught some flak for referring to the Iraqi people as "clowns" for their limited map-reading skills, a phrase I had adopted from Ben Miller that occasioned some debate in the pages of the *Times*.

One of Peter's turns of phrase was, I thought, particularly apt. Describing my transition from student of counterinsurgency to practitioner, Peter compared me to a paleontologist who suddenly had the chance to observe live dinosaurs. "But Nagl can't simply stand around and take notes. He is responsible, with the rest of his battalion, for taming an insurgency, which is as difficult as teaching dinosaurs to dance."[2]

The *New York Times Magazine* piece would attract a great deal of attention, including more journalists who stopped by Khalidiyah for visits over the course of 2004. One of the most interesting was Greg Jaffe of *The Wall Street Journal,* who, like Peter Maass, came to stay for an extended visit. I encouraged him to write a profile of John McCary, in an effort to draw attention to the pressing national need for more Arabic speakers. They remained my most closely guarded resource throughout our deployment, and for the next several years, I would continue to emphasize the importance of the Pentagon doing a better job providing talented, trustworthy interpreters.

It was at around this time that I received an e-mail from Newt Gingrich, who had read *Counterinsurgency Lessons from Malaya and Vietnam* at the suggestion of H. R. McMaster, a remarkable Army officer whose heroism at the Battle of 73 Easting in Desert Storm had been followed by the publication of his doctoral thesis on Vietnam. *Dereliction of Duty: Lyndon Johnson, Robert McNamara, the Joint Chiefs of Staff, and the Lies That Led to Vietnam* was a scathing indictment of the senior leadership of the U.S. military during Vietnam. H. R. had testified before Congress and gotten to know then-Speaker Gingrich, who had a longstanding interest in things military and asked H. R. what he should read about counterinsurgency. After taking H. R.'s reading suggestion, Speaker Gingrich sent a note in ALL CAPITAL LETTERS, telling me that it was a matter of national security that my book be published in paperback, an option that Praeger did not then provide, and asking for my permission to make that happen. Focused on other things, and a bit overwhelmed by attention from a former Speaker of the House, I quickly provided my assent and thanks and returned to the war.

In addition to Forward Operating Base Killeen on the south side of the Euphrates, the base camp to which I had retreated after the car bombing of the police station, we had established a position directly under the bridge on the north side of the river. It was manned by Blackhawk, our Humvee-mounted infantry company from the First Cavalry Division. Between Killeen and the Blackhawk position under the bridge, we were guaranteed protected access to the area of operations north of the Euphrates, where we were convinced AQI had established a base camp of its own. Todd Bryant had been killed because we did not control the bridge and the routes immediately around it, but Killeen and FOB Blackhawk allowed us to fight for that terrain. Our defensive positions and the freedom of maneuver they gave us guaranteed continued attention to both locations from the enemy.

One night I received word that we had intercepted conversations about an attack on a bridge. I radioed out to Blackhawk, telling them that we had information that they might be facing an attack, and I ordered them to disperse their forces and increase their readiness. The intelligence was good. The next morning at sunrise a water truck came barreling through the access-control point under the bridge at speed. An alert turret gunner in a Humvee opened up with his .50 machine gun, killing the driver before he was able to detonate the explosives in his truck. A tracer bullet ignited some of them, but they burned out rather than exploding, catching the Humvee on fire and burning it to the ground. The suicide driver's arm was handcuffed to the steering wheel of the truck, an encouragement to him not to bail out early. Good intelligence work combined with some great shooting by the Blackhawk trooper prevented what could have been a disastrous blow to the battalion. We nominated the gunner for a Silver Star medal for the valor he displayed.

Unfortunately, AQI wasn't giving up easily. It later targeted the bridge observation post with another car bomb, and this one was successful, killing three Blackhawk troopers at their most vulnerable moment during shift change, when they were exposed, away from the defenses that had shielded them from the earlier attack. (The AQI car bomb on the downtown Khalidiyah police station had also happened at shift change, for the same reason.) In the wake of these losses, we were ordered to collapse the Blackhawk position north of the river. Important as it was to enable access to the area north of the river, the price we were paying was too high to sustain. America was beginning to realize that the same point might be true across the broader theater of war in Iraq.

Another body blow was imminent. Immediately after the memorial service for the Blackhawk soldiers killed defending the bridge, Captain Matt August and his first sergeant, James Hoffman, departed Camp Habbaniyah to conduct reconnaissance of the banks of the Euphrates. We had given Bulldog, our attached engineer company, primary responsibility for the ammunition depot north of Camp Habbaniyah. Bulldog had overseen the contracts paying Iraqi citizens to restore concertina wire fencing around the depot, manned the guard posts overwatching the perimeter, and coordinated with artillery units that were tasked with methodically hauling away or destroying the ammunition inside. In fact, I had spent a pleasant hour in the ammo depot with Major Paul Yingling, my friend from the West Point Sosh Department, one day when his unit was tasked with that mission. But by this point Bulldog had the ammo depot under control and had begun searching for ammunition and weapons caches in sector. The banks of the river had proven particularly fruitful search areas, and Bulldog was progressively squeezing the ability of the insurgents to acquire weapons and ammunition, particularly those required to build improvised explosive devices.

But the war works in both directions. Somehow the insurgents had managed to slip an IED onto the main road in Khalidiyah, and Matt and his first sergeant didn't see it. The resulting explosion killed them both as well as their driver and gutted Bulldog Company. Matt had been an extremely popular commander, and First Sergeant Hoffman was also very highly regarded. Matt, of the West Point Class of 1997, had married one of his classmates who was also serving in Iraq at the same time. We had sent him on important coordination missions to her unit more than once, ensuring that the convoy schedule required him to remain overnight at her location. Matt felt guilty about having the chance to see his wife when the rest of us couldn't do the same, but we were pleased that someone in the task force got to do something pleasant every once in a while. Matt's wife stayed in theater and continued to fight after his loss, just one of any number of female soldiers and officers who demonstrated their mettle in this long decade of war that brought women in uniform the opportunity to serve in combat, which their performance indicated they deserved.

It wasn't just soldiers who were paying the ultimate price. Because of the small size of the Army and a lack of proper preparation for the war and its aftermath, a number of responsibilities that would have fallen to soldiers in other wars were performed by contractors in this one. While the vast majority of contractors were good people performing a difficult task under extreme challenges, not all were well prepared for the roles they were assigned, or well supervised, particularly early in the war. As in so much else, the system had to learn how to best employ contractors on the battlefield of a counterinsurgency campaign. The war took a tragic turn when four Blackwater contractors in our neighboring town to the east, Fallujah, inadvertently drove into the wrong neighborhood and were killed in an insurgent attack, after which their bodies were desecrated and hung from an overpass.

Major General Jim Mattis, commanding the First Marine Division, which now had responsibility for Al Anbar Province, recommended a deliberate approach to gather intelligence on those responsible for these attacks, followed by raids to bring them to justice, but he was overruled. Washington demanded a full-on assault. Mattis complied with his orders, conducted a massive attack on Fallujah, and received the result he expected: a general uprising, not just of all Sunnis in Al Anbar, but also of the Shia in the rest of Iraq. The United States had, through its failures to understand culture and power dynamics in the Arab world, accomplished the seemingly impossible: it had united all of Iraq behind a common cause. Unfortunately, that common cause was killing Americans.

Insurgents ambushed supply convoys and destroyed bridges. The ruling council of Iraq threatened to resign en masse, the few allies America had in the war effort expressed their dismay, and Washington called off the attack just as it was about to capture Fallujah from the insurgency. Mattis was livid, saying privately, "If you set out to take Vienna, TAKE [GERUND FORM OF EXPLETIVE THAT MARINES USE VERY FREQUNTLY] VIENNA." This was the worst of all worlds. We had lost a number of soldiers and Marines without accomplishing our objective of controlling Fallujah and bringing to justice those who had desecrated the Blackwater contractors' bodies. The makeshift solution—setting up an Iraqi governing council for Fallujah and forbidding American entry into the city proper—essentially yielded control of Fallujah to the insurgents, who celebrated their victory over the American occupiers by going on a killing rampage that cost us one of our most capable allies.

Lieutenant Colonel Suleiman was the commander of the local Iraqi Civil Defense Corps (ICDC) battalion. The ICDC was an attempt to exhume elements of the Iraqi Army that the United States had disbanded soon after the invasion. Within months, in an implicit acknowledgment that disestablishing the Iraqi Army had been a mistake, it was being rebuilt under the ICDC banner. The ICDC was in an impossible situation, reliant for training and equipping from the United States, and hated by much of the population for collaborating with what was increasingly seen as an occupying force. Equipping the ICDC was a continuous comedy of errors, as the United States scrambled to procure Soviet-built equipment that was familiar to the new Iraqi troops, many of whom had very recently been soldiers in the Iraqi Army that Paul Bremer's order had disbanded. But even when drawing upon individuals with prior service, it takes a long time to build a unit that can function effectively, particularly in a situation where the soldiers generally have to hide their occupation from their neighbors.

Inspecting ammunition with Iraqi Army officers in Khalidiyah in 2004.

Colonel Suleiman was a natural fighter. He argued with me continually—he wanted more weapons, better weapons, more radios, and real combat vehicles rather than the Nissan pickup trucks we provided to the ICDC. For my part, I wanted actions from Suleiman: more checkpoints set up by his troops, more intelligence from his troops and the sources he developed, and for his troops to stay awake when they were on checkpoint. (I'm funny that way.) A genuine respect developed between the two of us—the respect of two professionals who didn't always see things the same way but could understand each other's perspective.

Suleiman was crimping the style of the insurgents inside Fallujah. His ICDC battalion controlled the western exit from Fallujah, and he was essentially keeping the insurgents from attacking us. Eventually, the insurgents grew tired of his unit protecting our flank, and they kid-

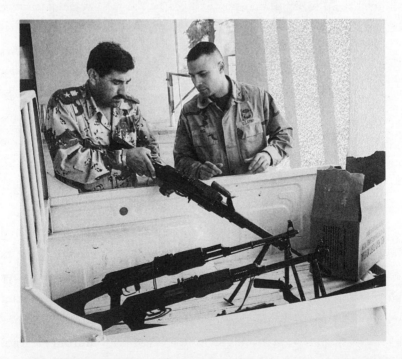

Inspecting machine guns with Major Hussein of the Iraqi Army in 2004.

napped one of his captains, holding him inside Fallujah, where Americans were forbidden to enter by terms of the peace treaty we'd signed ending the First Battle of Fallujah. They told Suleiman to come to a mosque to retrieve his captain, and he bravely did so. The insurgents beat him to death, documenting the beating on videotape and handing out CDs of his murder as a warning to other Iraqis not to cooperate with the Americans.

His ICDC battalion, predictably, dissolved. The weapons, equipment, trucks, radios, and ammunition that Suleiman had argued for, and that I had fought to get him, were captured by the insurgents and moved inside Fallujah, equipping the insurgents for the fight that they knew would eventually come. It did, after our departure from sector and just a few days after the American presidential election in November. The fight was absolutely necessary by that point to remove the tumor that Fallujah had become for all of Iraq—and it was made more difficult because of the weapons and equipment that we had provided to Suleiman and that his battalion had in turn given to the insurgents after his murder. The whole situation, of course, could have been avoided had General Mattis been listened to during the immediate aftermath of the Blackwater killings. Unfortunately, Mattis's sage advice had not been welcome in Washington at that point and would not be until the cumulative impact of mistakes made—on the ground in Iraq, certainly, but more critically in Washington—nearly led to the war being lost.

The ICDC took up a lot of my time, but another priority remained the police. The new police chief whom Khalidiyah received, after its second postinvasion one was killed during our transfer of authority with the Third ACR, was Brigadier General Ishmael, a former Iraqi Army officer who, like me, had experience in Desert Storm. We once did the math and found that his division had not been far from the Iraqi division that my First Cavalry Division had attacked on the opening day of the ground war. Like many veterans of long-ago wars, even those who served on opposite sides, we became friends. Veterans, even if they once tried to kill each other, have more in common with each other—and often, some of the most intense and important moments in their lives—than they do with many of their own countrymen who have not fought.

Ishmael was not at the police station the day the car bomber killed so many of his policeman, but he did spend a great deal of time in the office after we rebuilt it. He would occasionally come to Camp Habbaniyah for meetings, and I would frequently travel to his office, at least once for a feast that included roast chicken and the gift that keeps on giving. Immodium AD is a must for anyone practicing counterinsurgency; diarrhea is part of the job. Ishmael would provide information on insurgents only when there were no other Iraqis, including his own police majors, within earshot. This was yet one more indication of how dangerous his job was. Another came when an IED exploded on him in his own driveway—a strong suggestion that he did not control the town as well as he claimed. Ishmael was not badly hurt, although his driver was. And then came the fighting in Fallujah.

During that fight after the Blackwater contractors were killed, I received multiple credible reports that Ishmael was providing arms and ammunition to the insurgents fighting inside Fallujah. Although I believed the reports, I decided to do nothing at all about them. I knew that Ishmael had taken repeated risks to his own life and to the lives of his family in support of the American occupation, including surviving the recent IED strike. I concluded that if in fact he was providing material support to the insurgency inside Fallujah, he had to do so to remain in office and survive. I had no one with whom to replace him—I didn't trust any of his majors, in part because he didn't—and the stuff he was providing to the insurgents frankly wasn't that good. They got far better material when Suleiman's ICDC battalion collapsed and everything it owned poured into Fallujah. As if that wasn't bad enough, the Fallujah Brigade, which the United States created after the first Battle of Fallujah and officially provided with weapons and equipment, also donated its weapons and equipment to the insurgency. It was a hell of a way to fight a war, but not historically unique by any means. Mao remarked that the government forces opposing him were his armory, and the Vietcong acquired many of their weapons from the Army of the Republic of Vietnam that was opposing them. Still, it was a painful moment in my relationship with Ishmael.

In addition to Suleiman's dissolving the ICDC battalion on the eastern approach to Khalidiyah from Fallujah, we were working to stand up another battalion inside Khalidiyah proper. My interlocutor in this case was Major Hussein, a tall, handsome Sunni with presence and some flair. We had established a contract to rebuild dilapidated Iraqi Army barracks not far from the center of Khalidiyah for his forces, but the barracks were blown up as they were nearing completion. We provided more funds and rebuilding commenced, only to have the barracks again destroyed as the work was nearing its end. By this point, I understood what was going on and called Hussein into Camp Habbaniyah for a discussion.

"It is a sad day," I began. "The insurgents have again destroyed the barracks we were building for your brave soldiers so that they could protect the good people of Khalidiyah. If only I could find a contractor who could provide security for his work, so that we could push the insurgents out of Khalidiyah once and for all."

Hussein looked genuinely surprised. "Why, my brother is a contractor. If he received the contract, my troops could protect his work, and then we could protect Khalidiyah."

"Praise Allah!" I sang. "It is truly a great day for Khalidiyah. Bring your brother to me, and we will build a suitable barracks for your good men so that they can keep the people safe."

The mafia has nothing on Iraqis, but this time the barracks were not blown up, and Hussein's troops eventually moved into the rebuilt barracks. I'm confident that his kids will also be able to afford the tuition at Harvard on what we paid for rebuilding the barracks three times, but at least we got something for our money. And security did improve slightly, even as Khalidiyah remained a dangerous place. On one inspection visit of the barracks site, my truck rolled over an Italian land mine planted on the road median. Fortunately, the insurgents who planted it had not armed it properly, and the mine didn't detonate.

There were other close calls as well. During one late-night raid on a high-value target, we were just building up speed on the main road in Khalidiyah after pulling out of the airfield gate when a rocket-propelled grenade passed in front of my windshield, missing it by inches. Dragon Six, commander of the brigade scout troop, who was sitting in an overwatch position providing security for our operation, sent a radio call reporting that I had been hit. I was too overcome by the close call to correct him immediately but did manage to choke out after a long minute that I was still alive but had been forced to drop off the net to attend to a personal hygiene issue. Not literally true, but funny, and sometimes—as when an RPG has just missed your truck—you need to break proper radio protocol.

Unfortunately, the insurgents did not always miss. One episode in particular showed us both how far we had come and how far we had to go. Insurgents had somehow managed to wire a 152mm artillery round behind a guardrail on the southeastern side of the main bridge across the Euphrates River, putting it at the perfect height to inflict maximum damage. IEDs buried in the ground have much of their explosive force absorbed by dirt, but one suspended eighteen inches above the road would kill everyone within twenty-five meters. Whoever detonated

this one timed the explosion perfectly, killing Second Lieutenant Jeff
Graham, his radioman Roger Ling, one of our Arabic interpreters, and
an Iraqi policeman who was participating in the patrol. When I arrived at the scene, the wounded were still being evacuated, and we had
begun a cordon and search to gather information on the attack. Despite the loss of one of his colleagues, another IP who had been on the
patrol was participating in the cordon. He was on the team and was
not afraid to demonstrate this fact even in front of much of the population of Khalidiyah.

Jeff was a popular lieutenant, the son of an Army officer, as were
many of the officers serving in Iraq. Since the Vietnam War, serving in
the military has become something of a family business. Young men
and women who grow up on military bases following their parents'
careers often choose to attend a service academy or go to college on a
Reserve Officer Training Corps scholarship, and the West Point alumni
magazine, *Assembly*, was full of photographs of impromptu family re-
unions in combat zones. General Ray Odierno, who spent many years
in Iraq and later became chief of staff of the Army, has a son named
Tony who lost an arm while serving as a lieutenant in Iraq and now
works for the New York Yankees. General Petraeus's son was later to
serve as an infantry platoon leader in a tough area of Afghanistan while
Petraeus was the overall commander there. Tragically, the Grahams
lost not only Jeff, to combat, but also their other son, Kevin, to suicide.
Jeff's father, Mark, remained in uniform, serving the nation despite the
horrible price his family paid during the Iraq War.

Jeff had been in Cobra Company, which appeared to be the hard-
luck unit for platoon leaders, but the cruel hand of the insurgents took
officers from other units as well. One loss that struck close to home
was that of Doyle Hufstedler from the Bulldogs, our engineer company. Doyle and I had developed considerable rapport with each other,
often talking about fatherhood since I was a recent dad and he was

Briefing a mission to Lieutenant Doyle Hufstedler, 2004.

about to become one. He asked me to preside over his promotion from second to first lieutenant, a task I was honored to perform. I sent Doyle on a mission that took him over the bridge to clear Route Michigan for a supply convoy that was coming through, and a huge IED completely destroyed his armored personnel carrier. Responding to the attack, I found his helmet, with the sonogram of a baby he would never hold in his arms still inside the Kevlar. We lost every soldier in that vehicle and redoubled our efforts against AQI north of the river.

Late in our year, it was the lieutenants of Apache who suffered. Second Lieutenant Brian Smith was hit by a sniper's bullet while dismounted next to his tank and killed. Neil Santoriello was killed by an IED placed high on a pole that held a road sign, designed to target a tank commander exposed in his tank hatch ten feet off the ground. Neil was a compact fireplug of a man. I met him while he was waiting to report in to Lieutenant Colonel Swisher on his first day in 1-34, back at Fort Riley. Although I can't remember why, I know that as a result of our encounter, he was doing push-ups when Jeff came out to shake hands with him. Neil would regularly get down and knock out push-ups when he saw me coming after that, certain that I would find some reason for him to do so. He is buried in Arlington National Cemetery not far from Todd; it is reassuring to think of their shades on patrol together, Neil's tank protecting Todd, in his up-armored Humvee, from harm.

That deployment was a long, long year. We finally handed over Khalidiyah to an infantry unit that had been pulled out of an assignment in South Korea. Almost unbelievably, the Army was so short of troops by late 2004 that it had to remove units from Korea—a high-priority mission with the motto of "Fight Tonight" against an unstable North Korean regime that could quite literally go ballistic at any time—to meet the demands of the Iraq War. As we prepared to leave, we could point with pride to a better Iraqi police force, an ICDC battalion that was quartered inside Khalidiyah, a better understanding of the insurgency, and a vast number of dead or detained insurgents. Nonetheless, it was hard to argue that we'd won. In fact, in a final insult, the ammunition supply point at Taqquadam Airfield, from which many of us (including me) were scheduled to fly out after sector handover, was hit by a mortar round the night before our scheduled departure in what was clearly an inside job. The aim point was so precise that it detonated the entire ammo dump, raining down still-live munitions on the airfield and keeping us in Iraq for a week longer than we'd planned, until the mess was cleaned up and our airplane could take off from the damaged runway.

It somehow seemed an appropriate farewell. When we returned to Fort Riley, one of the battle captains had coffee mugs made that proclaimed, "IRAQ 2003–2004: We Were Winning When I Left."

But we weren't, and we knew it. Now I was about to get the rare opportunity to find out if Washington understood that we weren't winning, and why, and if anyone there had any idea what to do about it. I wasn't optimistic. It would turn out that the fight in the Pentagon would be in some ways even harder than the fight in Al Anbar; at least out there I'd had some idea who my enemies were.

4.

The First Washington Fight

Iraq

After reuniting at the Fort Riley airfield and hurriedly packing our things, Jack, Susi, and I set off for Washington. We stopped by my mom's house in Kansas City to celebrate Jack's third birthday and drove on to crash at my friend Chris Traugott's house in Arlington, Virginia, just a few miles from the Pentagon. Chris, who had been the head delegate of Wellesley College's Model United Nations team some fifteen years earlier, had obviously been fated to meet the guy running West Point's Model UN Team at the Georgetown conference during our respective senior years in college. We had remained close ever since that meeting in the Key Bridge Marriott not far from Georgetown, close enough that Chris was willing to have Jack, Susi, and me stay with her for a few weeks as we looked for a place to live in the environs of D.C. My orders to lieutenant colonel had come through in the interim, and in an impromptu ceremony in Chris's living room, Susi and Chris placed new silver epaulets on my uniform shirt the morning before I headed in to work at the Pentagon.

I had been hoping, after my return from Iraq, to use a Council on

Foreign Relations International Affairs Fellowship (IAF) in Washington to think and write about the counterinsurgency campaign I had just conducted, hopefully with an eye toward capturing some lessons learned that would be useful for the broader war effort. The Army supported the idea; I'd been selected as an IAF several years earlier but had postponed taking the fellowship in order to accomplish the tasks the Army expects of armor majors—typically, a year as an XO and a year as the S3 of a tank battalion or brigade. That had all been on track until Peter Maass's *New York Times Magazine* article attracted the attention of General Richard Cody, vice chief of staff of the Army, who decided that I would make a great speechwriter. I'd dodged this gig before— Secretary of the Army Louis Caldera had made a serious bid for my speechwriting services while I was teaching in the Sosh department, and I was able to evade that assignment only with great difficulty. Unlike Caldera, Dick Cody was unlikely to take no for an answer from a brand-new lieutenant colonel, and I resigned myself to my fate.

Rescue of the "from the frying pan into the fire" kind came from an unexpected direction. Brigadier General Frank Helmick, who had been the assistant division commander at Fort Riley while I was rebuilding tank nuclear, biological, chemical (NBC) protective systems, was now serving as the military assistant to Deputy Secretary of Defense Paul Wolfowitz. Dr. Wolfowitz was the man who had thought General Shinseki's estimate of "several hundred thousand" troops to maintain stability in Iraq after an invasion "wildly off the mark." Helmick wanted an Army lieutenant colonel to serve in the deputy secretary's office and remembered me kindly from the tank NBC imbroglio. Petraeus also weighed in on my behalf from Iraq, although I didn't know it at the time. Helmick placed a call to Task Force 1-34 in Al Anbar, told me that I was coming to work for Secretary Wolfowitz, and seemed completely unconcerned about the fact that the vice chief of staff of the Army, a four-star general, already had his eyes on me.

Helmick promised to take care of that little issue, and so it was not to the Council on Foreign Relations or to the office of the vice chief of staff of the Army that I reported on November 1, 2004, but to the belly of the beast, the office of the deputy secretary of defense.

I was replacing a Navy commander, as Helmick wanted more of an Army presence in the office given the weight the Army was carrying in Iraq. There was another Navy officer in the shop, a newly promoted surface warfare officer named Captain Sean O'Connor, who ran triathalons as well as a famously tight ship, both literally and figuratively. Sean, a member of the Naval Academy's Athletic Hall of Fame for his exploits on the lightweight football team as a midshipman, had as his top priority every day getting in a workout at the Pentagon Athletic Club. Given that every day was a twelve-hour workday, with first call at 0600, this was not only reasonable but necessary to stay sane, and I soon began jockeying for my gym time as well.

A one-star Army general, a Navy captain, and an Army lieutenant colonel would seem to be enough people to staff any one human being, but Paul Wolfowitz was not just anyone. I soon found him to be analytically ruthless, dedicated to finding answers, and completely and totally disorganized. Wolfowitz was a brilliant academic, a respected policy wonk, and an accomplished diplomat, but he may not have been the optimum choice for chief operating officer of the world's largest and most complicated organization.

In fact, Paul had originally been slated to be deputy secretary of state, a role for which he would have been much better suited. He had become close to George W. Bush as one of the original "Vulcans" who advised the candidate on foreign and national security policy, of whom the most important was Condoleezza Rice. Donald Rumsfeld, who had served as secretary of defense many years before, was not close to the new president but, like Colin Powell as secretary of state, was intended to provide foreign policy gravitas for a young president who was inexperienced abroad. The idea was that Wolfowitz would be Powell's deputy and Rich Armitage, another Naval Academy graduate and a man with a reputation for getting things done, would serve as Rumsfeld's deputy in the Pentagon. However, when Armitage reported to Rumsfeld for a discussion about the job, the new secretary of defense opened the conversation with the words "You know, Rich, there's about a ten percent chance I'm going to accept you as my deputy." Armitage, not easily bullied, replied, "That's okay, Don, there's about a zero percent chance I'm going to accept." And thus Armitage and Powell, who were great friends, served together at State, and Rumsfeld and Wolfowitz were to run the Department of Defense.

It was not a happy pairing. Rumsfeld had been selected in order to get control of Pentagon spending by applying business practices to the Defense Department; in between his tours in the Pentagon, he had run two Fortune 500 companies, G.D. Searle and General Instruments. He had succeeded in part by applying ruthless efficiencies to the companies, a practice he promised to repeat in what Rumsfeld saw as a bloated Pentagon. In fact, on September 10, 2001, Secretary Rumsfeld famously gave a speech in the Pentagon auditorium stating that the most serious threat to American national security was the Pentagon bureaucracy. Less than twenty-four hours later, with the Pentagon in flames, he was revealed to have been somewhat mistaken, if personally courageous, as he helped rescue the wounded, even as others made the critical decisions about whether to shoot down airliners that were potential threats on that dark day.

Rumsfeld might have been a good secretary of defense if, as almost everyone expected, the decade of relative peace after the end of the Cold War had continued and the biggest problem the Pentagon faced was downsizing while retaining the capabilities needed to hedge against a rising China. But he was the wrong man to serve as secretary of war in an irregular conflict against a very different enemy than the one his

*Paul Wolfowitz (right) in 2009 at our home in
Alexandria with Colonel (retired) John Collins,
neighbor and mentor.*

department had been prepared to fight. Defeating this opponent would require huge changes in the mental construct the department used to think about the world and its role in that world, and Rumsfeld was never able to make those adjustments.

Wolfowitz, a more agile thinker, was able to make them but was not particularly willing to do so. He had been a major—perhaps *the* major—voice urging the invasion of Iraq and the toppling of Saddam Hussein's regime, arguing to President Bush on the day after the World Trade Center and Pentagon attacks that Iraq must have been involved. After the invasion of Iraq in March 2003, when Saddam's regime crumpled even more quickly than he had dared hope, Wolfowitz rejoiced—but he, and the department he oversaw, were completely unprepared for what came next.

Rumsfeld had argued stridently before the invasion that it was the Department of Defense, rather than Powell's Department of State, that should be responsible for the postwar occupation of Iraq. But having won the right to take charge, he failed to follow through, appointing retired General Jay Garner as director of the Office for Reconstruction and Humanitarian Assistance far too late in the day and without adequate resources to accomplish his huge mission in a postwar Iraq. When Garner failed miserably, through little fault of his own, former ambassador Paul Bremer was given the job and a new acronym: the CPA, or Coalition Provisional Authority. The CPA exerted varying influence in Baghdad and essentially none outside it and had little direction from the Pentagon after the disastrous mandates Bremer issued almost immediately upon his arrival in Baghdad: disbanding the Iraqi Army, firing tens of thousands of Ba'ath Party members from Iraqi government employment (and most employment in Iraq was with government-owned industries or entities), and slow-rolling democracy.

Rumsfeld paid insufficient attention not only to the semicivilian responsibilities he had fought to gain control over but also to the military ones that were clearly in his domain. Army General Tommy Franks, the commander who had overseen both the initial fight in Afghanistan and the invasion of Iraq, retired from the Army while Baghdad was still burning. Command of an Iraq that was visibly in ruins was given to the most junior three-star general in the Army, the recently promoted Ricardo Sanchez. Sanchez's V Corps headquarters was neither prepared nor sufficiently manned to handle the political-military tasks required to rebuild a broken country and to get it up and running again, and he and his team had been given no warning that they would be taking on such a responsibility. Clearly out of his depth, Sanchez struggled to coordinate the actions of the Army divisions that were reporting to him, failing to create a comprehensive counterinsurgency strategy across the country.

Sanchez would be replaced, after a very difficult first year as the overall commander of the effort to pacify Iraq, by Vice Chief of Staff of the Army George Casey, who had preceded General Cody in that job. Casey was the son of the most senior Army officer killed in Vietnam. His father had been commanding the First Cavalry Division when his helicopter crashed into the side of a Vietnamese mountain in heavy fog, killing all aboard. Casey received notification that he would be assuming command in Iraq from President Bush while in Chief of Staff of the Army Peter Schoomaker's office. After Casey accepted the assignment and thanked the president, Schoomaker pulled a copy of *Counterinsurgency Lessons from Malaya and Vietnam,* which Newt Gingrich had encouraged the chief to read, from a shelf and told him that it was time to start studying. Casey read the book that weekend and would later admit that he had not previously done any reading on insurgency. Iraq was also his first combat experience. He, like Sanchez before him, was not set up for success by his institution and those above him in the chain of command, although just how grievously Rumsfeld and General Casey were out of step with the president himself would not become clear for some years to come.

General Casey's immediate problem was one left behind by his predecessor, but it was really the fault of the National Command Authority. By the time Casey took over from General Sanchez, Fallujah had become a bleeding ulcer in western Al Anbar, an internal sanctuary from which insurgents, including Al Qaeda in Iraq, staged attacks in Baghdad and out west. Lieutenant Colonel Suleiman had been beaten to death there precisely because his battalion had stood in the way of attacks on the rest of Al Anbar coming out of Fallujah. The Fallujah problem would have to be dealt with eventually, and eventually turned out to be immediately after the 2004 presidential election in the United States.

The fight was savage, not a twilight struggle against hit-and-run insurgents but a set-piece urban battle against enemy fighters who had no place to run. It was the toughest fighting American forces had done since Hue in Vietnam, the battle I later chose for the cover photo of the paperback edition of *Learning to Eat Soup with a Knife,* which would come out the following year. Second Fallujah was the bloodiest battle of the war in Iraq for Americans, with 95 killed and 560 wounded. As many as 2,000 enemies were killed in the fighting, which was complete by the end of December. But the second battle of Fallujah, while important in removing an insurgent sanctuary, was far from decisive in the Iraq campaign, and in fact the broader Iraq insurgencies continued to gain strength after the battle was over.

From my perch in the deputy secretary's office, I was making friends and building alliances in a quest to think differently about the situation we faced in Iraq and what we needed to do differently there. Jim Thomas had been Dr. Wolfowitz's student at the Johns Hopkins School of Advanced International Studies (SAIS) and had come to work for Wolfowitz as a special assistant. By the time I arrived in the Pentagon, Jim had been promoted to deputy assistant secretary of defense for strategy, a job for which he was well suited. Thin and intense, with bright eyes behind his glasses, Jim was a man who recognized and collected talent. He had heard an impressive presentation by an Australian Army lieutenant colonel some months previously and decided to bring the Aussie on his staff to work on the Quadrennial Defense Review, a comprehensive evaluation of U.S. strategy and force structure required by the Congress every four years—for which Jim was in charge of the evaluation team. He insisted that I meet Dave Kilcullen, certain that we would get along.

Jim was right. Kilcullen had also earned a Ph.D. in counterinsurgency studies, his at the University of New South Wales and focused on Indonesia. He was, as Jim Thomas had noted, hugely impressive, with a quick mind and a very persuasive manner about his speech; everything sounds smarter when a Brit or an Australian says it. After our first meeting, I immediately called Steve Metz, who had invited me to speak at the annual U.S. Army War College Strategy Conference at

*COINdinistas: David Kilcullen, Erin Simpson,
Janine Davidson, and me, July 2007.*

Carlisle Barracks, Pennsylvania, in April 2005, and volunteered to give
up some of my time to Kilcullen if Steve would add him to the
program.

We ended up driving to Carlisle in the same car. Kilcullen had a
son, Harry, who was almost exactly the same age as Jack. They would
become good friends over the next year, as would Dave and I. His performance at the Army War College was as impressive as I had expected
it to be, and Dave became a coconspirator in the emerging effort to
change the way the United States was thinking about the war in Iraq.

For my own talk, I pulled out the slides I'd used when working on
my thesis at Oxford, adapting them to the specifics of the current war
in Iraq. The title of the presentation was "Learning to Eat Soup with a
Knife: Counterinsurgency Lessons from Malaya and Vietnam for the
War in Iraq." I gave some version of this talk dozens and dozens of
times over the next five years, to audiences ranging from the office of
the deputy assistant secretary of defense for peacekeeping and stability

operations to the Defense Policy Board. In every talk, I emphasized the fact that conventional military forces had historically struggled with the need to adapt to defeat insurgencies, and those that succeeded in learning to protect the population did so because they were adaptive learning organizations. I made it clear that there was a lot of work to be done for the American military establishment to reach that category in Iraq. An e-mail summarizing my presentation and Kilcullen's similar one began to circulate after the Army War College conference, reinforcing points that I'd made in my book and that Peter Maass had suggested in his *New York Times Magazine* article: that counterinsurgency was hard, that conventional military forces were poorly trained and equipped to succeed in the tasks, but that they could learn and adapt to be more effective in this kind of fight if properly led and instructed. It was nice that someone had taken notes, but it often didn't feel like anyone was listening.

An important moment in the counterinsurgency learning process was a conference sponsored by Eliot Cohen, the bow-tie-wearing strategist from Johns Hopkins University, in the summer of 2005 in Basin Harbor, Maine. This conference brought together many old and new names in counterinsurgency, including Vietnam veteran and retired Army Colonel John Waghelstein, whose "Ruminations of a Pachyderm, or What I Learned in the Counterinsurgency Business" was one of the best articles I read while writing my doctoral thesis. Another ancient font of wisdom was T. X. Hammes, a retired Marine colonel who challenged and almost defeated Waghelstein in the competition for the contested title of "crustiest curmudgeon" at the conference. It was at Basin Harbor that I met for the first time Kalev "Gunner" Sepp, a retired special forces officer who had previously been an artilleryman, or "Gunner"—an unusual enough step en route to the Green Beret that his special forces peers christened him with the nickname.

Gunner had earned his Ph.D. at Harvard before teaching irregular warfare in West Point's history department. When General Casey had assumed responsibility in Iraq from Lieutenant General Sanchez, Casey quickly recognized that he needed a counterinsurgency campaign plan, and Gunner had been called to Baghdad from his post at the Naval Postgraduate School in Monterey, California, to help write it. As part of that work, Gunner researched the best and worst practices in past counterinsurgency campaigns—what worked, and what didn't. The answers would have come as no surprise to David Galula or Gerald Templer: emphasize intelligence; focus on the population, its needs, and its security; establish and expand secure areas; and don't concentrate military forces in large bases for protection or overemphasize killing or capturing the enemy rather than securing and engaging the populace. General Casey, who was unimpressed with the level of counterinsurgency knowledge in the force he was commanding, gave Gunner permission to publish his work in an unclassified format. It had just come out in the Fort Leavenworth journal *Military Review*, which was becoming an important outlet for dissidents writing about changes the Army needed to make to become more effective at counterinsurgency.

Held at a beautiful resort in Maine just before the summer season made room rates too expensive for Johns Hopkins to afford, the Basin Harbor conference played an important role in introducing people and ideas to each other. It was at Basin Harbor that David Kilcullen and I met "Hank," the CIA operator who had played a key role in bringing down the Taliban regime in Afghanistan after the September 11 attacks. On the last day of the conference, Hank would gain a last name, as the State Department announced that he was being named the ambassador for counterterrorism. Ambassador Crumpton soon hired Dave Kilcullen as part of his team.

The keynote speaker for the conference was Army Lieutenant General Ray Odierno, then serving as the assistant to the chairman of the

Joint Chiefs of Staff in the Pentagon, the building's liaison officer to the secretary of state. Major General Odierno's tactics while in command of the Fourth Infantry Division in Iraq in 2003–4 had drawn severe criticism for heavy-handedness, but he gave a speech at Basin Harbor that showed a growing appreciation for the cultural sensitivity and limited use of force that most of the conference participants agreed were essential to success in this kind of war. Odierno stuck around after his talk for a few beers in the Basin Harbor bar, partaking in a thoughtful exchange on some of the subtleties of counterinsurgency. He would later be appointed the operational level commander in Iraq, where under the command of David Petraeus many of these same ideas would be implemented in time, although there was lots of fighting and dying to be done before we got there.

It didn't help that we couldn't agree on what the problem was. Secretary Rumsfeld had banned the use of the word *insurgency* to describe the situation we were facing in Iraq, publicly correcting vice chairman of the Joint Chiefs of Staff General Peter Pace for using the word to describe current events in Iraq and even requesting that it be removed from the "National Strategy for Victory in Iraq" when that document was published in 2005. An alcoholic can't get better if he doesn't admit that he's an alcoholic, and a country can't defeat an insurgency if it won't admit that it's fighting one. Changing course in Iraq would require Secretary Rumsfeld's replacement, a difficult choice for President Bush, as Rumsfeld and Vice President Dick Cheney had been close friends for decades.

During a frustrating year, there was some good news when the University of Chicago Press got in touch, sent by Newt Gingrich, and asked to publish *Counterinsurgency Lessons from Malaya and Vietnam* in paperback. They immediately understood that *Learning to Eat Soup with a Knife* was the correct title for the book, not the subtitle, and asked me to write a new preface to the book based on my recent experiences in Iraq. That preface, which I titled "Spilling Soup on Myself," noted that while authors generally learn something about their subject matter, and then write about it, I had taken the opposite approach, writing the book before conducting counterinsurgency myself. It was, I now wrote, even harder than I'd realized, although I'd gotten many of the big ideas right: focus on protecting the population, prioritize intelligence and precision in targeting, and build mechanisms that allow the force to learn and adapt. The preface concluded by arguing that, to cope more effectively with the messy reality that in the twenty-first century many of our enemies will be insurgents, America's armed forces must continue to adapt to counterinsurgency warfare.

The University of Chicago Press also asked if there was anyone I could get to write a foreword to the paperback edition of the book. I knew that Speaker Gingrich had talked to General Peter Schoomaker, the chief of staff of the Army, about *Counterinsurgency Lessons from Malaya and Vietnam*. Schoomaker had then sent expensive hardcover copies of the book to all his subordinate four-star generals to read, spiking my sales on Amazon enough that I'd gotten a congratulatory email from the specialist at Fort Riley who still tracked my book's ranking from afar. A number of the generals, in turn, had handed the book to their resident smart guys to read and summarize for them, and several of the majors and lieutenant colonels, in turn, asked me for a précis of my own book so that they wouldn't have to read it themselves for their bosses! In good insurgent fashion, while he was waiting for a meeting with the habitually late Secretary Wolfowitz, I ambushed General Schoomaker and asked if he would be willing to write a foreword to the paperback. He quickly agreed and said nice things (or more likely, his staff said nice things) in the resulting foreword, calling the book "one that military leaders and interested citizens at all levels should read."

The rising interest in insurgency, as the Iraq War continued to spiral downhill, also led Praeger, which had printed many important books of the first counterinsurgency era during the Vietnam War (with the unacknowledged support of the CIA), to decide to reprint those classics. Praeger invited me to write a foreword to the book *Counterinsurgency Warfare: Theory and Practice*, written by the French counterinsurgent David Galula in 1963 but almost forgotten in the intervening forty years and long out of print. In fact, I had not read it during my doctoral work. I read it now and felt the same excitement I'd experienced when I met Dave Kilcullen. Here was a kindred spirit!

Galula provided the most concise and precise imaginable description of how to conduct a counterinsurgency campaign at the battalion level, drawing lessons from his own experience as a company commander and battalion operations officer in Algeria from 1958 to 1960. I wrote an enthusiastic endorsement of the book, noting in my first sentence that "the best writings on counterinsurgency share with the best sex manuals the fact that their authors tend to have some personal experience of their subject matter."

After a line editor's objection to this sentence was overruled by the series editor, who fell out of his chair laughing, Praeger internally referred to the series of reprints of counterinsurgency books they were pushing out as "the sex manuals." They included Roger Trinquier's book *Modern Warfare: A French View of Counterinsurgency*, with a foreword by Eliot Cohen; Napolean Valeriano and Charles Bohannan's *Counter-Guerilla Operations: The Philippine Experience*, with a foreword by Gunner Sepp; and George Tanham's *Communist Revolutionary Warfare: From the Vietminh to the Viet Cong*, with a foreword by Michael Sheehan, later the assistant secretary of defense for special operations and low-intensity conflict. All of these books helped popularize the idea that there was a body of knowledge available on how to fight wars like Iraq; there was no need to make up ideas about how to conduct

General Petraeus (fourth from left) with Sosh Alumns in Baghdad, August 2004.

counterinsurgency out of whole cloth. As it turned out, David Galula's ideas would play a particularly significant role in the learning process that was slowly gathering speed.

Lieutenant General Petraeus had by now completed nearly eighteen months in Baghdad running the Multi-National Security Transition Command–Iraq, or MNSTC-I, pronounced "Min-sticky." Wolfowitz had fallen under then–Major General Petraeus's spell during an early visit to Mosul after the initial invasion, and Petraeus had later recommended his deputy, Frank Helmick, to Wolfowitz as a suitable military assistant. I had visited General Petraeus in Baghdad before leaving Iraq in 2004, and he had repaid the favor, flying out to Khalidiyah to determine whether it was a suitable site for basing an Iraqi Army division. (It was, and he initiated construction of an Iraqi division base there.) Now Wolfowitz often spent an hour on Saturdays on the phone with Petraeus to get his views on the progress of Iraqi security forces, with Helmick and sometimes me listening in to take notes and render our assistance to the man in the arena.

Petraeus returned to the States via Afghanistan, where he did an assessment for Secretary Rumsfeld, concluding that winning in Afghanistan would be harder and likely to take longer than the campaign in Iraq. He swung through the Pentagon en route to Fort Leavenworth in the fall of 2005. Petraeus had earlier infuriated Secretary Rumsfeld by appearing on the cover of *Newsweek* magazine under the title "Can This Man Save Iraq?" The article within suggested that the answer was probably yes, and the secretary of defense was not amused. Rumsfeld wanted to get Petraeus out of the newspapers and was leaning toward sending him to the traditionally Army-career-ending job of West Point superintendent when Sosh department chair Colonel Mike Meese intervened. Meese talked with the Secretary of the Army, suggesting the Combined Arms Center at Fort Leavenworth for Petraeus's next assignment instead.

Kansas was even farther from major media markets than was upstate New York, so Rumsfeld let it go, giving Petraeus control over the Army's doctrine writing, branch schools, leader development, and training centers. It was a fateful choice. The Army was going to put its most experienced counterinsurgent in charge of what those at Leavenworth termed "the engine of change" for the Army. And the succinct guidance that General Schoomaker issued to General Petraeus was "Shake up the Army, Dave."

Though the secretary of defense had forbidden use of the word to describe the situation in Iraq, the Army, to its credit, knew that it was facing an insurgency there. It had recognized that it was not current on how to fight a counterinsurgency campaign soon after the statue of Saddam Hussein in Fardus Square crashed to the ground courtesy of a Third Infantry Division M-88 armored recovery vehicle. In the fall of 2003, the doctrine center at Fort Leavenworth assigned an Army officer

with no previous experience in counterinsurgency and without a combat tour in Iraq to rewrite its counterinsurgency doctrine. Under huge
time constraints, he made a commendable effort, and FM(I) 3-22.1,
Counterinsurgency, was published the day I arrived in the Pentagon from
Iraq on November 1, 2004.

The (I) stood for "Interim." It was a new designation, acknowledging
that the book was insufficient but declaring it was better than nothing,
and it came with a promise that a reworked final version would be published within two years. I had met the author, Jan Horvath, at the Army
War College conference at which Kilcullen and I had spoken, and I offered to help with the revision process but didn't have any official role
as he worked through a second draft. It had arrived just before Petraeus
visited the Pentagon en route to take command of the Army doctrine
center at Fort Leavenworth late in 2005.

Pointing to the second draft of the interim counterinsurgency field
manual on my desk, I told Petraeus that rewriting the manual—from
scratch—was the first and most important thing he could do when he
arrived in Leavenworth. I then provided a series of additional suggestions, including holding an open revision session on the rewritten manual to which key members of the defense press should be invited and
hosting a counterinsurgency essay contest at *Military Review*, the publication for which he was responsible at Fort Leavenworth. Petraeus was
noncommittal but took the proffered list of suggestions and promised
to think about them. He was true to his word, ultimately implementing all my suggestions, some sooner than others.

It was at about this time that the phone on my desk rang with a
cold call from Sarah Sewall. Sarah had been a Rhodes scholar at Oxford
a few years before me, although we'd never met. She had served in the
Pentagon as the first deputy assistant secretary of defense for peacekeeping, and a friend who had visited her in that role told me how
surprised he was to be offered herbal tea when he visited her Pentagon

office. He was further intrigued when she answered his questions sitting cross-legged on her sofa. Sarah was now director of the Carr Center for Human Rights at Harvard University and planning a conference
on counterinsurgency, to be held in Washington in November. Sarah
invited me to speak at the conference on "Counterinsurgency in Iraq:
Implications of Irregular Warfare for the U.S. Government," and I was
happy to accept.

It pulled together many friends from the Army War College, Basin
Harbor, and other counterinsurgency conferences, including Dave Kilcullen, T. X. Hammes, fellow former Sosh professor Rich Lacquement,
and Gunner Sepp. I gave an updated version of my dissertation talk,
focusing on the need to build an adaptive U.S. Army that could meet
the demands of the counterinsurgency campaign it was still losing in
Iraq, and I received polite applause. But the real work of the conference,
as so often at these events, came between the formal presentations.

Sarah knew Petraeus from her own time in the Pentagon and had
invited him to provide a lunchtime keynote address at her conference.
He spoke about lessons learned from his two tours in Iraq but made
news only during the question and answer session after his talk. Responding to a question about how well the Army was doing at adapting to the demands of counterinsurgency in Iraq, he replied that it still
had a long way to go—and that as a result I would be leading the effort
to write a new counterinsurgency manual for the Army!

This was news to me, but I wasn't in the habit of telling Petraeus
no and was frankly delighted at the tasking. After the conference
ended, I gathered together a few friends at a local watering hole called
the Front Page—former Sosh colleague Rich Lacquement, counterinsurgency theorists Erin Simpson and Janine Davidson, and fellow
Al Anbar combat veteran Kyle Teamey, whom we had literally bumped
into en route to the restaurant. Kyle was now out of the Army and
taking classes at Johns Hopkins SAIS under Eliot Cohen's mentorship.

Over burgers and beers, on a convenient napkin, we outlined the counterinsurgency manual that I had just been tasked to produce. The napkin is now lost to the ages, but I transferred its contents to electronic format not long after the event. They looked something like this:

1. Insurgency and Counterinsurgency
2. Unity of Command
3. Intelligence
4. Operations
5. Information Operations
6. Host-Nation Security Forces
7. Leadership and Ethics
8. Logistics

Already, at this early point, I wrote "annotated bibliography" on the napkin; it was important, I thought, for the Army to recognize that even the most comprehensive field manual couldn't possibly cover everything that its soldiers needed to know about counterinsurgency and that there was a long history of armies adapting to this kind of war. A list of additional books for consideration would be a great way to send that message. There had never been an annotated bibliography in any Army field manual to that time, to my uncertain knowledge, but it seemed like a good time to start encouraging the Army to read more of its own history.

The next morning, energized by the prospect of doing something a bit more directly connected to the conflict in Iraq than whispering in Secretary Wolfowitz's ear after receiving briefings on progress reports, I reported to General Helmick. I let him know that Petraeus had asked me to take the lead on writing the Army's counterinsurgency manual, probably by taking leave and being posted to Leavenworth myself, although we had not yet discussed the prosaic details. Although I wasn't used to telling General Petraeus no, Frank Helmick had worked for him in combat and, more important for the current situation, was used to calling on the authority of his current boss to outrank people with more stars than Petraeus had on his shoulder. He had used just that authority to wrest me away from General Cody's staff a year earlier, despite the fact that Cody had three more stars than he did. General Helmick picked up the phone and told Petraeus that, while I was certainly free to use my spare time between midnight and 0500 daily working for him, the deputy secretary of defense required my services from 0600 until 2000 daily and would not surrender me to a three-star, no matter how noble the task.

General Petraeus, unable to win a fight with Paul Wolfowitz and knowing that he had me in a backup role, decided to take Eliot Cohen's advice and put Conrad Crane in the writer's box. Con had been Petraeus' West Point classmate back in 1974, had later earned his doctorate in history from Stanford, and was now retired from the Army and teaching at the Army War College. Crane's prewar publication of a paper on "Reconstructing Iraq: Insights, Challenges, and Missions for Military Forces in a Post-Conflict Scenario" had proved prescient. Con had exactly the right skill-set to take lead on this mission and the perfect personality for it as well: low-key, self-effacing, quietly competent. With Con in the lead, I offered the outline we had scribbled out at the Front Page and a promise of help, including a suggestion that we get together at Leavenworth in early December at an information operations conference at which I would be speaking.

Petraeus led off that conference in similar fashion to the talk he had given at Sarah's get-together, going several hours over his allotted time. I gave my standard talk on learning counterinsurgency in Malaya and Vietnam. However, the conference was only an excuse to spend some time with Petraeus and Crane, so after my talk I slipped away with Con to the doctrine writers' conference room, joining Jan Horvath for the task of starting over on the counterinsurgency field manual.

Con came armed with a list of historical principles for success in counterinsurgency that drew heavily on Gunner Sepp's *Military Review* article along with a new set of imperatives that he believed applied in the modern era. Most important, however, he had a list of paradoxes that played up the counterintuitive nature of counterinsurgency: the best weapons do not shoot bullets; the more force is used, the less effective it is; the best response is doing nothing; and most important, decisions are not made by generals. The paradoxes were delightfully seditious, designed to illustrate just how different counterinsurgency was from conventional warfare and how much adaptation was needed for conventional forces to be successful in the endeavor, and a number of reviewers later described them as "zen." Although the elegance and simplicity of the initial paradoxes got watered down in the editing process by Petraeus, who thought them excessively confrontational to sacred Army shibboleths, these remained the most noted, and in many ways the most important, elements of the entire manual. Con was an effective insurgent against the machine, although he vetoed my plan for procuring conference coffee cups that featured the visage of Che Guevara—probably a good move in retrospect, although I protested volubly at the time.

My contribution was the outline from the Front Page. We posted it on an easel and then talked about selecting good primary authors for each of the chapters. Con took the first, defining insurgency and counterinsurgency. I suggested Rich Lacquement for the second, on unity of effort, and Kyle Teamey for the third, on intelligence. I would take the fourth, on counterinsurgency operations, in conjunction with Jan Horvath. I pulled out my phone and started making calls. Rich and Kyle immediately agreed to have chapter drafts done by New Year's, then just under four weeks away. It was a tight timeline, but we were constrained by Petraeus's embrace of my idea of a vetting conference, now also including the Marine Corps after Petraeus talked to his battlefield comrade and my former Al Anbar boss General Jim Mattis. Petraeus had already set the dates for a mid-February gathering despite the fact that he hadn't yet seen a completed sentence of the draft manual beyond my scribbled outline. We had promises to keep and people counting on us to come up with a way to win the war that was going even worse than it had been when I was fighting it directly.

5.

Clear, Hold, and Build

The field manual review conference grew far larger than I had initially envisioned. The guest list ended up at more than one hundred people, including many of the most impressive talents from Basin Harbor and from Sarah Sewall's conference. Sarah had agreed to cosponsor and cofund the draft review conference with Petraeus. The two of them sat together at the front of the room, while the bad kids (Janine Davidson, Dave Kilcullen, and I, along with *New Yorker* writer George Packer, who had written *The Assassin's Gate* and would later write *New Yorker* profiles of both Kilcullen and H. R. McMaster) sat in the back. The inclusion of Packer was an indication of Petraeus's media strategy. He invited several of the most thoughtful defense and foreign policy journalists, including *The Wall Street Journal*'s Greg Jaffe and the *Atlantic Monthly*'s Jim Fallows, to attend the conference in a background status; that is, they could use the information they gained at the conference in their later writings, but only if they didn't identify either the speaker or the location. In short, Petraeus was pre-seeding what hopefully would be positive coverage of the manual among some of the nation's most critical opinion leaders.

Con Crane was the ringleader and head inquisitor, actively supported by Petraeus, who iron-butted through the entire affair, a considerable sign of his commitment to the project. Con began the conference by handing out small rocks to each participant before explaining that the innocent-looking stones were actually copralite—fossilized dinosaur dung. He challenged us to write a document that, unlike most army doctrine, would actually be useful and used—not dried-up antique excrement. Con then successively shepherded the chapter authors to the front of the room to present and defend their chapters.

The chapters built nicely upon Con's principles, imperatives, and paradoxes. Two themes came through all of them: first, that in a counterinsurgency campaign, the top priority is not to kill the enemy but to protect the population from enemy intimidation. This was a dramatic change from U.S. policy that flew in the face of Secretary Rumsfeld's desires to continually reduce U.S. troop numbers. Protecting the population would require more troops, not fewer, although over time U.S. troops could be replaced by locally raised forces with American advisers to strengthen and assist them. But slow as it was, this was the best way to succeed in a counterinsurgency campaign; only the population could identify the insurgents in their midst, and they would do so only if they could be certain that they would survive the experience. This principle resounded through the history of previous counterinsurgency campaigns, and it was a strong pillar on which to build a manual.

The other pillar was more original. It centered on the need to build adaptive learning organizations to succeed in counterinsurgency campaigns, which the manual described as competitions in learning. The side that learned and adapted faster was more likely to win. This concept received a major assist from the Marine team that Petraeus invited to join the writing campaign. Petraeus's counterpart at Quantico was

Lieutenant General Jim Mattis, the hard-bitten but intellectual Marine for whom I'd worked in Iraq once the corps took over Al Anbar from the 82nd Airborne Division. Mattis had a brilliant "designated thinker" named Frank Hoffman, a Penn graduate and retired Marine reserve lieutenant colonel who was a prolific writer and thinker on military matters and who had held up the Marines' end of the discussion at Basin Harbor. Hoffman and General Mattis created the most intellectually innovative chapter of the field manual, the only one that I hadn't outlined at the Front Page but in some ways the most important chapter in the book. Ultimately titled "Designing Counterinsurgency Campaigns and Operations" and printed as Chapter 4, it proposed a continuous process of learning and adaptation in counterinsurgency campaigns that recognized the need to build a learning organization to succeed in this kind of war.

The diagram is closely related to the one that I stole from Richard Downie's dissertation on building a learning army and to one that Petraeus used describing his command at Fort Leavenworth as the Army's

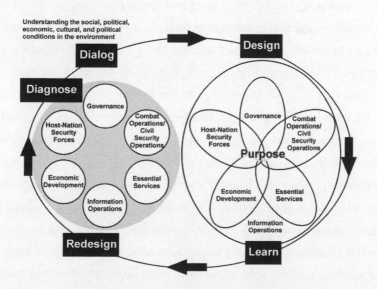

Iterative Counterinsurgency Campaign Design.

"engine of change." Both draw on the same requirement to understand the environment in which one is operating, and to delve deeper into the "black box" by which organizations come to a consensus that change is needed—that either doctrine itself or, in this case, a campaign plan for a particular counterinsurgency effort is no longer meeting requirements in the field and needs to be updated. The requirement to conduct continuous campaign assessments and change and adapt policies as additional information becomes available or as the situation on the ground changes has since become a part of Army doctrine more broadly and may end up being an even more important legacy of the counterinsurgency field manual than was the rediscovery of classic COIN principles it emphasized.

The chapter that followed "Designing Counterinsurgency Campaigns and Operations" was, cleverly enough, "Executing Counterinsurgency Operations." I had a hand in authoring this chapter, which drew heavily upon the work of David Galula. I was simultaneously writing the foreword for the new Praeger version of his masterpiece, *Counterinsurgency Operations: Theory and Practice*, and found Galula's instructions incredibly helpful as I thought through how to conduct COIN operations. Galula had worked the principles of counterinsurgency out on the ground during a campaign in Algeria forty years before, but they rang absolutely true to my experience in Iraq.

It took a long, long time for us to incorporate his instructions in the field. Simple lessons like "conduct a census of the population" and issue identification papers so that the occupying forces can tell friend from enemy, took years to implement, although in some ways we improved on Galula's instructions by incorporating biometric identification measures that hadn't existed during his time fighting in Algeria into the procedure we finally implemented across Iraq. These biometric techniques, along with other technological innovations, ultimately proved very useful in identifying insurgents more effectively and with less local input than had historically been possible.

Galula's influence is clear in the finished manual, and I would draw upon his work consistently while working on the drafts; in fact, a copy of his book was on my desk whenever I was writing, and I kept in mind his lament from *Counterinsurgency Warfare: Theory and Practice* throughout the writing process: "If the individual members of the organization were of the same mind, if every organization worked according to a standard pattern, the problem would be solved. Is this not precisely what a coherent, well-understood, and accepted doctrine would tend to achieve?"

In writing the "Executing Counterinsurgency Operations" chapter, we also relied upon a *Military Review* article by Major General Peter Chiarelli and Major Patrick Michaelis. General Chiarelli had come to the Pentagon in early 2005, upon his return from commanding the First Cavalry Division in Baghdad, and had given a talk on the Baghdad

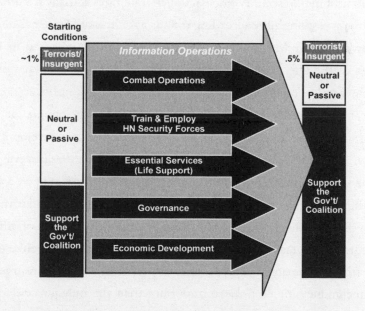

campaign that was an important step in my own learning process. Chiarelli, another Sosh veteran, described simultaneous counterinsurgency operations along a series of logical lines of operation in a slide that was later reprinted in *Military Review* and, still later, stolen lock, stock, and barrel and incorporated into the field manual. (The military doesn't allow copyright for military authors in military journals, so it was fair game.)

The brilliance of the diagram is in the recognition that most of the tasks required to succeed in a counterinsurgency campaign are not military and that all must be conducted simultaneously. David Galula had noted that counterinsurgency is only 20 percent military and 80 percent everything else—politics mostly, but also economics, development, and information operations. The Chiarelli/Michaelis diagram, which illustrated how they had thought about their mission to stabilize Baghdad over the course of 2004 and into 2005, lists only one exclusively military task (combat operations) and one *mostly* military task (train host nation security forces). Police training is actually a State Department responsibility according to U.S. law, although State has historically struggled with this task during combat situations and in Iraq most of the effective police training was done by the military, often military police units, or by contractors augmenting the MPs.

The other tasks—providing essential services to the population, encouraging good governance, and supporting economic development, all wrapped up in a comprehensive information operations campaign— were not primarily military, although in a combat zone military forces might well be the only ones who could even attempt to complete them. The division of labor in the diagram explains why "Unity of Effort: Integrating Civilian and Military Activities" was the second chapter in the final field manual. The nonmilitary tasks in a counterinsurgency campaign become even more important than the military ones once the initial clearing of insurgents is complete, and the challenge of just understanding all the tasks, much less coordinating and prioritizing among them, is a big part of what makes counterinsurgency "the graduate level of war," as the manual describes it. I would later see photocopies of the diagram everywhere I visited in Iraq in 2008.

One of the great failures of the field manual was the decision not to include a chapter on information operations (IO). The Front Page napkin outline included a separate chapter on information operations, and the Chiarelli/Michaelis diagram highlights information operations as encompassing and larger than all other logical lines of operation (LLO). The manual itself says (in acronyms only a doctrine maven could love) that "the IO LLO may be the most important one." Nonetheless, the final manual does not have a stand-alone chapter on information operations.

The lack of clear guidance in the manual on IO is an indication not of the insignificance of the field but of its overriding importance. In the complicated interagency realm of conflicting and competing cabinet agencies, information operations is seen as outside the military realm, with responsibility for the task residing somewhere between the White House and the State Department. The Army and the Marines were certainly not going to tell State and the White House how to do IO in an Army/Marine Corps field manual—and so this most important line of operations muddled by with no one in charge and no instruction manual on how to accomplish it.

During the Cold War, the U.S. Information Agency (USIA) conducted effective information operations against the Soviet Union, although that war was primarily economic, secondly military, and only thirdly an information war. USIA was closed at the end of the Cold War as a budget savings measure. The war against radical Islamic extremism, on the other hand, is *primarily* a war of ideas, but we have no organization in charge of fighting that part of the fight. The national failure to rebuild the U.S. Information Agency, which did such good work during the Cold War but was a casualty of the peace dividend, has cost lives and treasure over a decade of war that would have been far better fought with someone in charge of information operations.

This failing will outlast *The U.S. Army/Marine Corps Counterinsurgency Field Manual*. Alvin Toffler, the author of *Future Shock*, suggests that there have been just three revolutions in all of human history—the agricultural, the industrial, and the information revolutions. Each of these three revolutions has led to a profound impact on almost everything humans do, including how we wage war on each other. Agricultural-age warfare relied upon horseflesh and human muscle and reached its epitome under the leadership of Napoleon. Industrial-age warfare replaced animal muscle with the internal combustion engine and peaked in the Second World War; it took generations for agricultural-age generals to be replaced by those who understood this revolution in warfare, and the foot soldiers of the American Civil War and of the First World War paid the price in blood as their bosses struggled to understand the changing character of war. The information revolution changed warfare even more dramatically.

The first information-age war was the American war in Vietnam. Army Colonel Harry Summers was the author of the modestly named book *On Strategy* that became the Army's accepted version of why it lost in Vietnam. (Civilians had tied its hands behind its back, not allowing it to use firepower as widely and freely as it would have liked to.) In it, he tells the possibly apocryphal story of a discussion he had with a Vietnamese colonel at the Paris Peace Talks ending the war. Summers accosted the Vietnamese officer, telling him, "You know you never defeated us on the battlefield." The Vietnamese colonel considered this for a moment before retorting, "That is true. It is also irrelevant."

The power of the information age had allowed the Vietcong and North Vietnamese to defeat the United States without triumphing over its Army in the field, as had been required in all previous wars. Instead, the enemy went over the head of the Army to the American people, who decided that the war was no longer worth fighting. If a great power loses a small war, it does so for only one reason: because the national population loses the will to continue.

The full implications of the information revolution on warfare remain to be seen; proponents of the revolution in military affairs believed that information dominance would allow the United States to triumph bloodlessly (or at least without spilling *American* blood) in conflicts around the globe. They were wrong. In fact, the information revolution empowered the enemies of the United States to disseminate violent ideologies and recruit jihadis far more effectively than they could have in an earlier day, but locating these same insurgents continued to rely at least in part on personal knowledge that only close association with the population could provide.

Despite its failure to engage more directly with the requirements for success in information-age warfare, the field manual was a huge step forward, and the vetting conference an enormous success. James Fallows, of *The Atlantic Monthly*, offered the opinion at the end of the two days that he had never seen such an open exchange of ideas in any institution—government or private sector—and that the country would be the better for more such exchanges.

After the conclusion of the conference in February 2006, we optimistically estimated that publication of the field manual was still some months away. To get the ideas from the conference into the Army as soon as possible, Eliot Cohen, Con Crane, Jan Horvath, and I put together an article for *Military Review* titled "The Principles, Imperatives, and Paradoxes of Counterinsurgency" that drew heavily upon the first chapter of the draft manual. It was published in the next issue after the conference, in the March–April 2006 issue of the journal that (with Petraeus as "publisher") more than any other was the outlet for those who wanted to change the way the war in Iraq was being fought.

The meat of *The U.S. Army/Marine Corps Counterinsurgency Field Manual* is its middle chapters, which cover sociocultural intelligence, campaign design using that information to determine problem sets, and then execution along logical lines of operation to achieve solutions. Perhaps the most important influence of *Counterinsurgency Field Manual* on American doctrine has been through the concept of design, a contribution from the Marines that has become a part of all subsequent doctrine. Campaign design compels commanders to apply different combinations of information activities and combat operations, along with efforts aimed at improving governance and the economy, all in pursuit of a locally defined legitimacy that will sustain popular support. This complex and iterative plan must be conducted in concert with many partners, both from the host nation and internationally. While many of those partners have not yet developed the same degree of proficiency that the Army and Marines have displayed in recent operations in Afghanistan, efforts to increase civilian counterinsurgency capacity continue.

The process of campaign design allows U.S. forces to continually adapt to the demands of the neighborhood they are fighting in, determining the appropriate balance between killing the enemy and protecting the population on each block and at each moment. At times the priority will be on combat operations, as it is currently in Navy operations against pirates in Somalia. At other times and in other places, the focus will be on training host-nation security forces, as it is in campaigns led by U.S. Special Forces in Yemen and Pakistan. But the essence of success, and one of the two major pillars of the manual, was in being adaptive to changing circumstances in the theater of war.

That need was urgent in Iraq; in fact, all the dials were screaming red. On February 22, the first day of the Leavenworth field manual review conference, Al Qaeda in Iraq destroyed the Al Askari Mosque in

Samarra. The bombing collapsed the Golden Dome of one of the holiest Shia shrines, in a move expressly designed by AQI to accelerate the civil war in Iraq. For the Shia, it was the final straw. Recognizing the strategic importance of the attack, Dave Kilcullen immediately left the conference to get to Iraq.

The war had changed by now, from one in which Sunni revisionists upset with their loss of status and power targeted primarily U.S. forces, to one in which they also launched their car bombs and suicide bombers against increasingly Shia-dominated Iraqi security forces. The Shia had been remarkably tolerant of these attacks, but after the bombing of the Al Askari Mosque, the gloves came off. The Iraqi Army and Police, and the increasingly active Shia militia, engaged in all-but-open warfare against Sunni men, especially in Baghdad. The dark days of the Saddam Hussein era returned as the tortured bodies of young Sunni men were discovered every morning on the streets, many showing signs of torture administered by power drill. Sunni men began to get their home phone numbers tattooed on their thighs in the hope that when their bodies were discovered on the streets, someone would call their mothers to recover them. The Sunnis responded to the assassination campaign with more car bombs and improvised explosive devices, and the security situation deteriorated rapidly over the course of 2006 as we were tabulating revisions to the field manual from the conference.

The American commander in Iraq, General George Casey, was not oblivious to climbing Iraqi civilian fatality totals, but he was slow to understand that the nature of the war had changed from a Sunni insurgency directed primarily at U.S. forces to a full-scale civil war. General Casey had been dealt a hard hand after arriving in Iraq in 2004 to take command from the overmatched Lieutenant General Sanchez. Casey had never before seen combat and, like the rest of the U.S. Army, had not been trained or educated in counterinsurgency. Armed only with

the understanding of the subject he had gained from a weekend reading of *Learning to Eat Soup with a Knife*, General Casey was nonetheless
capable of recognizing that he needed a counterinsurgency campaign
plan, something his predecessor had not put together during his own
year in command. In fact, it was during the writing and revision of this
campaign plan that Casey had tasked Gunner Sepp to put together the
list of best and worst practices for counterinsurgency that had led to
his *Military Review* article and subsequent invitation to Basin Harbor.
Casey had also noted the British decision to establish a counterinsurgency academy during the Malayan Emergency and set up one of his
own at Taji in November 2005, after about a year of being unimpressed
with the counterinsurgency readiness of the forces he was receiving
from the Army.

But for all the disasters he had inherited—Casey was known to
mutter "George Bush has given me a pile of shit" under his breath—
and all the good things he did to improve his position, Casey suffered
from a fundamental misunderstanding of the situation in Iraq that his
boss, CENTCOM Commander General John Abizaid, had inflicted on
him. Abizaid, an Arabic-speaking infantry officer, had been stationed in
the Middle East in 1983 when the Beirut bombing left a Marine barracks in ruins and 241 American service members dead. Abizaid was
scarred by the experience, convinced that American troops evinced
such antibodies in the Middle East that even if they had been sent for
positive missions like peacekeeping, they would inspire more violence
than they tamped down. The lesson was imprinted in Casey's mind
through repeated interactions with General Abizaid, and over the
course of 2006, even as the dynamics of conflict changed and casualty
rates in Baghdad skyrocketed, Casey continued to press the case for
continued U.S. troop reductions.

The issue had been around at least since March 2005. Casey's strategy of focusing on shifting responsibility to the Iraqis inspired reserva-

tions in President Bush, who accused his commander of playing for a tie.[1] Casey was furious, but the president was right; his commander had no theory of victory, and no plan for how to reduce violence in Iraq to a level that could be handled by the Iraqis themselves. His focus was on turning over responsibility to the Iraqis as soon as possible, almost regardless of the consequences for the country.

Fortunately, other Army officers had a different view. H. R. McMaster was an armor officer who had earned the Silver Star in Desert Storm for destroying an entire Iraqi battalion with his cavalry troop in a few minutes at the Battle of 73 Easting; he had later earned his doctorate at the University of North Carolina for a scathing indictment of the leadership of the U.S. military in Vietnam, published as *Dereliction of Duty: Lyndon Johnson, Robert McNamara, the Joint Chiefs of Staff, and the Lies That Led to Vietnam.* H. R. was now commanding the Third Armored Cavalry Regiment in Tal Afar, where he applied the classic counterinsurgency techniques of isolating a piece of terrain, separating the insurgents from the population, and then holding the cleared terrain with a combination of his own forces and locally raised ones. We used the Third ACR's work at Tal Afar to illustrate the classic technique of "clear, hold, and build" in the fifth chapter of the field manual, and President Bush praised the technique in a nationally televised speech.

However, even earning the praise of the president of the United States wasn't enough to get H. R. promoted to brigadier general. H. R. had a way of telling the emperor that he had no clothes that rubbed many in the Army the wrong way, and a promotion board that was about to meet was likely to pass him over for the third time. That decision would have ended his career as a colonel despite H. R.'s extraordinary performance in two very different wars and his service as an academic thinker and innovator. H. R. was a hero not just to the president but also to many young officers who believed in his visionary leadership; if the Army failed to promote H. R., what hope did any of them have to make a difference in such a hidebound organization?

Paul Yingling and I published an article in *Armed Forces Journal* in October 2006, just as the field manual was going to final edits, titled "New Rules for New Enemies." The article drew heavily on the thinking I had been doing about the field manual and that Paul had done while working as H. R.'s deputy in Tal Afar. It presented a long list of recommendations for change in the Army but featured a plea based on our respect for McMaster and our belief that the Army would pass him over for promotion yet again.

"To win the Long War, the Army must develop a more adaptive organizational culture. To create such a culture, the Army must change its centralized, specialized focus on major conventional wars to a more decentralized and less specialized focus on full-spectrum operations. This shift in organizational culture cannot occur within existing organizations—indeed, these organizations can be an impediment to change. The best way to change the organizational culture of the Army is to change the pathways for professional advancement within the officer corps. The Army will become more adaptive only when being adaptive offers the surest path to promotion."[2]

Fred Kaplan later described me during this period as "wandering the halls of the Pentagon with a gaunt, hungry look on my face, desperately looking for someone to talk with about counterinsurgency." One of the few who were interested was Pete Geren. The former congressman, now a special assistant to Secretary Rumsfeld in the Pentagon, had procured an expensive hardcover copy of *Soup* after reading *The New York Times Magazine*'s depiction of "Professor Nagl's War." He later introduced himself to me at my desk in Secretary Wolfowitz's office. Geren was deeply concerned about the course of the war in Iraq, the casualties that we were suffering, and the general lack of understanding of what it was we were trying to accomplish and how. We grabbed lunch together several times in his office, more frequently once he became undersecretary of the Army. I hit Geren hard on two points: the need to promote adaptive Army leaders like H. R. McMaster, and the need to develop wheeled armored vehicles with V-shaped hulls that deflected IED blasts rather than flat-bottomed hulls that absorbed the impact and had cost us so many lives and limbs in Al Anbar. Geren listened politely, more politely than my enthusiasm probably deserved, although what I said went in. Unfortunately, fixing these problems had to wait until he was promoted to secretary of the Army by a new secretary of defense.

One of the arguments I often made to Geren and to anyone else who would listen was that the "sweep and clear" strategy that was being used by American units in Iraq was ineffective; the insurgents would return as soon as the American forces left, or would just lie low during our visits to their sector. I called it "clear and leave" and described the process as akin to mowing the lawn, because the terrain would have to be cleared again in the near future. This was one of many lessons that should have been learned from Vietnam but had been forgotten on purpose in the years after that war.

I was driving from the Pentagon to Carlisle, Pennsylvania, to give my "Learning Counterinsurgency in Iraq" talk at the Army War College on October 19, 2005, when Secretary of State Condoleezza Rice appeared before the Senate Foreign Relations Committee. She spoke of the need for a new approach in Iraq: "Our strategy has to be to clear, hold, and build: to clear areas from insurgent control, to hold them securely, and to build durable Iraqi institutions." My eyes filled with tears, and I had to pull over to the side of the road for a minute to get control of myself. The word on how to conduct counterinsurgency was finally getting through to someone close to the top. I later learned that the method of transmission was via H. R. McMaster and Lieutenant General Ray Odierno, who traveled with Secretary Rice in his new position as assistant to the chairman of the Joint Chiefs of Staff. Secretary Rumsfeld, of course, was apoplectic that a new strategy for Iraq was being briefed by the secretary of state, and sadly Secretary Rice's correct prescription for a better counterinsurgency strategy in Iraq was ignored in Baghdad and the Pentagon.

Our little band of insurgents inside the Pentagon was able to accomplish some good during the reign of Secretary Rumsfeld. The Defense Science Board, run by a small, brilliant man named Craig Fields, had focused its annual summer study on "Transition to and from Hostilities" in 2004. The report got mired in the bureaucratic muck of the Pentagon, but Deputy Assistant Secretary of Defense (DASD) for Stability Operations Jeb Nadaner refused to let it die. Nadaner was the successor in that office to Sarah Sewall several removed, although she had been called the DASD for "peacekeeping" under President Clinton. A deputy assistant secretary of defense is technically a three-star equivalent, but the real power of DASDs lies in their relationships with other political appointees—and with their military assistants. Jeb had invited me to speak to his directorate early in my Pentagon tenure. His subordinates included my old friend from Sosh Colonel Rich Lacquement, as well as civilians Vikram Singh, Colin Kahl, and Janine Davidson; all three of them would become DASDs themselves in President Obama's Pentagon, while Rich retired from the Army to become the dean of the Army War College. Jeb worked hard to turn the conclusions of the Defense Science Board study into something the Pentagon could get its arms around. The result was Department of Defense Directive 3000.05, signed by Gordon England on November 28, 2005. It stated:

> Stability operations are a core US military mission that the Department of Defense shall be prepared to conduct and support. *They shall be given priority comparable to combat operations* and be explicitly

addressed and integrated across all DoD activities including doctrine, organization, training, education, exercises, material, leadership, personnel, facilities, and planning. [Italics mine]

This was a huge change from the attitude in the Pentagon prior to the invasion of Iraq, which had all but forbidden the very activities that DoD 3000.05 now put on an equal footing with planning for, training in, and conduct of combat operations. But important as the words were, they would not be implemented by the man who was serving as the secretary of defense at the time the directive was signed.

My doctoral dissertation had centered on the importance of an individual leader at the top of the organization who recognized the need for organizational change, encouraged subordinates to innovate, and then drove the rest of the organization to adopt the best practices that had been identified. General Sir Gerald Templer had been such a change agent in Malaya, while William Westmoreland had stymied many innovations that showed great promise in Vietnam. By the time Creighton Abrams replaced Westmoreland, the American people had lost faith in the effort, and the changes Abrams was able to implement were too little, too late.

Even General Westmoreland, however, who has recently been labeled "The General Who Lost the Vietnam War" by former Army officer Bob Sorley, did not exert as pernicious an effect on organizational innovation during the Vietnam War as Secretary of Defense Donald Rumsfeld did during the war in Iraq. From his initial insistence on reducing the number of troops involved in the invasion well below the number that would be required to secure Iraq once the Saddam Hussein regime had crumbled, to his requirement that his Department of Defense rather than the Department of State be tasked to oversee postconflict operations followed by a complete failure to prepare to assume those responsibilities, Rumsfeld's role in the planning and preparation for the Iraq War was spectacularly bad. These mistakes were closely followed by his acceptance of Paul Bremer's decrees to disband the Iraqi Army, radically de-Ba'athify Iraq, and prohibit local elections; Bremer reported to Rumsfeld, and the secretary was therefore responsible for the decisions that created and inflamed the insurgency in Iraq.

Frustration with the war in Iraq and with the leadership of Secretary Rumsfeld peaked in the summer of 2006 with the publication of articles like Marine Lieutenant General Greg Newbold's "Why Iraq Was a Mistake" in *Time* magazine; the secretary's stubborn insistence that we weren't fighting an insurgency and refusal to send more troops to improve security or build a bigger Army and Marine Corps to relieve the strain on the force had boiled over.

But as Paul Yingling and I were discussing, it wasn't just the SECDEF whose performance was lacking; the Army's general officer corps had failed to prepare the Army for the war it was actually going to have to fight, and it had failed to rapidly adapt when the conventional Army they had built was required to conduct counterinsurgency. Our conversations often resulted in magazine articles, and this one was no different, but it was even more controversial than our previous writings had been. I tried to persuade Paul to publish this one anonymously, or under the pseudonyms "Willie and Joe," a reference to Bill Mauldin's iconic World War II soldiers, but he (probably correctly) pointed out that it wouldn't be hard to figure out that it was really the two of us who had written it.

In a decision that still troubles me, I reluctantly took my name off of the piece to preserve my limited Army career prospects, and Paul courageously published "A Failure in Generalship" as the cover story of the April 2007 *Armed Forces Journal*. The article was a collaboration between the two of us, as had been all the previous articles Paul had published; this was the first to have only his byline. I had written the part

*Lieutenant General Greg Newbold and Major General
Robert Scales, February 19, 2008.*

of the article comparing the performance of American generals in Iraq
with those who had served in Vietnam, and suggested calling on Congress to use its power to promote and prematurely retire general officers to reward good performance and punish failure; Paul's original
idea for a solution, creating an American version of the German General Staff, was unlikely enough to have reduced the credibility of the
article as a whole.

The article's best line was Paul's alone: "As matters stand now, a private who loses a rifle suffers far greater consequences than a general
who loses a war." Paul found out that a lieutenant colonel who signs
an article critical of the performance of generals in combat also suffers
greater consequences than a general who loses a war; he still took command of an artillery battalion shortly after the article was published

With Paul Yingling at the Council on Foreign
Relations, February 13, 2008.

only because of a phone call to the Army by House Armed Services Committee chairman Ike Skelton, warning the Army that it had better allow him to take command of his artillery battalion as scheduled. However, Paul was not selected to accompany his battalion to Iraq, a decision that was overturned only after intervention by General Petraeus, and he was promoted to full colonel only after intervention by General Chiarelli, then the vice chief of staff of the Army.

Paul has now retired as a lieutenant colonel, not having served long enough as a full colonel to keep that rank in retirement, and is pugnaciously teaching social studies at an international baccalaureate high school in Colorado Springs. In yet another mark of his strong character and general poor judgment, Paul does not resent me for throwing him under the bus, believing that had I kept my name on the piece, I would not have been able to continue advocating change in the Army. He received the Public Service Award from the University of Chicago in 2013 in recognition of his intellectual and moral courage.

Secretary Rumsfeld's continued refusal to acknowledge that there was an insurgency in Iraq—extending even to forbidding the use of the word *insurgency* to describe what was happening there—and his continued emphasis on withdrawing U.S. troops as rapidly as possible even in the face of the escalating civil war through the course of 2006, eventually became too much for President Bush to ignore. Secretary Rumsfeld was very close to Vice President Dick Cheney, who was determined to protect his old friend; Bush's decision to overrule Cheney and fire Rumsfeld in many ways marked the end of the six-year foreign policy string of errors that Tom Ricks correctly described as a *Fiasco*. It would remain for Rumsfeld's replacement, Bob Gates, to pick up the pieces and develop policies that would allow the United States to accomplish some of its core national security objectives and depart Iraq with a degree of honor and without leaving behind a Sunni–Shia civil war that might have consumed the entire Middle East.

6.

Proof of Concept

Iraq 2007–2008

With final revisions of the *Counterinsurgency Field Manual* under way at Fort Leavenworth, I departed the Pentagon in October 2006 to take command of the First Battalion, 34th Armor at Fort Riley, Kansas. 1-34 was the same unit with which I had fought in Iraq as operations officer. Giving lieutenant colonels command of units they had served in as majors had been anathema to the Army before the war, but given the constant churn of units deploying to and from Iraq, any stability or familiarity was a good thing. Returning lieutenant colonels to command their former units had now become official policy, and near the end of my first year in the Pentagon, I was delighted to get the news that I was returning to command of the Centurions from General Dick Cody, the vice chief of staff of the Army from whose speechwriting office Frank Helmick had delivered me.

I was not prepared for the next piece of information I received. The battalion had been slated to deploy to Iraq in 2005 but had been "off-ramped" as part of the Pentagon's continuing effort to minimize deployed troop numbers. Instead, a number of subordinate companies

*Everyone's favorite farewell gift from the Pentagon—a visitor's badge!
The photo is of me eating soup with a knife in the Pentagon
dining room, a joke that apparently never grows old, 2006.*

had deployed as Security Forces (SECFOR), escorting logistics convoys all over Iraq in up-armored Humvees. The work was important, but it wasn't tanking—and the deployment of the two SECFOR companies meant that the unit I was about to assume command of wasn't a complete, deployable tank battalion. Given that fact, the Army's decision to turn the First Battalion, 34th Armor into a training organization designed to build, train, and deploy military transition teams that would then embed with Iraqi or Afghan security forces almost made sense.

But the move was likely the kiss of death for my Army career, such as it was. My buddies would spend their battalion command tours preparing for and then deploying to combat, while I would never leave Kansas in an operational role. And as hard as I tried to convince myself that what we were doing to prepare the advisory teams that would train and fight with Afghan and Iraqi security forces was far more important for the overall course of both wars than was any possible contribution a deployed tank battalion could make, I was still very disappointed that I wouldn't get to lead troops in combat as a battalion commander.

Missing the chance to command in a war that had been the sole focus of the past three years of my life was a blow from which my love of the Army never really recovered; I had called the ball on counterinsurgency and received command of a tank battalion without tanks as thanks. Adding insult to injury, the Army not only took all our tanks away; it took all our weapons as well, underlining the truth that we were a training organization rather than a deployable combat formation. Some of our troopers joked that there were Girl Scout troops that were better armed than was our tank battalion.

I probably could have wiggled out of the assignment and gotten command of a real tank battalion, one with enough weapons to overthrow a small country rather than one that posed no threat to the average Girl Scout troop. I was in a powerful office, working for the deputy secretary of the entire Department of Defense; it wouldn't have taken much complaining to have my orders changed, sending another lieutenant colonel to the training mission. But the only time I had ever pulled strings to get an assignment was after my dad died, when I had asked for Fort Riley, two hours away from my mom. I'd said counterinsurgency was important, and now I was going to get the chance to demonstrate that I meant what I'd said.

Amid the disappointment, there was some good news. Although literally in the middle of nowhere, Fort Riley is a wonderful old frontier Army post, with big stone houses for command sergeants major and battalion commanders, and our house was one of the lovely, historic limestone dwellings built in a bygone era. More important, the fact that I wasn't deploying to the fight in Iraq gave me more time to fight to persuade the Army that it needed to take counterinsurgency seriously.

The deployable units at Fort Riley are all headquartered on the

Double-wide sweet double-wide, 2006.

ironically named Custer Hill, at which the Seventh Cavalry had been stationed for several years before its fateful rendezvous with Sitting Bull. When I arrived, the First of the 34th Armor was moving off the hill down to Camp Funston, the point of origin of the global influenza epidemic of 1919 that killed more people than had died in the First World War. Funston had been used again as a deployment site during the Second World War, and a number of wood-frame barracks from that period remained, but my battalion would be housed not in those drafty if historic buildings but in trailers. Battalion command posts were double-wides. Sergeant Shoe, my Desert Storm gunner from West Virginia, would have been right at home.

The Army had built two actual nontrailer steel-frame buildings to serve as barracks for the military transition team members. They deployed to Fort Riley for an eight-week training cycle. It was our job, during that time, to qualify them on their individual weapons, form them into vehicle crews, and train them to fire heavy weapons, includ-

Teaching COIN in a double-wide, 2007.

ing the M2 .50-caliber machine gun, the 7.62mm M249 machine gun, and the automatic grenade launcher. We also provided rudimentary Dari or Arabic training, some advice on how to advise Afghans or Iraqis, and the basics of counterinsurgency, a task I took on myself not just for the MTT teams assigned to my battalion but to all MTT teams trained by the other three battalions in the brigade as well. I relied, yet again, on the slides I'd made to defend my doctoral dissertation, although they were heavily modified by now with additions from David Galula and the writing of the counterinsurgency manual and featured the Chiarelli/Michaelis "lines of operation" slide.

One of the few benefits of commanding an MTT training battalion rather than a tank battalion deployed in Iraq was that I was in the United States when the *Counterinsurgency Field Manual* saw the light of day after what had to be the fastest drafting-to-publication schedule in Army history. When it was published on December 15, 2006, the international media outcry was astounding. In November Secretary Gates,

With Lieutenant Colonel (retired) Art DeGroat and Secretary of Defense Robert Gates (center), after his lecture at Kansas State University, November 26, 2007.

when asked whether the United States was winning the war in Iraq, at his confirmation hearing to replace Secretary of Defense Rumsfeld, had correctly answered "No, sir," and the world was watching to see whether Gates, quickly confirmed as secretary, could turn the war around. New personnel are the punctuation point on new policy, and the commander in Iraq would also soon change. General Petraeus was widely viewed as the likely candidate to replace George Casey in command, and the *Counterinsurgency Field Manual* was the way he would go about doing it if given the chance. There is no comparable moment in history when a general has taken the time to plan out how he intends to fight a war that is currently being lost, publishes the plan publicly, and then goes to war to execute the playbook he has written.

The manual was downloaded more than a million times in the first month after it had been published. Ultimately, copies were even found in Taliban training camps in Pakistan, and it was translated and critiqued on jihadi Web sites. Our enemies were reading it; we had to get *our* guys to read it. In support of that effort, General Petraeus asked me to do some of the publicity associated with the launch, and I participated in a number of interviews, including one on National Public Radio. It had far-reaching consequences.

A week or so after the interview aired, I received a phone call from a man I didn't know who told me that I had been a "driveway moment" for him: although he'd arrived where he was heading, he didn't turn his car off in order to hear the end of my discussion of the counterinsurgency manual on his car radio. He had me at "driveway moment."

He told me that he worked for the U.S. Naval Institute, which was putting together a national security conference at the end of January in San Diego and had scheduled Admiral William "Fox" Fallon to speak. Fallon had just been nominated to replace General Abizaid as the commander of Central Command and had dropped the speaking engagement to prepare for his confirmation hearings. Would I fill in for the admiral and talk about the new counterinsurgency doctrine? I pointed out that he was replacing a full admiral, an officer with the pay grade of ten, with literally half the man, an Army O-5 whom he'd never met. He told me that I'd be fine, based on what he'd heard on the radio. I agreed to give the talk and decided to take Susi along on my dime as she'd never been to San Diego. We left Jack with my mom in Kansas City.

San Diego in January is a nice place, and there was a good-size crowd for my breakfast talk, including a retired Marine three-star general I knew. I introduced him to Susi before I gave my talk, and afterward he called me over for a chat. Cutting straight to the point, the general said, "Son, you need to get out of the Army."

I was surprised. Was the talk that bad?

No, he said, it was fine—in fact, he offered, I could probably do more for the Army out of uniform than in it at my current pay grade. Moreover, he sensed that my wife was ready for me to get out of the army, and he'd seen too many officers lose their families and their careers. Save yours, he advised, making it clear that my family was the one he meant.

Thus began a yearlong discussion with my wife and the hardest decision of my career. Susi had never been a good fit in the Army. While personable and fun-loving, she didn't truly warm to the women for whom being married to the Army was a career in itself, and in all honesty, they didn't warm to her. Still, she'd been a good sport, as Paul Yingling said when I told him that I was thinking of getting out. Beyond that, I sensed I'd have little trouble finding another way to contribute. Then–Lieutenant General Peter Chiarelli weighed in hard from his perch as senior military assistant to Secretary of Defense Gates to get me to stay in the Army and almost succeeded with a five-page handwritten letter. He was a good man facing hard challenges, including retaining the Army's talent after a decade of grinding war. As I told General Chiarelli later, if I'd been sleeping with him instead of Susi, he would have won the fight.

In addition to the visit to San Diego, I also answered an invitation to speak on the manual at the Center for Naval Analysis in Washington at the request of my Al Anbar Province friend Carter Malkasian, like me a product of Bob O'Neill's supervision at Oxford. After that talk, the director of program analysis and evaluation at the Pentagon asked a hard question about my day job, training military transition team members. I was fairly critical in my response, and he asked whether I had a better answer to the problem of providing advisers to the Iraqi and Afghan Armies that I could put in writing. I wrote it that weekend, sent him a draft copy, and then submitted "Institutionalizing Adaptation: It's Time for a Permanent Army Advisor Corps" to *Military Review*, which had published so many articles to such good effect over the

preceding five years. *Military Review* said that they'd be happy to publish it but were backlogged; would publication in a year be acceptable?

It would not. The article I'd written was based on my experience
commanding one of the battalions preparing advisers for service in
Iraq and Afghanistan. I was furious at the ad-hocracy that underlay everything the Army was doing in adviser selection and training; our
consensus at Fort Riley was that they were picking the wrong people
(those who had not yet deployed to combat, rather than the most talented who had), sending them to the wrong place (a Kansas prairie to
prepare them to operate in deserts and mountains, when we had a
superb training area with mountains and deserts at the National Training Center in California), training them with the wrong people (tank
drivers rather than the Special Forces Green Berets who actually knew
how to execute a train and advise mission), and then disbanding
trained, battle-tested adviser teams a year later, only to create new ones
from scratch to replace them.

It was no way to run a railroad. When asked about the Army's performance of this critical mission by Lieutenant General Doug Lute,
then serving at the White House as the deputy national security adviser for Iraq and Afghanistan, I told him, "We only need to do better if
we want to win."

I mentioned *Military Review*'s reluctance to rapidly publish the
piece on standing up permanent adviser forces to Jim Miller during one
of our periodic talks. Jim had just taken on the arduous job of director
of studies at a new defense policy think tank in Washington, the Center
for a New American Security (or CNAS, so named because the Old
American Security wasn't working out so well in the post–September
11 world). CNAS had been spun out of another Washington think tank,
the Center for Strategic and International Studies, by two former deputy assistant secretaries of defense, Kurt Campbell and Michèle Flournoy. They were convinced that what Washington needed was yet

another think tank, and they courageously decided to stand up an organization that they dedicated to the promotion of strong, principled,
pragmatic defense and security policies. While CNAS was officially
nonpartisan and included scholars from both political parties, both
Kurt and Michèle had served in the Pentagon for President Clinton.
Furious about the shortcomings of defense policy under George W.
Bush, particularly the Iraq debacle, they believed that they could take
national security policy away from the Republicans as a campaign issue
in the forthcoming presidential election season.

I had met Kurt and Michèle before and was impressed by both, but
it was Jim Miller who pulled me into the CNAS orbit through the
mechanism of my article on improving the foreign military advisory
effort. Under the title "Institutionalizing Adaptation: It's Time for a
Permanent Army Advisor Corps," it became the first piece CNAS published in June 2007, released at a conference attended by many Washington policy wonks. The idea of a standing Army adviser corps would
gain appreciable attention, including endorsements by both Senator
John McCain and Senator Barack Obama during the 2008 presidential
campaign, but it has still not been fully implemented—a grievous failure to understand the strategic environment and build the forces necessary to succeed in it that now puts at risk everything the nation and
international community have invested in Afghanistan.

However, Afghanistan was not perceived to be the risk of the
moment in 2007. There was room in the national conversation for only
one war at a time, and that war was Iraq. The American effort there
was clearly in trouble. Stung by the loss of both the House of Repre-
sentatives and the Senate in the 2006 midterm elections, President
George W. Bush had replaced Secretary Rumsfeld with former director
of central intelligence Bob Gates, a low-key Kansan who described his
priorities as "Iraq, Iraq, and Iraq" at his confirmation hearing. He
headed to Iraq on December 18, the day after he was sworn in as secre-

tary of defense and just three days after the publication of the *Counterinsurgency Field Manual*. The president had decided to double down on Iraq, against the advice of almost everyone concerned, and needed new people to implement the new policy: Gates and David Petraeus, whom he subsequently nominated for a fourth star, would implement the new counterinsurgency strategy that Petraeus had been thinking about continually for the past year. When Petraeus met with the president, he corrected his boss's statement that he was "doubling down" in Iraq; no, Mr. President, he said, you're going all in. And, he added, we need the rest of the U.S. government to go all in with the military.

The metaphor was apt, even if it did become an unfortunate title for the biography of Petraeus written by Paula Broadwell in 2012. The president committed additional troops to implement the new strategy—literally all the ground troops the nation had available to deploy to Iraq: five Army brigades, with deployments stretched from the usual twelve to fifteen full months, two Marine battalions, a Marine expeditionary unit, and a variety of other elements, including an aviation brigade, a division headquarters, and other combat support and logistical elements. The Army units would be used to clear and hold in Baghdad and the "Baghdad Belts" around the city that the insurgents were using as staging grounds, while the Marines would be sent to Al Anbar, then apparently in danger of slipping completely into the hands of insurgents.

The story of the origins of the surge, as this additional deployment of more than 25,000 troops was called, is an extremely unusual one. General Casey had taken aboard his boss General John Abizaid's belief that American troops deployed to the Middle East inspired such significant antibodies that fewer American boots on the ground was almost always the right answer, even as violence spiraled over the course of 2006. This was music to the ears of Secretary Rumsfeld, who had fought to prevent the deployment of a large number of American troops to Iraq in the first place and had not changed his mind simply because things hadn't worked out as planned. The Joint Chiefs of Staff were concerned about doing fatal damage to the all-volunteer force, which was clearly creaking under the strain of repeated deployments; the default answer thus was to draw down American troops as soon as possible, an answer perhaps prompted by the fact that they knew it was the one the secretary of defense wanted to hear.

In this context, the most critical voice arguing for the deployment of more troops to Iraq was someone with no official standing whatsoever. General Jack Keane had recently retired as vice chief of staff of the Army, turning down a promotion to chief of staff officially because of his wife's health problems, although many speculated that he did not want to work for Secretary Rumsfeld. Himself a Vietnam veteran, Keane fumed at the prospect of America losing another counterinsurgency campaign. He was extremely close to Petraeus, at whose side he had been standing when a trooper from the 101st Airborne tripped and accidentally shot then–Lieutenant Colonel Petraeus in the chest during a training exercise. Major General Keane had flown with Petraeus in the medical evacuation helicopter and ensured that the best surgeon in the region—a certain Dr. Bill Frist, who later became Senate majority leader but on this day came straight to the operating room from the golf course—was the person who sewed his subordinate back together again. Keane now became the de facto senior military adviser to President Bush, advocating powerfully for more troops, a new commander, and a new strategy for Iraq, all against the express wishes of the serving chairman of the Joint Chiefs, Marine General Peter Pace, and theater commander General George Casey.

Bush's decision to deploy an additional 20,000 "surge" troops (which grew to well over 25,000) to Iraq in an attempt to end the escalating Sunni–Shia civil war was the bravest of his presidency. He made the decision against the advice of almost all his advisers as well as the Joint

Chiefs of Staff, who eventually bought in only in return for a long-over-due presidential decision to increase the size of the Army and Marine Corps to begin to relieve the increasing strain on the force. It is hard to remember now how bad the situation looked in Iraq at the time. At his confirmation hearing for the position of overall commander in Iraq, General Petraeus had to remind the Senate Armed Services Commit-tee that "hard is not hopeless." The president has enormous freedom of action in foreign policy decisions. Against their better judgment, the Senators gave Bush one last chance in Iraq and confirmed Petraeus for his fourth star.

Although many of the COINdinistas went to Baghdad to work with General Petraeus, including Dave Kilcullen and H. R. McMaster, I was not called. Petraeus thought my battalion command too import-ant to my career, and my role helping train, educate, and inspire future advisers to the Iraqi and Afghan security forces too critical, to pull me out of that role. Instead he asked me to serve as his surrogate explain-ing and defending the *Counterinsurgency Field Manual* to the American people.

That role had started when the field manual was released with the NPR appearance that ultimately resulted in the conversation in San Diego and led to my retirement from the Army. It went in directions that no one expected, however, on a January 2007 visit to the Univer-sity of Chicago to give a talk on the principles of counterinsurgency and their application in Iraq. I dropped by the University of Chicago Press to meet the editors I'd worked with on the paperback edition of *Learning to Eat Soup with a Knife.* When asked what I'd been doing for America lately, I proudly noted that the *Counterinsurgency Field Manual* had been downloaded more than a million times in the month since we had posted it online. Editor John Tryneski, sensing a bestseller, asked who held the copyright. When I couldn't answer, he inquired whether I'd be willing to write a foreword to a paperback edition if Chicago could garner the publication rights. I readily agreed, and when John discovered that the government allows open publication of all field manuals, Chicago jumped on the opportunity.

It became only the second field manual to be published by a university press, the first being the Marine Corps' *Small Wars Manual* of 1940, published by the Sunflower Press of Kansas State University, not far from Fort Riley. The finished University of Chicago version, published in a World War II style cover complete with rounded corners to fit into fatigue pockets and simulated "dirt" ground into the creases, featured an introduction by Sarah Sewall that began, "This counterinsurgency manual challenges much of what is holy about the American way of war. . . . Those who fail to see the manual as radical probably don't understand it, or at least understand what it's up against." Con Crane later said that Sarah's introduction was as good as the whole rest of the book put together. She decried the lack of a broader U.S. counterinsurgency strategy, describing the field manual as a "moon without a planet to orbit" in the absence of national-level counterinsurgency guidance, and also presciently expressed concern about the staying power of the American public, which she thought unlikely to "supply greater concentrations of forces, accept higher casualties, fund serious nation-building and stay many long years to conduct counterinsurgency by the book."

I wrote a foreword that explained both the evolution and the importance of the manual, beginning by noting that when an insurgency began in Iraq in the late summer of 2003, the Army was unprepared to fight it. The foreword concluded with praise of David Galula's thinking:

> Of the many books that were influential in the writing of Field Manual 3-24, perhaps none was as important as David Galula's *Counterinsurgency Warfare: Theory and Practice*. Galula, a French Army officer who drew many valuable lessons from his service in France's unsuc-

cessful campaign against Algerian insurgents, was a strong advocate of counterinsurgency doctrine. He wrote, "If the individual members of the organizations were of the same mind, if every organization worked according to a standard pattern, the problem would be solved. Is this not precisely what a coherent, well-understood, and accepted doctrine would tend to achieve?"

The University of Chicago Press released its edition of the manual on July 4, 2007, just as the surge forces were beginning to make progress in breaking down the wall of resistance from Iraqi insurgents and militia members. The press did a great job of getting it out to media outlets for reviews to expand its reach. The field manual was reviewed favorably by Sarah Sewall's colleague at Harvard, Samantha Power, on the front page of *The New York Times Sunday Book Review*—the first time a military doctrinal manual had risen to the attention of the *Times*, which called it a "landmark."

Chicago also sent a copy of the field manual to *The Daily Show with Jon Stewart*, as I discovered while running Machine Gun Range 8 at Fort Riley one sunny Monday in August. As military transition teams were qualifying on the range, my cell phone rang with a New York number, and a young woman invited me to appear on *The Daily Show* that Thursday night to discuss the field manual with Jon Stewart. *The Daily Show* had never even appeared on my radar screen as a lifetime stretch goal. I agreed immediately, then had to convince the Army that letting me fulfill that promise was a good idea.

Fortunately, I knew the Army's chief of public affairs, Brigadier General Tony Cucolo, from giving a talk about counterinsurgency to his team at Joint Force Headquarters in Norfolk, Virginia, the previous year. He knew something was up when I called (I think his exact words were "This can't be good"), and I got to the point quickly: I was going to appear on *The Daily Show* to talk about the *Counterinsurgency Field Manual* on Thursday night, either in uniform with the Army's permission or in a suit and tie without it. I mentioned *The Daily Show*'s status as the number-one news source among under-thirties in the United States in case General Cucolo had any interest in getting the Army in front of that demographic.

He asked for twenty-four hours to work the problem and called back the next day with official permission and an admonition: "Nagl, don't [mess] this up." Interestingly, that was the exact same advice that First Infantry Division Commander Carter Ham had given me when I assumed command of the Centurions; apparently, I had that effect on Army generals.

Almost anything goes in Manhattan, but not many people walk around in Army greens in August. I received a few stares in the hotel lobby, took a ride over to the taping in a *Daily Show* limo, and then cooled my heels in the green room. Jon Stewart came by a few minutes before taping began, carrying his young son. He apologized for getting only about halfway through the manual, and I told him that that was all I'd read of it, too, but that I thought we'd still have plenty to talk about.

We did. The audience was friendly at the start but cooled off quickly when I described the manual in a phrase attributed to General Jim Mattis: "Be polite, be professional, be prepared to kill." I pointed out that this was a good rule to follow in New York as well, and Jon agreed.

The experience was surprisingly enjoyable and helped buy General Petraeus some support at a rough time in the fight for Baghdad. He'd taken command of the American effort in Iraq from General Casey in Baghdad on February 10, 2007. The security situation he faced was dire, but he had additional resources with which to attack it: five Army brigades plus the two Marine battalions and the Marine expeditionary unit for Al Anbar.

Far more important than the number of additional troops deployed was the mission change they were given by Petraeus and the operational-level commander, Lieutenant General Ray Odierno. As Petraeus would often note later, "the most important surge was the surge of ideas, not the surge of forces," and the biggest of the big ideas was captured in the new mission, which, in accordance with the dictates of the new field manual, emphasized the imperative of securing the population first. A big step in this direction was the creation, during 2007, of seventy-seven new joint security stations and combat outposts throughout Baghdad, manned by American troops and their Iraqi Army and Police counterparts. American casualties rose as the Army cleared neighborhoods controlled by insurgents or militia fighters, but the locals benefited from a higher level of security. As the field manual suggested, when security improved, economic and political progress soon followed.

Napoleon famously said, "All my generals are good. Give me ones who are lucky." Petraeus was both good enough and lucky enough to take advantage of the Sunni Awakening, the decision of several Sunni tribes to switch sides and fight against the Iraqi branch of Al Qaeda after being assured the support of American forces. This development, which was similar to those earlier in the war that literally died due to lack of support in Baghdad, was years in the making. It marked a dramatic change in American policy, which had until then stubbornly ignored tribal power structures in favor of democratic processes for which Iraq was simply not ready.

Petraeus had, himself, overseen reconciliation with Sunnis in the summer of 2003, only to see the hope of a broader negotiated settlement evaporate due to nonsupport in Baghdad. Now he had the wisdom to recognize this opportunity and the courage to seize it— interestingly, without asking for permission from his superiors in Washington. He felt the conduct of the war and negotiations with America's enemies in it were all within his span of authority. And stating often that it was not possible to kill or capture your way to success against an industrial-strength insurgency, he returned to Iraq knowing that he would need to foster reconciliation with those insurgents and their supporters willing to reject Al Qaeda and the Sunni insurgent leaders.

With Petraeus directing a new strategy to nurture the "shoots" of the nascent awakening, it quickly grew from its origins outside Ramadi, throughout Al Anbar province, and in subsequent months, into Baghdad's Ameriyah neighborhood, itself no rose garden. My West Point classmate and senior-year roommate Lieutenant Colonel Dale Kuehl, who was commanding 1-5 Cavalry in the area, was able to back Sunni leader Abu Abid with support directly from Petraeus (who happened to go for a run with Kuehl's executive officer at a key moment) when that brave Sunni leader chose to turn against AQI in late May 2007.

In the months that followed, this process was repeated throughout the Sunni areas and then commenced in Shia areas, where U.S. forces supported tribal leaders who wanted to oppose the militia elements that had made life difficult in their neighborhoods. Adversaries became allies in a vivid illustration of the classic principle "The enemy of my enemy is my friend." A platoon leader in Kuehl's battalion described the overnight transformation in Ameriyah with dramatic understatement: "It was weird." Petraeus, briefed on the possibility of a switch in the Sunnis' allegiance by Kuehl's number two, had two instructions: "Do not let our Army stop you" and "Do not let the Iraqi government stop you." It was that kind of war.

Neither the U.S. Army (in which some commanders did not initially like the idea of reconciling with those who had our troopers' blood on their hands) nor the Shia-led Iraqi government (leery of accommodating the Sunnis who had once dominated Iraq) was able to stop what eventually became the "Sons of Iraq" concept, which spread like wildfire across the Sunni west and center of the country.

Getting Dale Kuehl ready for a parade at West Point.

The effective end of the Sunni insurgency and the implementation of Petraeus's joint security stations also eliminated the need for the Shi'ite militias that had sprung up to defend their sect against their old enemies—and that then carried out many of the sectarian attacks on Sunni areas in Baghdad and much of the crime in southern Iraq. And in March 2008, Iraqi prime minister Nouri al-Maliki deployed the Iraqi Army to clear the militias from Basra and Sadr City, tasks in which it succeeded thanks to considerable support by U.S. forces. By the time Petraeus left Iraq in September of that year, the net result of the surge was a decrease in violence by nearly 80 percent and the lowest American casualty rates of the war.

There is now a significant debate over the extent to which Petraeus's leadership, and the doctrine he authored and then implemented, was in fact responsible for the incontrovertible change on the ground. Doctoral dissertations will be written on the subject for decades to come, but the best work so far was an article written by my friend Steve Biddle and two accomplices for the respected journal *International Security* in 2012. In it, Steve, Jeffrey Friedman, and Jacob Shapiro conduct exhaustive quantitative analysis to determine whether more troops or the new employment of the troops mattered more. They find it hard to isolate the independent variable that caused the change:

> It is difficult, however, to distinguish which surge component—reinforcement or doctrinal change—was most important in Iraq, primarily because there was little variation in force employment during this period. After February 2007, General Petraeus strove to enforce consistent methods across the theater, and none of our interviewees reported tactical choices at odds with prevailing doctrine. The modest scale of reinforcements in 2007 suggests that doctrine may have been the decisive factor.[1]

The debate over what caused the dramatic reduction in violence in Iraq is of more than academic interest. If counterinsurgency strategies that focus on protecting the local population are in fact effective, as Steve Biddle and his friends say the data suggest, then people who know how to conduct it should be protected and promoted in the armed services, particularly the Army.

One of the most important innovators in counterinsurgency practice was H. R. McMaster, who had commanded the Third Armored Cavalry Regiment in Tal Afar and earned the praise of the president as well as ink in chapter 5 of the field manual for his use of the classic principles of "clear, hold, and build." However, H. R. had been passed over the first time he was considered for promotion to brigadier general despite his many contributions to the Army in intellectual and actual combat, a fact that had been noted by many younger officers who were concerned about the direction the Army was taking. McMaster was the canary in the mine shaft, and everyone below the rank of colonel was watching what would happen in his second opportunity. I was fortunate to have the opportunity to weigh in on his potential for stars.

I had made a firm argument to now–Secretary of the Army Peter Geren in early 2007, during an unusual one-on-one dinner during his visit to Fort Riley to check on the advisory training mission, that the Army needed to be appreciably bigger. A primary reason for the inability of the nation to successfully execute the ground wars in Iraq and Afghanistan simultaneously was the stubborn refusal of the Bush administration to increase the size of the Army and Marine Corps despite the continuing demand for ground troops. My argument was based on my own perception that young officers and senior noncommissioned officers, burned out after repeated yearlong combat tours with only a year off in between, were bailing out on the Army, seeing no improvement of this unsustainable pace in their future.

A bigger Army would not only relieve the strain on the force but would also be a huge psychological boost. It would show that someone in the Pentagon understood the problem and was taking action to fix it. Not long after our discussion at Fort Riley, and undoubtedly after others provided similar input, Pete Geren persuaded Secretary Gates to increase the size of the Army by 50,000 troops over the next several years. That decision, coupled with the drawdown in Iraq, over time relieved the constant pressure on the troops, but the long-term effects of fighting two prolonged counterinsurgency campaigns would scar the Army for at least a decade to come, with the damage visible in high divorce, suicide, and misconduct rates.

I'd mentioned McMaster more than once to Geren during our Pentagon meetings and again at Fort Riley and told him that a whole generation of junior officers saw H. R. as a hero. The fact that the Army had chosen not to promote McMaster to brigadier general was a collective slap in all their faces. Partly as a result of those discussions, in the

summer of 2007 Geren refused to sign a proposed list of Army generals to conduct the promotion board for the next crop of Army briga-
diers, seeing in the list few veterans of the current conflicts in Iraq and
Afghanistan. Instead of approving business as usual, Geren took the
very unusual step of requesting that General Petraeus return to the
States from command in Iraq in order to sit on and chair the board
(despite there being a more senior four-star on the board).

In a sign of how important the secretary of defense considered the
selection of the next crop of Army one-stars, Gates gave his permission
to Geren to pull Petraeus out of combat at a time when progress in
Iraq was still uncertain at best. The board—which also included Lieutenant General Stan McChrystal, then the JSOC Commander and also
brought home from Iraq; Lieutenant General Pete Chiarelli, Gates's
senior military assistant; and Lieutenant General Ann Dunwoody, the
Army's senior female officer—was known in the Army as the "H. R.
McMaster promotion board." It selected H. R. for his star at long last.

It did something else that was arguably just as important, selecting Sean MacFarland for his first star as well. MacFarland was the
brigade commander in Ramadi who had provided the initial support
for what became the Al Anbar Awakening that created the Sons of
Iraq. MacFarland's efforts were multiplied by the heroic work of Captain Travis Patriquin, the Arabic-speaking tribal engagement officer
who was killed by an IED on December 6, 2006. Travis was in many
ways the Lawrence of Arabia of America's war in Iraq; possessor of a
larger-than-life personality as well as a flamboyantly exuberant and
well-out-of-regulation mustache, he was loved by the tribal leaders he
came to know in Al Anbar.

Travis was not the first to reach out to the Sunni tribes to convince
them that their future lay in efforts not to overthrow the Shiite government by force but to fight their battles at the ballot box. Nonetheless,
his successful campaign in Al Anbar was the seed corn that Petraeus

nurtured early in his new command after visiting MacFarland in his first week back in Iraq. Those who suggest that any commander would have taken advantage of the nascent Sunni Awakening are unfamiliar with the many previous efforts by Sunni sheikhs to gain American support for their efforts against Al Qaeda in Iraq. They withered on the vine without high-level American and Iraqi support, resulting in the deaths of many brave Sunni leaders and dampening future enthusiasm for rebellion against Al Qaeda.

Meanwhile, back at Fort Riley, it was getting easier to train military transition teams for service in Iraq as the situation on the ground improved. The system remained suboptimal, as it would have been far better to have standing advisory units to deploy and redeploy; but when the individual members of a transition team arrived at Fort Riley, we were by then at least able to tell them where in Iraq they would be deploying and to put them in touch with the unit they would be replacing. We could offer no such assurances to Afghanistan-bound teams, headed for a critically underresourced theater. The frustration of the mission was real, but I enjoyed discussing counterinsurgency theory and practice with the teams during their training and gave my pitch literally scores of times during the twenty-two months I spent in command.

When in June 2008 I gave up command of 1-34 Armor, the tank battalion with which I'd fought so hard in Khalidiyah, after a little more than twenty years in uniform, I also retired from the Army. To its credit, the Army pokes and prods you when you join and again when you leave, and it pays compensation for whatever damage has been inflicted on you in the interim by the vagaries of military service. At my exit physical, the counselor looked at my test scores and said, "Wow, your wife takes good care of you." Blood pressure and cholesterol levels were fine, and even my knees and back, the traditional bane of career tankers, were not much the worse for wear—no doubt helped by the

*Giving the flag symbolizing command of 1-34 Armor to
Colonel Jeff Ingram at Camp Funston, June 2008.*

fact that my last command was on the plains of Kansas and involved
getting into and out of a Humvee rather than jumping off a tank in
Baghdad clad in seventy pounds of body armor, Kevlar helmet, and
other gear.

From Kansas, we moved to a home we'd purchased in Alexandria,
Virginia, not far from the neighborhood in which we'd rented Admiral
Jim Stavridis's house during my previous Pentagon tour. On July 15 I
showed up for my first day at work at the Center for a New American
Security in company with my new officemate, Nate Fick, for whom
this was also coincidentally his first day on the job.

Jim Miller, the director of studies at CNAS, had called a few weeks
earlier to check to see whether I would be willing to share an office
with Nate even though other senior fellows had offices of their own.

Although I didn't know Nate well, having met him in person only a few times, first through the good offices of newswoman extraordinaire Martha Raddatz, I leaped at the chance to spend time with a man I'd already written I would be proud to work for despite the fact that he was a decade younger than I was. We'd spend about six months together in a small office at the back of the CNAS office complex, which we occasionally noted was the side where the actual work got done, with Nate focusing on Afghanistan and me splitting my time between that war and the windup of the one in Iraq. I knew when Nate had been in the office because driving home on those days, my sides hurt from laughing so hard.

While still on what the Army calls "terminal leave" (probably because in its worldview there is no life after the Army), I returned to Iraq in the summer of 2008 at General Petraeus's invitation and struggled to comprehend the extraordinary reversal in Iraq's fortunes in the three and a half years I had been gone. I was simply unable to process the facts in front of me, befuddled by the contrast between my memories of a destroyed society and the reality of one that was being reborn right in front of me. The most vivid illustration of the change was the jewelry shops that I saw in Baghdad, overflowing with gold clearly visible through plate-glass windows. Security in a city has to be pretty good for that business model to be effective.

I traveled in the company of former Marine Bing West, whose book *The Strongest Tribe* I had reviewed for *The Washington Post* just prior to getting on a plane with him. I had liked it, which made it even harder to keep secret the fact that I'd read the book throughout the trip. Cotravelers were CNAS colleagues Colin Kahl and Shawn Brimley and *New Yorker* writer and New America Foundation president Steve Coll, whom I hadn't previously known. Coll was the author of *Ghost Wars*, the Pulitzer-Prize-winning history of the American role in Afghanistan between the Soviet departure and September 10, 2011. He was a gracious traveling companion and took the opportunity to interview me for a profile on Petraeus he was then writing for *The New Yorker*.

This was my first experience of the "battlefield circulation" think-tank trips that Petraeus pioneered in Iraq in an attempt to create a better-informed punditocracy and thus public back home. Our guide was Army Lieutenant Colonel Joel Rayburn, a silver-haired intelligence officer and former West Point history instructor who ran Petraeus's strategic advisory group, a sort of internal staff think tank that dealt with issues including measuring progress in the counterinsurgency campaign. Although Bing was a former four-star-equivalent assistant secretary of defense for international security affairs, Petraeus made me the senior member of the trip for protocol purposes. Bing was less concerned about the briefing slides titled "Nagl plus four" than about the fact that for the first time ever on one of his trips to Iraq (this was number nine), he hadn't gotten shot at. Unlike the rest of us, he refused to wear body armor and Kevlar helmets when outside the armored vehicles, preferring his well-loved Red Sox baseball cap.

The trip was a revelation. We met members of the Awakening Councils who had decided to side with the Americans and then work for the Iraqi government in order to protect their communities from the Iraqi government's Shia-dominated security forces. They were a bit rough, but they were effective. These so-called Sons of Iraq were aided by massive concrete T-walls, which separated Baghdad neighborhoods into easily controlled, mostly single-sect enclaves. Good counterinsurgents make good walls; the history of counterinsurgency is filled with barriers that serve to concentrate populations like the "new villages" of British Malaya, and the T-walls were the modern evolution—creating what Petraeus called "gated communities." We also visited some of the joint security stations that enforced the peace throughout Baghdad, manned by Iraqi Police and Army soldiers who had come a long, long way from those I had helped stand up in Khalidiyah what seemed a lifetime earlier. Local security forces remained as important as they had always been in these fights—they were the exit strategy in our counterinsurgency campaign in Iraq just as they had been for the British in Malaya and the Americans in Vietnam.

I came back from the trip inspired, almost unbelieving. Before I left Baghdad, I'd written a piece that reflected on the changes in Iraq since my long year in Al Anbar. Remembering how I'd felt at the end of that tour, I titled this Sunday *Washington Post* article "Back in Baghdad: This Time, Things Are Looking Up" and illustrated it with a picture of the coffee mug that Gary Belcher had created in Fort Riley almost four years earlier.[2] Slides that Petraeus's staff put together later show the number of attacks, civilian and military deaths, and car bomb attacks falling dramatically after the summer of 2007.

Washington was still several months behind the reality on the ground in Iraq, as it had been when the situation spiraled downward earlier in the war. The same was true now when the trajectory was in the opposite direction and Washington was denying the success of its policy. The Democratic presidential candidate, Senator Barack Obama, had defeated his primary opponent in part because Hillary Clinton had supported the invasion of Iraq in 2003 from her perch in the U.S. Senate and because he outflanked her to the left on the issue. She had over-learned the lesson from a decade earlier, when Sam Nunn had torpedoed his chances at becoming secretary of defense by voting against the authorization for the use of force in Desert Storm.

Obama campaigned against the war in Iraq, calling Afghanistan "the good war," while his Republican opponent, Vietnam war hero John McCain, used progress in Iraq as a rallying cry. The result was overdetermined, with the collapse of the American economy reinforcing the foreign policy errors of the George W. Bush administration, and Obama won going away.

Although CNAS was technically nonpartisan, many of the staff

Attacks in Iraq

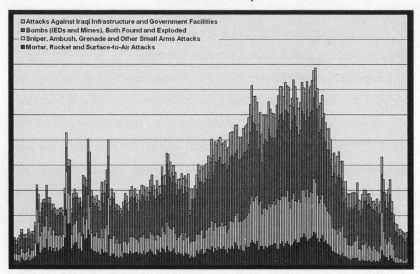

Civilian Deaths

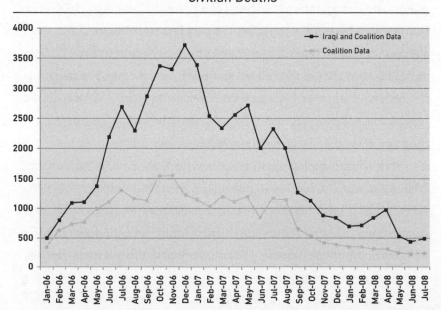

ISF and U.S. Military Deaths in Iraq

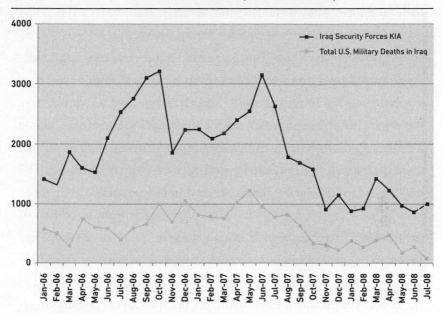

High Profile Attacks (Explosions)

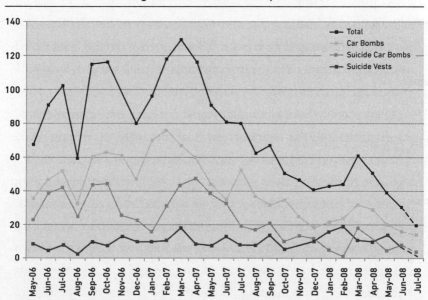

were not just Democrats but also working on the Obama campaign on their own time. They were delighted with the result. McCain had lost my support when he chose Sarah Palin as his vice-presidential candidate, giving up the "ready for leadership from day one" argument. He'd wanted Joe Lieberman as his number two and should have chosen him; McCain would probably still have lost, but he would have done so with a much greater degree of integrity. Lieberman would have been a credible presidential replacement from day one, and beyond that, he was an unusual, beyond-partisan-politics leader who did much good for the nation during his time in the Senate.

The Obama transition team named Michèle Flournoy as cochair of its Pentagon transition, which was no surprise. All of us at CNAS had expected Michèle to go into the administration, but we thought Kurt Campbell was going to stick around to run the Center. He intended to do so until the president-elect made his "team of rivals" decision to select Hillary Clinton as secretary of state. Kurt was very close to Senator Clinton and couldn't say no when she offered him the dream job of assistant secretary of state for East Asia. With Director of Studies Jim Miller tagged as Michèle's deputy undersecretary of defense for policy and Chief Operating Officer Nate Tibbets en route to the National Security Council staff, CNAS was suddenly in free fall without noticeable leadership.

I hadn't really been emotionally ready to leave the Army the previous summer and was excited about the possibility of serving in the Pentagon in a political position, but I could hardly say no when Michèle asked me to fill her seat as president of CNAS. I took the position on condition that Nate Fick be selected to replace Kurt Campbell as chief executive officer, which was not a foregone conclusion by any means. Nate was widely viewed as too young (he had just turned thirty-two) and inexperienced in Washington to take on the role, but I was adamant. From my first meeting with him, I had been enormously im-

pressed by his leadership skills, integrity, and sense of self. His book *One Bullet Away: The Making of a Marine Officer* was, I thought, the best memoir from the wars in Iraq and Afghanistan. The self-awareness and maturity evident in his memoir were a big part of the reason I had jumped at Jim Miller's offer to share an office with Nate. The bonds we formed in that office would pay off handsomely as he and I learned together how to run a think tank in Washington.

We had a lot to learn—everything from where the money comes from to where it goes. We had to hire people to replace those Kurt and Michèle took with them into the administration and establish a research agenda, demonstrating that CNAS was still open for business under new management. It was a great adventure. An early good decision was the one to hire Kristin Lord to replace Jim Miller as our director of studies. I'd met Kristin at a conference on information operations in Florida hosted by Doug Wilson, who later became the assistant sec-

With General Petraeus at the 2009 CNAS Annual Conference.
© Getty / Win McNamee

retary of defense for public affairs. (Former CNAS head of external relations Price Floyd was his deputy; it was an incestuous little circle.
Secretary of Defense Robert Gates, who repeatedly turned down re-
quests to address CNAS over the next two years, reputedly said, "If I
want to talk with CNAS, I'll call a staff meeting.") Kristin had blown
me away with her clear thinking, her excellent writing skills, and her
organizational ability. With her addition, the leadership team was
formed, and as March 2009 began, we were ready to get started preparing for the annual conference in June that was the high point of the
CNAS calendar every year.

CNAS's long-range calendar hadn't extended much beyond the November elections, so with no plan for the conference, there was a lot of
work to do. My research assistant Brian Burton went to work on a
paper projecting a future direction for American policy toward Iraq

that would ultimately serve as the basis for a public discussion between George Packer, Jack Keane, the Iraqi ambassador to the United States, and me. However, the real coup was getting General Petraeus, now the commander of U.S. Central Command (which oversaw an area of responsibility from Egypt to Pakistan), to agree to give a public address at the conference. Both the ballroom and the overflow room of the Willard Hotel in Washington were jammed as Petraeus provided a masterful discussion of recent events and prospects in the CENTCOM area of operations. CNAS was back in business.

Although CNAS had come into existence in no small part in reaction to the misguided invasion of Iraq and mishandled occupation that followed, CNAS 2.0 would focus on another war that was also not going well, although unlike the invasion of Iraq, it had at least been necessary: the war in Afghanistan.

7.

The Second Washington Fight

Afghanistan

Counterinsurgency is messy and slow under the best of circumstances, and Afghanistan was a long way behind Iraq in almost
every way that mattered. The human capital in Iraq was far better; by
2009, the Afghan people had been shattered by thirty continuous years
of war. The Soviet invasion of Afghanistan in 1979 was followed by a
bitter guerrilla war in which mujahedeen, supported by the CIA, fought
to expel the invaders, an almost unbelievable true story well chronicled
in George Criles's book *Charlie Wilson's War*. After the Soviets' departure came a civil war in which the Taliban eventually seized control of
most of the country, although the central government survived as long
as funds from the Soviet Union kept coming. The Afghan government
fell only when the Soviet Union collapsed, some three years after the
last Soviet troops crossed the Termez Bridge out of the country. The
Taliban made the error of providing a home for Al Qaeda and its leader,
Osama bin Laden. That didn't work out well for the Taliban, as the
American invasion in 2001 drove the remnants of both organizations
into the frontier regions of Pakistan, where they almost immediately

resorted to plotting an insurgency inside Afghanistan against the American forces there.

As a result of the decades of constant fighting, good leaders and administrators were even harder to find in Afghanistan than they had been in Iraq. Iraq also had the advantage of substantial and increasing oil revenues, meaning that it could largely pay for its own security forces and development, and impressive infrastructure. Afghanistan was going to be a ward of the international community for the foreseeable future, and those in power had much more temptation to try to grab aid money to line their own pockets while the getting was good. They knew that the wartime funds were not going to last forever, unlike the prospect that Iraq's leaders enjoyed: a share of substantial long-term oil revenues if they governed that country reasonably well.

Afghanistan faced other challenges as well. It was a rural rather than an urban insurgency. The success rate of rural insurgencies is far higher than those fought largely in urban areas because the population in an urban insurgency is already concentrated in cities and easier to separate from insurgents, using expedients like the T-walls that divided ethnic factions in Baghdad. Furthermore, the population of Afghanistan was largely illiterate. I had explained the impact when briefing my classes of future advisers at Fort Riley: "In Iraq, they knew how to read; we had to teach them how to fight. In Afghanistan they know how to fight; we have to teach them to read. Unfortunately, it takes a lot longer to teach someone how to read than it does to teach them how to fight."

But the biggest problem in Afghanistan was, and remains, Pakistan. The initial U.S. mistake of providing too few American troops to pin down Osama bin Laden in the Tora Bora Mountains allowed Al Qaeda and much of the Taliban's leadership to escape from Afghanistan. They settled in Pakistan, which either willingly or through lack of control over its own territory provided bases for both organizations to lick their wounds and regenerate. This they did with a vengeance. The Taliban regained strength in Pakistan and began reinfiltrating into Afghanistan in the mid-2000s while the attention of the United States was focused on the escalating disaster in Iraq. By 2008, when I had been shocked at the positive progress of the war in Iraq during my summer visit but disappointed to see the opposite in our other war, the Taliban clearly had the upper hand in Afghanistan. I reported this fact to Admiral Michael Mullen, who had replaced General Peter Pace as chairman of the Joint Chiefs of Staff, in an office call upon my return from Afghanistan in the fall of 2008. Not long afterward he correctly told the Senate Armed Services Committee that "In Iraq, we do what we must; in Afghanistan, we do what we can," with whatever resources we had left over after we had sent to Iraq what was needed there to prevent full-scale civil war in the heart of the Arab world.

I had visited Afghanistan for the first time in early 2007, while training U.S. Army, Navy, and Air Force teams at Fort Riley to serve as advisers to the Afghan Army and Police. It seemed like a good idea to have actually been to Afghanistan at least once before standing on a podium telling American soldiers, airmen, and sailors what their war would be like. I found a critically underresourced war, starved of the soldiers, dollars, and attention required to beat back a resurgent Taliban. It was difficult to return to Fort Riley and send advisory teams to a war that I knew was an economy-of-force effort.

Although central Kansas was a long way from the Pentagon, there were still a few things I could do to help. I was astounded during my 2007 visit to find that many of the counterinsurgency lessons that had been painfully relearned in Iraq had not been transferred to the Afghan theater. Chief among them was the need for an in-country counterinsurgency academy to teach tactics, techniques, and procedures to those arriving for a tour of duty. General Casey had established one in Taji, Iraq, back in 2005, but two years later there was no comparable effort in Afghanistan, where knowledge of Afghan culture and the principles of counterinsurgency were sadly lacking among the troops we deployed there.

I got in touch with a friend from my Pentagon days who was now working as a strategic adviser to the head of the Afghan training mission and suggested that he establish a COIN academy in Afghanistan, explaining how effective General Casey's effort in Iraq had been at improving the counterinsurgency performance of U.S. units sent there, at relatively low cost. I was pleased to find a friendly ear. The idea was quickly adopted, and I was invited to head over to Afghanistan to set up the Counterinsurgency Academy myself, but Fort Riley and the First Infantry Division, in which I was then serving, denied permission. As a battalion commander training advisers for two wars, I couldn't be released for this mission.

Fortunately, I knew just the man for the job. Captain Dan Helmer had just completed the makeshift adviser training at Fort Riley and been deployed to Afghanistan as a combat adviser. Dan was a West Pointer and Rhodes scholar who had taught himself Arabic during a previous Iraq rotation, had read and internalized the counterinsurgency literature and philosophy, and was completely impervious to conventional views on the proper role of a captain in the U.S. Army. On my recommendation, he was given the mission of standing up the COIN Academy–Afghanistan. Working on a shoestring, Dan lied and stole to accomplish the mission, acquiring officers senior to him as meat puppets to put more authority behind his pronouncements and generally making miracles happen. When he left Kabul after a year, the COIN Academy–Afghanistan was fully up and running. At my encouragement and to the detriment of his Army career, Dan then came back to Fort Riley to train future advisers for Afghanistan, bringing with him a boxed flag for me that had flown over the COIN Academy in Kabul. He inscribed the flag box "To the architect of the counterinsurgency insurgency—the wheels are in motion."

Captain Dan Helmer teaching at the COIN Academy–
Afghanistan he helped establish.

I visited Afghanistan again as a civilian senior fellow working at CNAS in late 2008 and again found an underresourced theater of war, although General David McKiernan, who was now commanding the effort there, at least appeared to have a good handle on what it was he was supposed to accomplish. One of the highlights of my visit was a short session at the Counterinsurgency Academy that Dan Helmer had set up outside Kabul. The stage was set for an increase in American attention to the Afghan theater of war.

Senator Barack Obama, who had campaigned in part on refocusing attention from Iraq to the war in Afghanistan, was elected to the presidency a few days after my return to the United States from my Afghan visit. Upon assuming office, President Obama recognized that the situation in Afghanistan was even more dire than he had thought as a candidate. When he took office, he found waiting for him a request for tens of thousands more troops to secure the Afghan presidential election scheduled for the summer of 2009. The request was already several months old, but the George W. Bush White House had not acted on it. Sending the additional troops to Afghanistan as General McKiernan had requested would have revealed the truth of then-candidate Obama's argument that "the good war" in Afghanistan was being neglected. If General Casey had been correct that "President Bush has given me a load of shit" in Iraq, President Obama could perhaps be forgiven for feeling the same way about Afghanistan.

President Obama faced an immediate decision about Afghanistan even before the Senate had confirmed his whole defense team. Important voices in the debate included Michèle Flournoy, recently confirmed as the top policy official in the Pentagon, and my former West Point student Craig Mullaney, who after fighting in Afghanistan and leaving the Army had handled Afghanistan for Senator Obama during the campaign and been given a job in the Pentagon with responsibility for that war. With Michèle and Craig's encouragement, President Obama immediately established a review panel headed by Brookings Scholar and South Asia expert Bruce Reidel, and within three months ordered the deployment of 30,000 additional U.S. forces to the fight there. Nate Fick and I attended the troop increase announcement at the White House and were heartened by the new president's commitment to counterinsurgency principles and to success in Afghanistan.

Changes in strategy often require changes in personnel to implement them. General David McKiernan understood the war in Afghanistan far better than any of his predecessors save Lieutenant General Dave Barno, who had run the war there in 2003 and 2004. Barno had worked to implement counterinsurgency principles despite being poorly resourced—he had only one Army brigade at his disposal to cover the requirements in all of Afghanistan. General Barno would later tell me that he'd kept his hardback copy of *Learning to Eat Soup with a Knife* on his desk during his command in Kabul, and he had me sign it in General Helmick's backyard after the Army ten-miler upon Barno's return from theater in 2005. In a sign of how little the Pentagon cared about the Afghanistan conflict, Lieutenant General Barno was given the job of running Army installation management after commanding the U.S. effort in Afghanistan. He retired from the Army to teach at National Defense University, and I later hired him to run the CNAS Afghanistan program.

McKiernan was judged to be too conventional and not energetic enough by Secretary Gates, who relieved him in favor of Stanley McChrystal in June 2009. General McChrystal had impressed the Pentagon through his leadership of Joint Special Operations Command for the past five years, making significant contributions to the kill/capture part of the counterinsurgency effort in Iraq and Afghanistan, and through his focus on supporting our efforts in those wars during his subsequent appointment as director of the Joint Staff in the Pentagon.

While he was serving in the Pentagon in 2009, I helped General McChrystal implement the long-overdue creation of "AfPak hands," developing officers and sergeants specially trained and educated in counterinsurgency, regional languages, and local culture. Admiral Mullen dedicated the AfPak hands to repeated assignments to the region, either in theater or back in the United States in between deployments. That it took until 2009 to stand up a small corps of a few hundred military experts on the region was another indication of the Iraq War stealing all the oxygen from the Afghanistan effort. Despite significant flaws in execution—many of the people selected as AfPak hands had been "voluntold" that they would be participating in it, and the education they received has varied widely in quality—the program at the very least requires repeated assignments to the same region to build enduring relationships between Afghan and American leaders, a lesson that took far too long to learn.

Upon being given command in Afghanistan, General McChrystal set up a strategy review panel and invited me to be a part of it. Although I dearly wanted to accept, I had just taken the position of president of CNAS and couldn't afford to take the time away from my new responsibilities of hiring talent and raising money. For the first time I understood fellow defense policy analyst Mike O'Hanlon's incredulity that I had accepted the promotion to head CNAS; he told me that I would no longer be able to serve as a thinker and opinion leader because of the administrative burdens of my new role. I wasn't smart enough to figure out that he was right until I had to tell McChrystal no. In my stead Nate and I sent Andrew Exum to serve on the Afghanistan strategy review panel. Ex was a former Army Ranger with time in both Iraq and Afghanistan who was finishing his doctoral dissertation on the strategy of Hezbollah; he was one of the first people Nate and I had hired.

General McChrystal's strategy review panel included not just Ex but also Fred Kagan, who had been an important thinker behind the decision to "surge" troops to Iraq, and Steve Biddle, with whom I'd traveled to Afghanistan a few months earlier, visiting the COIN Academy in Kabul for the first time. The review panel found a situation that was "deteriorating," as the first sentence of their assessment noted, and recommended "an integrated civil-military counterinsurgency strategy" to turn things around, which would require another significant troop increase on top of the one that had just been decided upon.

This caused real consternation in the White House, which had only a few months earlier signed off on the troop increase for Afghanistan that the Reidel study group had recommended. McChrystal's ultimate request for an additional 40,000 troops began a long period of delibera-

In a helicopter in Afghanistan with Mike O'Hanlon.

tions in the White House that became quite public. I had the chance to influence the debate when I testified before the Senate Foreign Relations Committee on the prospects for fighting "a better war in Afghanistan" on September 16, 2009. I argued that the United States was trying to accomplish the ends of keeping continued pressure on terrorist groups in the region, preventing a sanctuary for terrorists (as was the case before 9/11), and ensuring that there was no regional meltdown—code for Pakistan losing control of its nuclear weapons to radical Islamists. The ways I suggested were the same clear-hold-build strategy that had worked in Iraq, and the means required to do it was a U.S. troop surge to create space in which to build and professionalize more Afghan troops and police. I also suggested a renewed effort to conduct more effective information operations—in Afghanistan, in the region, and here at home.

My fellow expert witnesses included Rory Stewart, who had walked across Afghanistan in 2002, soon after the fall of the Taliban, and written about the journey in a book titled *The Places in Between*. He had later set up a nonprofit, Turquoise Mountain, to encourage economic development in Afghanistan. The other was Steve Biddle, freshly back from McChrystal's review group; Biddle noted correctly that the answer to the question of whether Afghanistan was worth the cost of a fully resourced counterinsurgency campaign was "a close call on the merits." Nonetheless, he came down in favor of more civilian and military resources for Afghanistan, applied in the same manner as they had been in Iraq, where Biddle's support for the surge had played some role in influencing President Bush's decision to implement the strategy.

In addition to rather publicly advocating a counterinsurgency strategy for Afghanistan before the Senate Foreign Relations Committee, I also had the chance to make the argument before a smaller but more influential audience. Vice President Joe Biden played a major role in the decision over troop levels for Afghanistan that occupied much of 2009. He was not an advocate of a fully resourced counterinsurgency strategy, believing that a smaller footprint of American troops focused on counterterrorism operations would be sufficient. I was invited to the White House to try to change his mind, spending ninety minutes in his office explaining that counterterrorism by itself would do nothing to change the dynamics that led terrorists to decide to wage war against the Afghan government and its American supporters. A counterterrorism strategy by itself was a recipe for endless war; it was necessary to resource improvements in governance, economic development, and the provision of services to the population to persuade Afghans not to support a Taliban insurgency that promised it would do all those things if it regained power. The other problem with a counterterrorism strategy was that it offered little to the Afghans themselves in return for basing rights; in order to get them to permit us to conduct such operations from their territory, I believed that we had to offer them something in return—economic development, greater security, and the prospect of eventual peace through the defeat of the Taliban. The vice president was unconvinced, but I appreciated the chance to make the argument in person.

The White House debate over a second increment of troops for Afghanistan in 2009, in which the vice president played a major role, took place against the background of the summer Afghan presidential election that President Karzai won in an election aided by significant ballot stuffing on his behalf. He would have won without cheating, so the effort cost him in international credibility for no real gain. It also made it harder for American advocates to argue that the fragile democracy in Afghanistan was worth an increased investment of our blood and treasure.

The Obama administration had inherited the summer elections in Afghanistan from the Bush administration, which pursued a "freedom agenda" throughout both of its terms in office. This was one of the critical errors of President Bush's foreign policy and was ironically based on an overly simplistic understanding of international relations theory. The Democratic Peace Theorem notes that mature democracies do not wage war with each other very often. The key word is *mature*. Countries going through the process of democratization are actually more likely to wage war than are autocracies or established democracies. The essence of mature democracies is not honest voting to determine the will of the majority; it is effective institutions to protect the rights of the minority, even if the majority doesn't like them. These institutions play a major role in establishing peaceful relations both internally and externally, but building them can take decades.

The Bush administration's misreading of international relations theory had real-world implications in many countries, including Iraq and Afghanistan. By moving too quickly to create democracies without doing the hard work to create institutions to protect the rights of minority groups—work that can literally take generations, as it did during the development of strong democracies in Taiwan and South Korea—the Bush administration simply made it more likely that the most ruthless and best-organized thugs would seize power in the Palestinian territories, in Iraq, and in Afghanistan. We have since seen similar results in Libya, Egypt, and in the insurgency in Syria.

The Bush administration's "freedom agenda" mistake was even more consequential than it might appear at first glance. In Malaya, Gerald Templer had essentially embodied political and military power. He had no need to negotiate with the government of Malaya—he *was* the government of Malaya for the duration of the Emergency, during which Britain suspended the normal political order. In both Iraq and Afghanistan, the United States and the international community granted sovereignty to regimes that didn't yet have the capacity to exercise it and encouraged democratic elections before founding and nurturing the political parties and other institutions that underlay all functioning democracies worldwide. In both Iraq and Afghanistan, American commanders and ambassadors would have to cajole actions from the local political leaders that General Sir Gerald Templer could have simply ordered to happen. It is a crippling distinction in the history of counterinsurgency campaigns, and it was a self-inflicted wound for our efforts in both Iraq and Afghanistan—imposed at the national command level, well outside the control of military leaders.

However, in 2009 it was far too late to undo the Afghan constitution, and so after the flawed elections of the summer, the Obama administration was stuck with President Karzai for another five years. Rather than making political decisions unilaterally, or even in consultation with junior Afghan partners, American ambassadors and generals were forced to plead with Karzai to fire corrupt governors and replace them with more capable successors. Improving governance and encouraging economic development would have been a challenge in Afghanistan in any case, given the limits of human capital in the country after three decades of war. Accomplishing these tasks when it was impossible for American leaders to independently fire or prosecute Afghan leaders who stole development funding (just one of many examples of corruption and malfeasance) added a degree of difficulty to the task that would prove almost insurmountable.

The political decision to allow democratic elections so early in the lifespan of the new Afghanistan was far from the only error of U.S. policy there. The lack of significant, well-resourced U.S. effort in Afghanistan over the eight years preceding President Obama's two decisions in 2009 to increase troop strength there had given the Taliban a second chance. They took the opportunity to regain strength both in the south around Kandahar, where their movement had begun, and in the east, close to their sanctuaries in Pakistan. General McChrystal's request for 40,000 additional troops provided sufficient resources to take on both problem areas nearly simultaneously, but it would prove too big a bill for the president to swallow in the fall of 2009 after already doubling down on troops for Afghanistan earlier in the year.

Along with several other think-tank denizens, I was invited to the White House Situation Room to hear the results of the months of Afghan policy deliberations on the afternoon of December 1, 2009, as *Marine One* was preparing to ferry the president to West Point for the announcement. The troop numbers were about 10,000 short of what I had recommended, which seems like a small "commander in chief tax," as some in the White House called it, but was actually hugely important. The president's decision to send just 30,000 American troops—and to pledge to get the rest from coalition countries—meant that the effort to defeat the Taliban could not be carried out simultaneously Afghanistan-wide but would instead have to be sequential—focusing effort first on the south and swinging to the east later.

Although America's allies in the Afghan effort did, over time, promise an additional 10,000 troops, they came in packages of varying size, capability, and thus utility. And the sad truth was that only American soldiers were consistently effective enough in an offensive role to clear the Taliban from their sanctuaries in the south and east; the additional allied troops might be able to hold areas that Americans cleared, but that was about it. The International Security Assistance Force (ISAF) consisted of troops from nearly forty countries, and they varied widely in degree of commitment to the fight. While some were excellent—the Canadians for many years paid a heavier toll in blood per capita than did the United States, while the Brits, Australians, and French were also great fighters—the many jokes about the acronym ISAF, such as "I Suck at Fighting" and "I Saw Americans Fight," hint at a bitter truth about which nations were willing to pay the high cost of doing the hard work of clearing the Taliban.

The Afghan "surge," to be announced that evening at West Point, suffered from another problem. In Iraq, the fight to build host-nation security forces began in earnest not long after the Iraqi Army had been disbanded. Real assets were devoted to the effort to rebuild it, including, already in June 2004, putting Lieutenant General Petraeus in charge of the effort, although it took some six months to assemble the organization he needed, and many of the troops under his command who were assigned advisory and training duties were not the first tier. But unlike in Iraq, in Afghanistan the effort to build an Afghan Army and Police force was cursory at best. I had discovered this at Fort Riley in my last assignment in the Army, when I could tell advisers assigned to Iraq exactly where they would be assigned even before they arrived in Kansas, while their counterparts assigned to Afghanistan literally got their assignments when they landed in Kabul. As a result, the American soldiers who cleared Baghdad during the Iraq surge had capable, well-advised Iraqi forces to help hold what they had cleared with U.S.

forces, while the effort to build a decent Afghan force began roughly simultaneously with the commitment of American forces to clear southern Afghanistan. There would be no Afghan troops trained and ready to hold what Americans cleared, much less to build a better country in the newly purchased free territory.

But the biggest flaw in the president's decision to commit more forces to Afghanistan was not in the sequencing of building Afghan forces simultaneously with the commitment of American surge forces (a decision that had effectively been made for him by the neglect of the advisory effort under the previous administration) or the commitment of insufficient U.S. forces to clear both the south and the east simultaneously. Instead, the critical error was the decision to announce that the "surge" troops for Afghanistan would begin their withdrawal in just eighteen months, during the summer of 2011.

When this fact was briefed to the think-tankers in the White House Situation Room on the afternoon of the president's West Point speech, our reaction was immediate and unanimous: this was a disaster of the first order. In Afghanistan, and just as important in Pakistan, the announcement of an increased American troop commitment to the war would be instantly overshadowed by the announcement of the time limit on the American troop commitment. The only words that our allies, and our enemies, would hear from the president's speech would be the withdrawal date. The president was cutting his own policy off at the knees before it had even gotten up on its feet.

The cause for this self-defeating policy decision was domestic politics. The president paid a heavy price with his Democratic base for the increased troop commitment to Afghanistan. They apparently hadn't believed his repeated promises on the campaign trail to increase the U.S. troop commitment to Afghanistan. I explained to Rachel Maddow that night on her program on MSNBC that the president had done exactly what he had promised to do in Afghanistan, at some cost to his popularity among Democrats. Announcing that the Afghan surge would be limited in duration was in part at least a commitment to his political base to start ending the war in his first term, before the 2012 election.

But nothing is free. The president undercut the value of the increased U.S. troop commitment by announcing its withdrawal date, giving both the Taliban and Al Qaeda a finish line in sight: if they could hold on for eighteen months, the American tide would recede. The Afghans were listening as well, and the lesson they took was similar: *The Americans are going to abandon us again, just as they did after we defeated the Soviet Union in the 1980s, so get everything you can now while the getting is good.* Announcing the withdrawal date in advance was a grievous self-inflicted error, or "own goal" in the British parlance.

The White House would claim that Secretary Gates, Admiral Mullen, and Generals Petraeus and McChrystal agreed to or at least accepted the president's decision to announce the date to begin drawing down the surge at the same time as he announced the additional forces. However, some of those involved stated later that there was no true discussion; rather, they were confronted with a "take it or leave it" moment, and they decided to take it, knowing that leaving it would have given no chance to achieve our objectives. General McChrystal had no choice but to comply with the president's directives, and he set to work attempting to implement a fully resourced counterinsurgency strategy for the first time during our decade of war in Afghanistan—at least in the south, as he didn't have the resources to simultaneously get started with a fully resourced COIN campaign in the east.

The process began in Helmand province, which had been the responsibility of the British Army, who called it "Helmandshire," but was now being buried under the weight of Marines. They were no longer responsible for Al Anbar Province in Iraq, my old stomping grounds. The first test of counterinsurgency in Afghanistan was slated to be the town of Marjah, where on February 13, 2010, Marines poured in to clear out the Taliban. General McChrystal made the mistake of over-promising, telling *The New York Times*'s Dexter Filkins, "We've got a government in a box, ready to roll in."

We didn't. Afghan forces were not yet developed enough to hold what the Marines had cleared, and there were insufficient political and development specialists in Afghanistan to roll into Marjah for the build phase. The fight in Marjah, which had been scheduled to take just a few weeks, dragged out for the rest of the year, consuming vast resources and attracting far more attention than it deserved. It became an early indicator that Afghanistan was not going to "flip" as quickly as had Iraq under General Petraeus. Afghanistan was harder because of the insurgent sanctuaries in Pakistan, insufficient Afghan human capital, the lack of adequate governance and institutions, and limited infra-structure and government revenues.

McChrystal was deeply concerned about civilian casualties in Afghanistan, correctly understanding that counterinsurgents who killed the innocent created recruits for the enemy. This was a primary tenet of the *Counterinsurgency Field Manual,* and the war in Afghanistan was one of the cases we were thinking about when we wrote it. John Paul Vann, a famous counterinsurgent during the Vietnam War, had noted of that conflict, "This is a political war and it calls for discrimina-tion in killing. The best weapon for killing would be a knife, but I'm afraid we can't do it that way. The worst is an airplane. The next worst is artillery. Barring a knife, the best is a rifle—you know who you're killing." Unfortunately, given how underresourced the fight in Afghan-istan had been, there were too few rifles available, and when troops got in trouble, often the only option available to bail them out was airpower, which sometimes went astray and killed the innocent. McChrystal imposed firm restrictions on the use of airpower and artil-lery in his attempt to win over the Afghan population, dramatically reducing civilian casualties—but perhaps overcorrecting, at least in the eyes of subordinate commanders.

General Petraeus had done a good job of underpromising and overdelivering in Iraq, but McChrystal took the opposite approach. He also misread Petraeus's skill in managing members of the media. Although Petraeus worked the media constantly, answering press e-mails at all hours of the day or night, he was very careful about how he talked with members of the press and how much he revealed to them. Between his time at grad school at Princeton and in the Social Sciences department at West Point, he had gotten to know a large number of writers, and he worked assiduously to show them only the sides of him that he wanted revealed on the front page of *The New York Times*.

McChrystal hadn't had the same developmental experiences during his long career in the special forces and didn't have the same natural caution. When, encouraged by his staff, he allowed Michael Hastings, a stringer with *Rolling Stone* magazine, to embed with him for a few days in early 2010, he let Hastings inside the circle of trust. A veteran of many years of service inside the close-knit special operations community, knowing almost no one who did not adhere to his personal code of loyalty to mission and command, it was beyond Stan McChrystal's ability to imagine that a fellow American would report things that would hurt him.

He was wrong. The *Rolling Stone* article that was published that summer under the title "Runaway General" featured comments by members of McChrystal's staff about Vice President Biden that were deeply disrespectful and, according to Hastings, encouraged by the general. McChrystal was recalled to Washington and, on June 23, tendered his resignation to the president, who accepted it and announced on the same day that Petraeus would step down from his position at Central Command in order to take responsibility for the war in

Afghanistan. Petraeus hadn't had time to tell his wife, Holly, that he was going back to war.

He did so on July 4, almost immediately overriding his predecessor's overly restrictive guidance on the employment of lethal force in the counterinsurgency campaign. Although counterinsurgency is mostly political, there are committed insurgents who cannot be persuaded to quit and who have to be captured or killed. Even those who are persuadable are more likely to abandon their objections if they face a real threat of being killed or captured; one of the indices of progress we tracked in Khalidiyah in 2004 was the rising price the insurgent leaders had to pay to get a poor subordinate to fire a rocket-propelled grenade at one of our tanks. The cost went up in consonance with the likelihood that the RPG firer wouldn't survive to enjoy his earnings.

McChrystal had overinternalized the guidance in the *Counterinsurgency Field Manual*. Only *some* of the best weapons for COIN don't shoot bullets, and although dollars are weapons in this kind of fight, bullets work pretty well in a lot of circumstances. McChrystal's guidance had limited the ability of American units to call in air support or artillery fire even when they were under enemy fire, but Petraeus restored firepower to its proper place in a counterinsurgency fight, noting that "protecting the Afghan people does require killing, capturing, or turning the insurgents."

This change was enormously popular in theater, and the results were almost immediate, as the employment of air strikes and of joint special operations raids increased rapidly. Petraeus and his team implemented a number of other changes, including the commencement of the Afghan Local Police program, support for an insurgent reintegration program modeled on the one that had paid off in Al Anbar, an anticorruption task force led by newly promoted Brigadier General H. R. McMaster, a huge increase in the program to train and equip Afghan forces, and an effort to build capability and capacity to expand the rule of law led by Brigadier General Mark Martins. All made progress in key areas, but time was always the limiting factor.

Petraeus succeeded in putting more pressure on the Taliban and in rapidly increasing the size and capability of the Afghan security forces, but he was fighting an opponent as implacable as Afghan government corruption: the Washington clock. He would later tell me, "We didn't get the inputs even close to right in Afghanistan until the late fall of 2010. . . . And, in the end, we only had the benefit of all the forces for some six months or so, with the drawdown commencing in the summer of 2011." By the time he left his position in Afghanistan in July 2011, the drawdown of U.S. surge forces from Afghanistan had already begun. President Obama was true to his word; he announced the end of the Afghan surge in June 2011, exactly eighteen months after it had begun, and began bringing the troops home in July.

General Jack Keane, longtime mentor of Petraeus and intellectual godfather of the Iraq Surge, urged Petraeus to resign in June 2011 when President Obama announced the drawdown would be carried out at a more rapid pace than Petraeus had recommended. General Petraeus, already nominated to become the CIA director, felt that he had been given every opportunity to make his case to the president and chose to continue to serve despite his disagreement with the decision to end the Afghan surge as originally promised.

In fact, Afghanistan was harder than Iraq in some key respects, even though it was never anywhere near as violent as Iraq was in 2006 and the first half of 2007, and the outcome of the campaign was very much in doubt when he departed. The results on the ground were as mixed as we think-tankers would have predicted that afternoon of December 1, 2009, in the White House Situation Room. On the glass-half-full side of the equation, the U.S. troop increase had been substantial, and it did have a huge impact in the south and the west, where the main effort was led by the Marines and an Army division. The clear-hold-build transfer strategy proved its effectiveness on the ground, not for the first time in the history of counterinsurgency campaigns. After years of neglect, the Afghan National Army grew in both size and capability and was able to hold areas that had been cleared by U.S. forces with only a minimal advisory presence. The Afghan Police also improved, albeit from a lower base, and the Afghan Local Police program initiated by Petraeus was scaled across Afghanistan in an example of a historical COIN best practice that was eventually adopted across the campaign.

Kill/capture operations to take down high-value targets proved successful as a result of improvements in the links between operations and intelligence gathering and some very innovative intelligence fusion operations. With our forces and those of our NATO and Afghan allies, we came tantalizingly close to the 1:50 ratio of counterinsurgency forces to the local population that the *Counterinsurgency Field Manual* noted had proved a tipping point in past COIN campaigns. The numbers were staggering: 600,000 troops would be indicated to protect the 30 million in Afghanistan's population. At the peak in 2011, NATO had as many as 150,000 troops, with Afghan security forces still building to an expected total of 354,000 and an Afghan Local Police force of some 40,000. Unfortunately, Afghan forces were still being built up even as the NATO drawdown began, long before the Taliban had been defeated. Afghan forces will have to confront a challenge that may be more than they can handle.

Five years after President Obama doubled down on troops to Afghanistan and the AfPak hands program was stood up, the results are mixed. The greatest successes have come in the military field, but that is not the most important battlefield in this kind of war. David Galula said that COIN is 20 percent military and 80 percent everything else—political, economic, and information operations. It is possible to get everything right in the military domain and still lose the war, and there is some danger of just that outcome.

Counterinsurgency is as much political as military, of course, and the political shortfalls in Afghanistan are also significant. The most pressing is the continued disappointment of Afghan governance, which remains marred by corruption that is excessive even by Afghan standards. Brigadier General H. R. McMaster was given the task to reduce corruption, and the fact that even he wasn't able to put much of a dent in the problem shows what a significant—and potentially decisive— obstacle Afghan governance is to achieving our objectives there. Promoting democracy in the short term can perversely make it harder to achieve stability in the short term and human rights in the long term, and there are many indications that this will be the result of American and international decisions to move directly to democracy in Afghanistan.

And if Afghan governance is troubling, Pakistan's is worse. The most dangerous country in the world for the United States continues to allow the Taliban to operate from its territory, although it is unclear whether this failing results from a lack of ability to control its own territory or from a lack of will to do so; most likely it is a mix of both. The Pakistani deterrence triad has been described as nuclear weapons, the conventional Pakistani Army, and irregular forces including the Pakistani Taliban, which has turned into something of a Frankenstein's monster that now threatens its own creator. Pakistan is the core of the problem in the region, the main driver of U.S. interests in Southwest Asia, and the keystone to solving it—but not for many years to come. It is worth underlining the fact that the success or failure of the Afghan security forces remains perhaps the most powerful lever to influence Pakistan's strategic calculus.

The long-term presence of Osama bin Laden inside Pakistan for some five years prior to his dispatch by a SEAL team underscores the problems that the country poses. And the killing of Bin Laden, ironically, increased the challenge for the United States of staying the course in Afghanistan. U.S. public opinion, never much engaged in the Afghan War, turned even more negative toward the effort after the killing of Bin Laden and the effective dismantling of Al Qaeda by drone strikes inside Pakistan. Public opinion could be summarized as noting that Bin Laden is dead, Al Qaeda is no longer a threat to the United States, and it's time to go home.

The war in Afghanistan is likely to end with a negotiated settlement that allows the Taliban some role in the Afghan government in return for verifiable Taliban commitments to renounce violence and Al Qaeda (and that will be easier to do as Al Qaeda fades more deeply into irrelevance) and to adhere to the terms of the Afghan constitution. As long as the United States remains committed to the security of the Afghan government over the long term, we are likely to accomplish our core national security objectives in the region, although at a much higher price than would have been necessary had we not taken our eye off the Afghan War for eight years to focus on an unnecessary one in Iraq.

America will leave a force of some thousands of troops to conduct counterterrorism operations, to support the Afghan government, and to advise Afghan security forces, particularly with intelligence assets, airpower, medical evacuation and assistance, and logistical support. These forces will be sufficient to prevent the Afghan government from falling to the Taliban, largely by making it too expensive for the Taliban to mass forces for a frontal assault on Kabul. Although the United States will no longer conduct counterinsurgency directly in Afghanistan, the Afghan government in Kabul will, with American help, continue to counter the Taliban's insurgency. The remaining U.S. troops will focus on counterterror operations—part of counterinsurgency, and a part that can continue only if the Afghan government remains in control of its capital and airspace.

In 1975 Saigon fell not to guerrillas but to conventional forces from North Vietnam; a tank, the very icon of conventional war, broke down the gate at the U.S. embassy in Saigon. There is no danger of a conventional Taliban invasion of Afghanistan from its bases in Pakistan, only of continued infiltration and subversion—serious threats, to be certain, but ones that the Afghan forces, if enabled by American support, will likely be able to contain. The outcome will not be pretty; however, it should be marginally acceptable if we continue to provide sufficient support.

Great powers lose small wars for only one reason: they run out of will to continue the fight. After more than twelve years in Afghanistan, it is understandable that America is tired of war. But the commitment of a very small number of American troops and a relatively small investment of dollars may make the difference between the survival of a representative government in Afghanistan post-2014 and the return of the Taliban. At the end of the movie *Charlie Wilson's War*, after American-backed mujahedeen have expelled the Soviet Union from Afghanistan, the Texas congressman and Naval Academy graduate pleads for a small investment in the future of the country. He failed. America chose to ignore Afghanistan after the war in that country had broken the Soviet Union, and in the power vacuum we left behind, the Taliban came to power and provided Al Qaeda with a base of operations that enabled it to attack us. It would be a shame to repeat that particular crime of neglect in the same place just a generation later.

This question of American support for Afghanistan over the long term may be the longest-lasting impact of General Petraeus's affair with Paula Broadwell. I met Paula at a CNAS event sometime in 2009 and saw her around Washington at other events, including Dave Kilcullen's wedding to Janine Davidson and a party at her brother's house; I found her both impressive and ambitious.

I was apparently not the only one. Paula was writing her doctoral dissertation on leadership at King's College, London, with General Petraeus as a case study; when he was unexpectedly assigned to take command in Afghanistan, she adroitly decided to turn her dissertation research into a book. Most of us do it in the opposite order, although I have been accused of similarly writing my book and then doing the research afterward, in Al Anbar. Petraeus developed a closer relationship with Broadwell than was proper over the course of her writing what became the biography *All In* and resigned from the CIA when it came to light.

The affair with Paula surprised many of us who had known Petraeus for decades and who believed him to be invulnerable. If an M16 round in the chest during a training accident and a collapsed parachute that resulted in a shattered pelvis couldn't slow him down, what could? I was shocked to discover that Petraeus was human; I knew my own faults, but had imagined none in him.

And so one of the great Americans of our time was brought down by a sin that appears to have been more notable by its absence than by its presence in the great men of all eras past. Petraeus's reputation will recover as, like President Clinton, he continues to serve the public interest. My friend and fellow baseball fan Paul Yingling has described Petraeus as having the most "wins above replacement" (the acronym WAR is particularly appropriate here) of any general officer in his generation. It is hard to imagine anyone else buying the time and space to turn Iraq around, or performing better than he did in the Afghan theater.

The real cost of Petraeus's infidelity is the loss of a compelling advocate for the people of Afghanistan at a critical time in America's involvement in that nation's history. Over the course of 2014, the Obama

administration decided how many American troops to commit to the
security of Afghanistan after the formal end of combat operations in
December 2014. The need is clear; without American help to check
them, the Taliban are likely to regain control of much of rural Afghanistan and even threaten Kabul. Those concerned about stability in the
region, the security of Pakistan's growing nuclear arsenal, and the re-
sidual elements of Al Qaeda central want Afghan bases from which to
conduct counterterrorism operations and intelligence gathering. The
cost of those bases will be enough American advisers and airpower to
give Afghanistan's own security forces a fighting chance against the
Taliban.

Petraeus would have been a powerful advocate for a strong and enduring American presence of perhaps some 15,000 troops; if the absence of his voice results in a considerably smaller force, the price of
his private sins will be heavy indeed—and much of it is likely to be paid
by the innocent people of Afghanistan, who have already suffered so
much.

8.

Counterinsurgency Revisited

Learning from Our Mistakes

My military life began in Operation Desert Storm, a war that was heavily influenced by perceived lessons of Vietnam: fight with overwhelming forces, win the military conflict decisively, then withdraw rapidly regardless of the mess you leave behind. Desert Storm was the war that the Pentagon had wanted to fight ever since Vietnam—a war against a conventional enemy on a battlefield all but devoid of civilians and without jungles, mountains, or cities in which her enemies could hide from America's overwhelming firepower. My first war was, on the surface, an enormous success, as tanks and airpower reduced the Iraqi Army from the fourth largest in the world to the second largest in Iraq in just one hundred hours. Satisfying as it seemed at the time, however, Desert Storm was a military triumph without a political victory; Saddam Hussein remained in power to threaten his neighbors, a low-level air war continued for a decade, and ultimately America chose to fight again to topple him from power, adding another decade of war with Iraq to the historical ledger.

The costs of the second Iraq war were staggering: nearly 4,500

Americans killed and more than 30,000 wounded, many grievously; hundreds of thousands of Iraqi civilians wounded or killed; more than $2 trillion in direct government expenditures, with the possibility of another $2 trillion in indirect costs over the generations to come, and the significant weakening of the major regional counterweight to Iran and consequent strengthening of that country's position and ambitions. Great powers rarely make national decisions that explode so quickly and completely in their faces, and the nation and the world will pay a heavy price for our arrogance and hubris for many decades.

The first Iraq war, in which I led a tank platoon, was necessary; the second one was not. The second Iraq war was one that we did not need to fight but fought for dubious reasons that were eventually proved false. Iraq was not, as we were repeatedly told, developing weapons of mass destruction; even if it had been, deterrence, which prevented war with a nuclear-armed Soviet Union, might have worked against a nuclear Iraq. There was no substantive link between Al Qaeda and Saddam Hussein and no Al Qaeda presence in Iraq until the American invasion, which caused social order to collapse and provided the terrorist group with a powerful recruiting message and a dangerous new base from which to attack.

The invasion of Iraq and its bitter aftermath should remind politicians for generations of the high cost and unpredictable results for those who roll what Otto von Bismarck called "the iron dice," and it should forever discredit the notion of "preventive war." Reluctance to send American ground troops to intervene in Libya and Syria, while providing different levels of political and military support, gives some hope that the country will think more than twice before fighting another unnecessary war. Good intentions do not always lead to favorable outcomes.

In Vietnam, the U.S. military was typically slow to recognize and adapt to the demands of the counterinsurgency campaign it confronted. Over time it improved its performance under the command of General Creighton Abrams, who took command from William Westmoreland and changed his search-and-destroy strategy to clear, hold, and build too late, after the American people had already given up hope. But the lessons learned too late in Vietnam recur again and again in the pages of successful counterinsurgency campaigns, from the Philippines to the Malayan Emergency. They include the importance of building capable local forces, linking political and military lines of effort, conducting information operations, protecting the population rather than focusing exclusively on killing insurgents, and holding the terrain you've cleared rather than allowing the insurgents to reoccupy it. These old lessons had been codified in the *Marine Corps Small Wars Manual* of 1940, painful learning drawn from the Marines' experience in the Banana Wars that had to be learned again in Vietnam at an enormous cost in blood and treasure.

Tragically, all these lessons were forgotten yet again in the wake of the Vietnam War. In fact, after Vietnam, the United States intentionally turned away from the counterinsurgency lessons it had repurchased, certain that it would never again fight a counterinsurgency campaign and instead deciding to focus on a kind of war it knew how to fight well, conventional tank wars against another tank Army. The American military can be justly proud of its renaissance after the debacle of Vietnam and subsequent triumph in the Cold War, but its historical amnesia left it grievously unprepared for the wars of this century.

The British historian Michael Howard noted that it is impossible to perfectly prepare military forces for the next war; what is important is to make sure that you have not gotten the preparations so wrong that the military cannot quickly adapt when it is next needed. The Department of Defense failed that test in both Iraq and Afghanistan. It ignored preparations for counterinsurgency operations and was all but

criminally unprepared for the demands of occupying Iraq after the invasion caused its government to collapse and Saddam Hussein to disap-
pear into hiding. American actions, including the disbanding of the
Iraqi Army and excessive use of force early in the occupation, contributed to the raging insurgency that threatened to pull Iraq down into
civil war.

After the American people made clear their displeasure with this
state of affairs in the midterm elections of 2006, transferring both the
House and the Senate from Republican to Democratic control, President George W. Bush made the bravest decision of his presidency, firing Secretary of Defense Rumsfeld and doubling down on Iraq under
the leadership of Bob Gates and David Petraeus. Petraeus, who had
written his doctoral dissertation on Vietnam and had prepared his
whole career in case America needed him to conduct an irregular warfare campaign, applied the lessons of Vietnam to the Iraq campaign.
The Army, which had too long neglected the need for a deep understanding of languages and cultures, changed its spots in a remarkable
example of organizational adaptation under extreme pressure. Winston
Churchill said that you can always count on the United States to do the
right thing when it has exhausted all possible alternatives; with Petraeus's selection to command in Iraq under Gates's leadership in the Pentagon, it adapted in the nick of time.

As history would suggest, the principles of counterinsurgency
worked, albeit at great cost and just as American patience with the war
effort in Iraq was about to expire. American support for the Sunni
Awakening proved crucial in rebalancing the forces on the ground that
eventually changed the course of the Iraq conflict, and Petraeus received well-justified accolades for turning around a war that had
seemed destined to be America's second consecutive loss in the irregular warfare category. The cost was excessive, the pleasure momentary,
and the posture ridiculous, as British diplomat Lord Chesterfield is re-

puted to have described another activity, but the outcome was far better than could have reasonably been expected.

Petraeus later had the chance to practice counterinsurgency in Afghanistan, which had been starved of resources for many years by the overwhelming demands of the debacle in Iraq. Counterinsurgency worked where it was resourced, particularly in southern Afghanistan, albeit slowly and at great cost, as T. E. Lawrence and any other student of counterinsurgency would have thought likely to be the case.

The question is not whether the classic counterinsurgency principles of clear, hold, and build work; the fact that they do has been demonstrated repeatedly. The question is whether the extraordinary investment of time, blood, and treasure required to make them work is worth the cost. The answer to that question depends on the value of long-term stability in the country afflicted by an insurgency, and that answer varies by time and place.

The attempt to unify Vietnam under the North's leadership was not, as the Kennedy and Johnson administrations argued, an attempt to expand Communism across all of Southeast Asia; it was instead largely a nationalist expression of anticolonialism and a desire for independence that should have sounded familiar to Americans who were themselves products of such emotions a scant two centuries prior. Ho Chi Minh quoting from the Declaration of Independence in 1945 should have been an indication that perhaps we were backing the wrong side. But the Democrats, who had absorbed the blame for "losing" China to Communism under Harry Truman, were not about to let another domino fall on their watch. Ironically, when South Vietnam did ultimately fall to North Vietnamese tanks, it was Democrats on Capitol Hill who refused to uphold obligations in the Paris Accords that we would come to the aid of our South Vietnamese allies in their hour of need.

The fall of Vietnam, despite its horrible repercussions throughout

Southeast Asia, did not signal the triumph of global Communism, and ironically it was a similar counterinsurgency campaign in Afghanistan that ultimately exhausted the Soviet Union. Stability in Afghanistan was not as essential to Soviet security as the Politburo had believed it to be, but the costs of the war in blood and treasure were crippling. Afghanistan fell when the Soviet Union could no longer pay the bills to support Afghan security forces some three years after the last Soviet soldier had left the country, a lesson that should resound as we contemplate the future of our own efforts in Afghanistan twenty-five years later.

Unlike Vietnam for us or Afghanistan for the Soviet Union, a degree of stability in Iraq was a vital national interest for the United States. Even with the threat of Saddam Hussein's bellicosity confined to the dustbin of history, Iraq's impact on the pre-fracking global oil market and its position in the heart of the Muslim world meant that America could not simply withdraw her forces and hope for the best when a civil war erupted in the power vacuum we had inadvertently created. After invading the country and toppling the government, not just morality but hard national interest demanded a degree of stability in Iraq that appeared unachievable in 2006 but that was clearly visible in the streets when I visited in the summer of 2008. It was hard to comprehend the change. The curbstones that had been shattered by bombs were already rebuilt and painted jaunty colors, and the guardrails we'd ripped out with tanks after an IED planted behind one killed Roger Ling and Jeff Graham had been reinstalled. Iraq mattered a lot, and although the invasion had been unnecessary and the subsequent occupation was a debacle, cleaning up the mess we'd made was the least bad option available.

Afghanistan is a rather different case. Sitting next to me before the Senate Foreign Relations Committee in 2009, Steve Biddle had testified that continuing to invest in stability in Afghanistan after the toppling of the Taliban and scattering of Al Qaeda was a close call on the merits. An unstable Afghanistan would not disturb the global oil markets, and the neighborhood was not as susceptible to the contagion of Sunni-Shia conflict as had been Iraq's. There was and is a danger that absent American support, Afghanistan could again be conquered by the Taliban and provide a new home for terrorists, including ones who might further destabilize nuclear-armed Pakistan. That danger was worth making an investment in counterinsurgency in Afghanistan, but the case was never as clear as had been the decision to surge in Iraq in 2007, and even that had been something of a long shot.

Still, candidate Obama had campaigned on Afghanistan as the good war, and to demonstrate his seriousness about national security despite his criticism of the Bush administration's conduct in Iraq, he could hardly allow the Afghan presidential elections scheduled for the summer of 2009 to fail. During Obama's first term, Democrats were still tainted with weakness by the long shadow of Vietnam. Determined to escape those ghosts and make the Democrats seem strong on national security, President Obama judged counterinsurgency to be the least bad option available during two separate rounds of White House deliberations over Afghanistan strategy in his first year. He nearly tripled U.S. forces committed to the war but simultaneously imposed a definite deadline of summer 2011 as the endpoint of the Afghan surge.

Much to the surprise of the U.S. military, he meant it. Obama was willing to give counterinsurgency a try, but the costs of the war clearly weighed on him, and he began the drawdown as scheduled. He was able to do so over the resistance of Secretary Gates and General Petraeus in no small part because of the killing of Osama bin Laden by a SEAL team in April 2011, the climax of an intensive counterterrorism campaign that had effectively defeated Al Qaeda as a strategic threat to the United States. Although Al Qaeda's affiliates in Somalia, Yemen, and Iraq still had the ability to conduct local strikes of some significance, they had proven unable to replicate the effects of the September 11, 2001, attacks. They were unlikely to be able to regain that global reach given the more effective American intelligence and counterterrorism capabilities we had developed in the decade that followed.

Obama had proven his national security bona fides, and the Democrats actually earned an advantage on the issue over their Republican adversaries during the presidential campaign of 2012. The president was free to overrule his military advisers who recommended a larger and longer-term troop commitment to Afghanistan, and American-led counterinsurgency in that country came to an end early in his second term. Even at its peak the counterinsurgency campaign had not been sufficiently resourced to be applied across all of Afghanistan, and where the main effort was made in the south, American forces were withdrawn and Afghan troops thrust into the lead more rapidly than many would have recommended. Whether the Afghans will be able to hold what Americans and NATO troops have cleared of insurgents at such cost will depend largely on the American commitment to Afghanistan after the formal transfer of authority in 2014.

The endgame remains unclear. Will Afghanistan end like Vietnam—in an abject, helicopters-flying-out-of-Kabul, people-hanging-on-the-skids defeat—or in an unsatisfying and untidy sort-of victory like Iraq? While neither option seems particularly attractive, President Obama would welcome an Iraq-like end to Afghanistan. America can live with the current Iraqi government and its policies, and Iraq's increasing oil output will help the global economic recovery. This is an unsatisfying return on the blood and treasure we poured into Iraq, but it is not a complete loss—and it is far better than we could have imagined in 2006, when Iraq was descending into civil war and Al Qaeda had established an important foothold there.

It is not unlikely that 2015 will see a similarly reasonable Afghan government that will hold together with American money and advisers—an unsatisfying end, but not a failure, and not without promise of greater stability to come. Like any successful counterinsurgency, Afghanistan's is likely to end somewhat unsatisfyingly for Americans, with a corrupt but gradually improving government in Kabul, advisers helping Afghan security forces fight a weakening but still dangerous Taliban, and a schizophrenic Pakistan alternately helping Afghan and Taliban fighters. If not a good return on our huge investment in the country, it would be a reasonable outcome given the advantage we gave our enemies by taking our eye off the ball in Afghanistan for eight years while Iraq burned.

A reasonable outcome in both wars, unsatisfying as it seems, is about the best we can hope for in what is likely to remain an age of unsatisfying wars. This unsatisfying but not catastrophic outcome, however, is one of the reasons that modern critics of counterinsurgency have such an uphill battle in front of them, and why their critiques have failed to take hold of the military imagination the way Colonel Harry Summers's book *On Strategy* did after the Vietnam War.

Summers argued that the reason the United States lost the Vietnam War was that it had practiced too much counterinsurgency in Vietnam, fighting with one hand tied behind its back; "A War is a War is a War," he thundered, and only the complete use of all available force was acceptable. This attitude ignored the changes in the character of warfare since the deployment of nuclear weapons and the Cold War context in which the Vietnam War had been fought, as a smaller proxy war in a longer and larger global conflict against the Soviet Union. Never mind; it was a simple answer that made sense to Army officers, and *On Strategy* became for many years the Army's answer to itself to why it had lost a long, hard war in Southeast Asia.

There are modern applicants to fill Harry Summers's role for the more recent wars in Iraq and Afghanistan. They are hobbled not just because the outcomes of those wars are much more likely to be unsatisfying sort-of wins rather than abject defeats—indeed, the Army is rightly proud of its turnaround in Iraq after a horrible start that was largely bequeathed to it by its political leadership, and Afghanistan's outcome is still too close to call—but also by the intellectual incoherence of their own arguments.

Thus Army Colonel Gian Gentile, the most strident voice against modern counterinsurgency doctrine and implementation, alternately claims that his own battalion was already implementing classic counterinsurgency principles in Baghdad in 2006 and that counterinsurgency is an inherently flawed policy in which the United States should never again engage. While he is certainly correct that the invasion of Iraq was a mistake and that the United States has reaped a most meager return on the extraordinary investment of lives and treasure it made there, he has never said what the United States should have done once the decision to invade Iraq had been so unwisely made and so poorly implemented. The counterinsurgency campaign in Iraq, once comprehensively implemented under the leadership of General Petraeus, was imperfect and left behind a deeply troubled country that remains violent and unstable, but absent the implementation of counterinsurgency best practices, it would have been far, far worse. Large-scale counterinsurgency is rarely a great option—it is in fact messy and slow and hugely expensive—but it may sometimes be the least bad option available.

Critics of counterinsurgency must do better than say that they would not have invaded Iraq in March 2003; I argued against the invasion as stridently as a serving officer could. But once Iraq had been invaded against my wishes, its government destroyed, its security forces disbanded, and fundamental splits in Iraqi society exposed and exacerbated by the occupation's incompetence and willful blindness, there was no better alternative than a full-blown counterinsurgency campaign. As the great historian Arthur Schlesinger, Jr., liked to say, the right question is often, "Compared to what?" No critics of counterinsurgency have examined the situation in Iraq in early 2007 and presented an alternative answer that can be subjected to a cost and benefit comparison.

That absence matters, because there is every chance that America will fight another full-scale counterinsurgency campaign, in a generation or perhaps much sooner. This is true despite and perhaps even because of the Defense Department's Strategic Guidance released at the Pentagon on January 5, 2012. Standing with Secretary of Defense Leon Panetta, who had recently replaced Gates at the Pentagon, President Obama held a press conference to emphasize the importance of the Strategic Guidance. The document, titled *Sustaining U.S. Global Leadership: Priorities for 21st Century Defense,* explicitly ordered "the end of long-term nation building with large military footprints."

That goal seems laudable, but it ignores the reality that the United States is currently involved in a number of counterinsurgency campaigns: fighting insurgents in Afghanistan, Pakistan, the Philippines, and the Horn of Africa, and rather halfheartedly supporting insurgents in Syria after having recently helped other insurgents topple the government of Libya. Insurgency and counterinsurgency are not going away, and it is essential that the Pentagon remembers that postinvasion stability operations, including counterinsurgency, are core military tasks for which America's armed forces must always be prepared.

Iraq and Afghanistan were not the only insurgencies to challenge the United States during the first decades of the twenty-first century. In fact, in the wake of the asymmetric September 11 attacks, challenges to state power in much of the world increasingly took the form of insurgencies, as conventional state-on-state warfare receded further into the realm of history. As rebellion and insurgency roiled the planet,

the United States supported some insurgents and engaged in counterinsurgency campaigns against others, often by supporting the host nation in its efforts to defeat the rebels. There is no sign that the future
holds anything but a continuation of this trend toward less conventional conflict and more insurgency and counterinsurgency.

The reasons are multifaceted and mutually reinforcing. They begin
with a single big idea: that the information revolution is changing
our world as dramatically as did the agricultural revolution of some
five thousand years ago and the industrial revolution of 250 years ago.
Both these revolutions strengthened the state against the individual,
and for the three hundred years following the Treaty of Westphalia in
1648, the state became the dominant force in international politics and
in organizing the affairs of human beings.

However, that power dynamic changed with the beginnings of
the information revolution in the wake of the Second World War. The
rapid growth of computing power at an ever-decreasing cost—as
described in Moore's Law, which notes that computing capabilities
double and costs are cut in half every eighteen months—shows no sign
of diminishing and has given individuals and small groups a degree of
power that has formerly been restricted to states. The ability of lone
wolves like Bradley Manning and Edward Snowden to single-handedly
damage international relations between the United States and her allies
and expose intelligence operations and operatives worth billions of
dollars is just one indication of the changing direction of the balance
of power between the individual and state for the first time in three
centuries.

The impact of the information revolution on the relative power of
the state and the individual is not yet clear. Technologically sophisticated states can use digitized information to track the actions and locations of individuals within and sometimes even outside their borders;
the raid that killed Osama bin Laden inside Pakistan was made possible

only because some of his intermediaries were sloppy with their use of cell phones. But information technology also gives power to individuals who are wise in its use to apply that power against their own state or others in the international system; the Vietcong and North Vietnamese used the power of television to undermine U.S. support for the war in Vietnam, and the Green Revolution in Iran used Twitter and other social media to organize powerful (although ultimately unsuccessful, at least for now) demonstrations against the Iranian regime.

In fact, the entirety of the so-called Arab Spring revolutions against authoritarian or semiauthoritarian regimes can be seen as a consequence of the information revolution. With easy access to personal, demand-pull rather than command-push information technology, it became increasingly hard for regimes like Mubarak's in Egypt, Qaddafi's in Libya, and Assad's in Syria to control their populations' access to information about the performance of their government. Once they knew the truth, the Egyptian, Libyan, and Syrian publics could use that same information technology to mobilize demonstrations against the regimes they had detested for years but had never had the power to effectively confront. An earlier form of information technology, the photocopier, contributed to public discontent against the Soviet regime throughout the Communist bloc in the 1970s; photocopied *samizdat* versions of dissident manifestos like Aleksandr Solzhenitsyn's *The Gulag Archipelago* fermented discontent in an earlier spring of rebellion against autocracy, and the trend has only accelerated as technology to rapidly disseminate information has improved.

But globalization—the essentially instantaneous, essentially free transfer of information around the globe—is just one of the factors driving the new era of insurgencies around the globe. Others include nuclear weapons, conventional U.S. military superiority over any conceivable state enemy, urbanization and population growth, climate change, and resource depletion. Judged against the backdrop of the information revolution, this series of factors strongly implies a period of rapid strategic change, of which the Arab Spring is only the beginning.

In *The Better Angels of Our Nature*, Stephen Pinker argues that human-on-human violence of all kinds has been declining over the course of history, particularly since the end of the Second World War. One does not have to fully buy into his argument to note that the seventy years since the end of that conflict have seen an impressive decrease in the number of conventional, state-on-state wars that saw their climax in the First and Second World Wars. In fact, since V-E and V-J days, the United States had engaged in only two significant primarily conventional wars against other states—the Korean War against North Korean and Chinese armed forces, and Desert Storm against Iraqi armed forces. Vietnam, Lebanon, Somalia, Bosnia, Operation Iraqi Freedom, and Operation Enduring Freedom have all included significant combat against irregular nonstate actors.

At least one reason behind the decrease in conventional combat has been the existence of nuclear weapons, which impose a kind of force cap on how far great powers are willing to pursue military objectives. It was his request for nuclear weapons that led to the relief of Douglas MacArthur by Harry Truman, who knew something about the employment of those systems; Dwight Eisenhower similarly refused to employ nuclear weapons in support of the French at Dien Bien Phu. John F. Kennedy's refusal to face nuclear Armageddon correctly limited U.S. options during the Cuban Missile Crisis; LBJ similarly refused to escalate the Vietnam War to a point that threatened nuclear war with North Vietnam's backers in the Soviet Union. In short, nuclear weapons have put a cap on how far nuclear powers have been willing to push the use of conventional force and have in some ways made the world safe for irregular war. There are now those who believe that the United States should turn away from the lessons of the past decade and focus on preparing to invade other great powers' sphere of influence, despite their improved anti-access area-denial capabilities (A2AD in Pentagon parlance), using our Air Force and Navy comparative advantages in a strategy called AirSea Battle. They ignore the lessons of the Cold War, in which nuclear weapons made impossible conventional conflicts that would result in thousands of casualties directly attributable to another great power; instead, the Soviet Union and the United States engaged in expensive but indirect proxy wars. China and the United States are far more likely to do the same than to fight a single climactic battle in the Strait of Taiwan, no matter how much more the Pentagon and military-industrial complex would benefit from World War III in the Pacific.

Similarly, conventional U.S. military superiority has reduced the incidence of conventional state-on-state wars like Operation Desert Storm, which cast a heavy shadow across the military capabilities of lesser powers that realized conclusively that they could not compete with the United States in tank-on-tank warfare. Ironically, this very superiority of U.S. military muscle made the world safe for irregular warfare, particularly in the decades since the collapse of the Soviet Union after its own foray into irregular warfare in Afghanistan. The triumph of American arms in Desert Storm demonstrated the likely result of any conventional military aggression against American desires anywhere in the world. The very fact that we are so good at the American way of war makes it almost impossible for anyone to compete against us on a conventional battlefield—another factor behind the decrease in conventional combat in the decades since the end of the Cold War, and another factor making AirSea Battle more of a dream of defense planners than a real challenge worthy of primacy in Pentagon war planning.

That's the good news. The bad news is that a number of factors are increasing the likelihood of irregular war, and those trends will only increase in years to come. A number of them have contributed to the uprisings of the Arab Spring. In addition to the information revolution that has empowered individuals worldwide with more and more easily accessible knowledge than has ever been available in human history, populations continue to increase in urban areas as people flock to cities for employment and the hope of a better life. However, living in cities exposes people to vast inequalities that mark the globalized world, and increased concentrations of humanity put more pressure on governments and make demonstrations larger, more frequent, and more dangerous.

Population growth continues in many of the least developed parts of the world, putting yet more pressure on governments that have to feed and house them or risk rebellion. The increased environmental energy infused into the global climate system by global warming is increasing the frequency and violence of weather patterns, further pressuring some of the world's least capable governments; Bangladesh is likely to be a victim of all of these mutually reinforcing trends, but it is only the most obvious site of future unrest. Pakistan is another, with far more serious implications for global stability as a result of its nuclear weapons.

So, in a classic good news/bad news scenario, the world is less likely to see conventional conflict of uniformed armies clashing with peer or near-peer forces for the foreseeable future. Instead, we are likely to experience more of the kinds of rebellions and insurgencies that have marked the Arab Spring.

In this world, one of the critical questions the United States will face is when, whether, and how to intervene in the varieties of insurgencies and rebellions that are likely to be the face of conflict in this century. The complicated answer is "sometimes" with nonlethal assistance and advisers, and "seldom" with U.S. combat forces and then only when vital U.S. national interests are affected. The Afghanistan and Iraq interventions are instructive on this point, but so are the more recent conflicts in Iran, Egypt, Libya, and Syria.

Afghanistan was, to use Richard Haas's excellent construction, a war of necessity. After the attacks of September 11, 2001, when the leaders of Afghanistan refused to hand over the members of Al Qaeda responsible for the costliest foreign attack on U.S. soil, the United States had no choice but to use force to capture or kill the Al Qaeda leadership in simple self-defense. Because the Taliban resisted American efforts to accomplish those tasks, and could not be trusted to prevent Al Qaeda from using its territory to plan and execute future attacks, the Taliban also had to go and be replaced by a government that would pursue policies more supportive of U.S. interests, with the minimum standard being one that would fight rather than support Al Qaeda. This intervention was legal and necessary and remains likely to accomplish its core objective of preventing Afghan territory from again being used to attack the United States or her interests, although the campaign has been longer and harder than anyone would have predicted when it began more than a dozen years ago.

The two factors that have prolonged the Afghan campaign are instructive as the U.S. contemplates future interventions, hopefully with a "once bitten, twice shy" attitude. They are the presence of sanctuaries in Pakistan and the endemic corruption of the Afghan government that was established in the wake of the Taliban's initial defeat. These two factors are historically among the most important in predicting the success or failure of a counterinsurgency campaign; both have a strong negative correlation with success, with invulnerable foreign sanctuary that shares a difficult-to-control border the single factor that is most likely to promote the success of an insurgency.

Still, important as foreign sanctuaries are, there are reasons to believe that the sanctuary Pakistan provides to the Taliban and to

Al Qaeda central will not be decisive in determining the final outcome in Afghanistan. Pakistan, which created the mujahedeen who expelled the Soviet Union from Afghanistan with U.S. and Saudi Arabian help (including Osama bin Laden) in the 1980s, is paying a heavy price for allowing the Taliban to use its territory to continue attacks inside Afghanistan; indeed, it has lost more of its own soldiers to the Pakistani Taliban than has the government of Afghanistan. Pakistan has made some efforts to regain control of the Frankenstein's monster it unleashed, with enthusiastic if not particularly sophisticated counterinsurgency efforts in places like the Swat Valley that have at least complicated the efforts of the Taliban to seize control of the nuclear-armed country.

The United States and her NATO allies in Afghanistan have not been able to conduct ground operations inside Pakistan but have used airpower in new ways to take on the Pakistani Taliban and, especially, Al Qaeda central. Drone strikes have decimated Al Qaeda inside Pakistan, rendering it essentially irrelevant as a global threat able to plan, prepare, and conduct strikes outside Pakistan's borders. Drone strikes have not been as effective against the Afghan and Pakistani Taliban but have limited their effectiveness and imposed additional complicating factors on their ability to recruit, train, and conduct operations in both countries. Thus, as important as the Pakistani sanctuary has been for the insurgent groups based there that threaten regional stability, the new technologies being used to identify, locate, track, and disrupt their operations have essentially stalemated the insurgents at the strategic level. The Pakistani-based insurgent groups can continue to operate and cause casualties, but they are unable to mass in attacks of true strategic significance that threaten the government of Afghanistan. As long as the United States provides airpower in support of that government, even after the withdrawal of U.S. ground troops, the Pakistani-based insurgents will be limited to guerrilla attacks that are unlikely to lead to the fall of Kabul. It is worth remembering that Saigon fell in 1975 not to insurgents but to North Vietnamese tanks that would have been easy pickings for American airpower had it still been on station; in the forty years since, the advent of precision weapons empowered by the information revolution has only increased the costs of conventional invasions and attacks for lesser powers.

The corruption of the Afghan government is another factor that has complicated the counterinsurgency campaign there, but it is also unlikely to be strategically decisive. Corrupt and ineffective host-nation governments are the stock in trade of counterinsurgency campaigns; effective governments regarded as legitimate by their population do not give rise to insurgencies in the first place. And as bad as the Afghan government under President Karzai is by Western standards—often ranking as the worst or next to worst in the world—it is more effective and better regarded by the Afghan population than the despised and repressive Taliban regime that preceded it. Partly because Afghanistan was in such a dire place when the September 11 attacks occurred, life there has improved dramatically for most people despite twelve years of war. A country that had fewer than one thousand telephones in 2001 now has more than ten million, and the population in school has exploded, particularly among girls and young women. The people of Afghanistan do not hate their government, and as long as it remains able to pay its security forces—a question much more for the international community than for the Afghans themselves—the state will hang together. The people do not want to return to the days of the Taliban; bad as the Karzai government is, the Taliban, within the living memory of most Afghans, was far worse.

The invasion of Afghanistan in 2001 was a necessary war, and the need for continued counterterrorism operations to be conducted from Afghan territory for the foreseeable future required a counterinsurgency campaign to build and strengthen an Afghan government to a degree sufficient to protect American bases in the country. Operation Desert Storm was also a necessary war, required to prevent Iraq from controlling Kuwaiti oil supplies and to demonstrate that the international community would not tolerate changing borders by the open use of conventional force; if international law is to mean anything, than the occupation of Kuwait could not and did not stand.

The invasion of Iraq in 2003, on the other hand, was an unnecessary war of choice, fought on intelligence that proved to be false and on logic that was prima facie flawed even if the intelligence had been correct. If Iraq did have weapons of mass destruction, the American-led invasion force should have been large enough to secure those weapons sites rather than barely large enough to topple Saddam's government, much less police the postwar chaos that many, including Conrad Crane, predicted. As a result of inadequate postwar planning and insufficient troop strength, when my battalion arrived in Al Anbar in September 2003, we found acres of weapons depots completely unguarded. The United States was fortunate that all that escaped from the weapons depots—which Saddam had guarded far better than we did in the immediate wake of his fall—were artillery shells to make roadside bombs; if there had been chemical weapons in the storage sites, the invasion of Iraq could have been far more of a disaster than it proved to be.

Worst of all, because it was a war of choice, the United States had extraordinary freedom of action to choose when, where, with what forces, and how to conduct the invasion, making the failure to plan for the subsequent occupation even more inexcusable. Iraq presented no imminent threat to U.S. or allied interests in March 2003, and I opposed the invasion at the time, as did most serious students of U.S. foreign policy; John Mearsheimer and Stephen Walt are just two of the political scientists who published articles arguing that the planned invasion was not in the American national interest. They were right, and the costs of the operation to topple Saddam Hussein will constrain American foreign policy and affect intervention decisions for decades to come, in the United States and among our allies, as the reluctance to intervene in Syria even by the British has shown.

Some defenders of the decision to invade Iraq in 2003 argue that the invasion and the subsequent creation of an admittedly flawed democracy there contributed to the popular uprisings across the Middle East sometimes collectively referred to as the Arab Spring. This claim is hard to conclusively support or refute; as with the relationship between global warming and individual disasters like Hurricane Sandy, putting more energy into a complex system is likely to have extreme and unpredictable results, but it is hard to draw a direct line to any individual event in a complicated region that the United States struggles to understand.

However, it is not hard to make a connection between the shattered expectations of quick success in Iraq and subsequent American reluctance to use force to accomplish U.S. national security objectives abroad. The Obama administration's foreign policy has been marked by reluctance to intervene abroad with ground forces, but even the final days of the George W. Bush administration showed some welcome learning about the uncertain consequences and heavy costs of military intervention, as President Bush refused to support Israeli plans for a strike on Iran.

Bush's successor, Barack Obama, was elected to the presidency in no small part because of his predecessor's poor decisions on Iraq, and because Hillary Clinton, his primary opponent, had voted in favor of the invasion. The extraordinary energy that the Iraq fiasco injected into the American political system was a once-in-a-generation event; America had not been so riven over a foreign policy issue since Vietnam. But even Barack Obama, elected because of his opposition to the invasion, could not afford to overlearn the lesson about the costs of foreign intervention.

A cat that sits on a hot stove once learns not to sit on any stove, hot or cold. But the United States is too important an actor in the international system, with global interests and global responsibilities, to sit out hard foreign policy choices for the next generation. Indeed, expensive as was the Iraq intervention for his predecessor, President Obama spent much of the first year of his first term focused on two separate decisions to increase troop strength in Afghanistan—unpopular decisions that cost him support from his political base, a fact that contributed to his decision to announce the date of the drawdown of the Afghan surge simultaneously with its commencement. That announcement undercut the effectiveness of the troop surge and betrayed the president's profound unease with the deployment of military forces to achieve national security objectives abroad in the wake of Iraq—a "half pregnant" attitude that marked many of his subsequent foreign policy decisions as well.

He would have plenty of decisions to make (or avoid). Population growth and resource scarcity in much of the developing world continued to stir discontent among the populations of poorly governed countries, but the burgeoning information revolution gave new tools to people who in decades past would have suffered in silence and isolation. Thus when Tunisian merchant and frustrated college graduate Mohamed Bouazizi immolated himself on December 18, 2010, just over a year after the Afghan surge announcement at West Point, Tunisian revolutionaries were able to seize the moment to protest their inadequate government's policies. The resulting electronic-enabled protests led not only to the fall of Tunisian president Zine El Abidine Ben Ali barely a month later but, in quick succession over the following year, to changes of government in Egypt, Libya, and Yemen. All were driven by popular protests against corrupt and inefficient governments; all posed varying dilemmas to American foreign policy.

Tunisia had relatively little impact on American policy other than as a tinderbox that sparked the revolutions that shook the foundations of U.S. policy in the Middle East. Egypt was an entirely different issue; it is the largest and most important country in the region and has been a pillar of American policy in the Middle East for decades. Hence the Obama administration initially hesitated when popular rebellion broke out against the administration of President Hosni Mubarak after thirty years of repressive rule that had been one of the driving forces behind the ideology of Al Qaeda—but that also had permitted Mubarak, for all his manifest flaws, to run a foreign policy that was not broadly supported by his population but that was in the interests of the United States and Israel. Mubarak's fall was a victory for democracy, but democracy in the absence of institutions is merely mob rule—and the mob in Egypt did not support Egypt's peace agreement with Israel. After initially supporting Mubarak against the popular rebellion, President Obama's team eventually shifted against him in a move that shocked the other rulers of the Middle East who had longtime alliances with the United States but repressive tendencies toward their own population, chief among them the Al Saud family that governs Saudi Arabia.

Washington harbored no such concerns about Libya's Muammar Qaddafi, who had committed the fatal error of demobilizing his WMD program in the wake of the invasion of Iraq in 2003, believing that his country was next. Having given up the invasion insurance that protected North Korea and that Iran was desperately seeking, Qaddafi was vulnerable to outside pressure when a revolt against his regime garnered international support. A coalition led by Britain and France, but with significant support from the United States, operated under a UN Security Council mandate to support the rebellion with airpower. It proved decisive in a country where the vast majority of the population lives within fifty miles of an international seacoast, and Qaddafi's regime fled the capital city of Tripoli (but continued fighting) on September 1, 2011. The dictator was himself killed on October 20, but the air campaign was longer and more difficult than Britain or France had expected, and only American logistical support, refueling planes, and ammunition stores allowed it to continue through to completion. Both European powers were chastened by the difficulty of the endeavor, with Britain in particular, decreasing her armed forces for budgetary reasons, demonstrating less inclination to intervene in future military operations abroad.

If Libya showed the difficulty of small-footprint, no-boots-on-the-ground military interventions in support of insurgents, international unwillingness to intervene in Syria was proof that the lessons had been internalized. Protests against the regime of President Bashar Al Assad began in January 2011, a few weeks before those in Libya, but Syria was a much tougher nut to crack than Libya had been. Assad proved willing to use indiscriminate violence against his own people, including even violating the long-standing international prohibition on the use of chemical weapons, in order to remain in power, while an exhausted international community remained indecisive about whether to intervene in support of the rebels as it had in Libya or even to punish the use of chemical weapons in support of that international norm.

The Obama administration's foreign policy team, including Secretary of State Hillary Clinton, Secretary of Defense Leon Panetta, and Director of Central Intelligence David Petraeus had recommended a program to arm and train the Syrian rebels in the summer of 2012, but President Obama, facing an election in which his own base was already disenchanted with the surge of American military force into Afghanistan, decided against this limited intervention. The rebels suffered mightily as a result, not just from attacks by the Assad regime but also from internecine warfare within their own ranks. As often happens in these cases, the most violent and best-organized groups scramble to power over the bodies of their rivals, and by the time the question of arming and training the rebels had risen to the top of the American policy agenda again a year later, in the summer of 2013, that window had closed. The rebels were now led by members of the Muslim Brotherhood, many linked with Al Qaeda, and there were no good policy options left for the United States: it didn't want Assad to remain in power, but it had no guarantee that what replaced him would be better—and the real risk that it might be worse.

President Obama, who was elected to the presidency in no small part because he had opposed the invasion of Iraq in 2003, retained an ambivalence toward the use of military power in the service of U.S. interests throughout his tenure. While willing to use remotely piloted aerial vehicles, or drones, to attack members of Al Qaeda wherever they presented themselves, but particularly in Pakistan and Yemen, and even to authorize the Navy SEAL team mission to kill Osama bin Laden, Obama had internalized lessons about the effectiveness of American power to protect populations and build good governance in countries afflicted by insurgency that were not dissimilar to those learned by T. E. Lawrence a century before, in another war in the Middle East: counterinsurgency operations are messy and slow and extremely expensive.

And yet insurgency remained a vibrant force in the international system, perhaps the dominant factor in the international relations of the early twenty-first century. The counterexample may appear to be China, the rising power of East Asia, whose ascent carries with it a promise of a return to primacy of the diplomacy empowered by ships and planes that the United States understood so well when it confronted the Soviet Union's armed forces around the globe. But even China faces significant internal rebellions and the prospect of widespread protests against the legitimacy of its government. The anger and frustration that incited the protests in Tiananmen Square twenty-five years ago have been temporarily diminished by two decades of double-digit economic growth, but when that slows, the barricades will return, made more potent by information-sharing devices that are, ironically, often "Made in China." It is to protect her own ability to use whatever degree of force is necessary that China so often vetoes interventions in the internal affairs of states like Syria; allowing the Libyan intervention to pass the UN Security Council was a mistake that China will not soon make again.

The age of counterinsurgency cannot be over as long as insurgencies roil the globe. And so the challenges of insurgency and counterinsurgency will continue. The United States should intervene in them with ground forces as seldom as possible, only when vital national interests are threatened, and only when she can be confident that the peace that will follow the conflict will be an improvement over the prewar situation. Whenever possible, the United States should follow a light-footprint policy, sending advisers and equipment in support of people fighting for freedom rather than putting large numbers of American combat troops on the ground.

Humanitarian intervention to protect people from harm when vital U.S. national interests are not involved should be conducted only when there is an international coalition willing to intervene and a UN Security Council resolution in support of the operation—and even then only when there is a commitment to build a better peace in the wake of the war. Both the 2011 Libyan intervention and the planned but not implemented Syrian punishment strikes fail to rise to this standard, as does the 2003 invasion of Iraq; of recent American military operations, only the Afghan War is justified by this test.

And yet the need for future large-scale counterinsurgency operations may arise again. The United States may again be attacked from a country that harbors terrorists, need to topple the government that supported them, and be determined to prevent that ground from again being used to attack the homeland. In that case, the options are unpalatable, but it is unlikely that the nation will choose the Roman technique of making a desert and calling it peace. We must, therefore, retain the ability to conduct counterinsurgency operations among the peoples, with all the requirements for cultural competence, linguistic skills, and organizational learning that that implies, even as we strive to avoid the messy, slow operations that have cost us so much over the past decade.

Saint Augustine taught that the purpose of war is to build a better peace, but we have not built the capacity to create that better peace in the American national security establishment. The historical record reveals that the United States engages in ambiguous counterinsurgency and nation-building missions far more often than it faces full-scale war. Similar demands will only increase in a globalized world, where local problems increasingly do not stay local and where, as Secretary of Defense Gates once noted, "the most likely catastrophic threats to our homeland . . . are more likely to emanate from failing states than from aggressor states."[1]

Trends such as the youth bulge and urbanization in underdeveloped states, as well as the proliferation of ever more lethal weaponry into more hands and the radicalization of individuals and small groups over the Internet, point to a future dominated by chaotic local insecurity and conflict rather than to confrontations between the armies and navies of nation-states. This future of persistent low-intensity conflict around the globe suggests that American interests are at risk not from enemies who are too strong, which was the case throughout the twentieth century (Germany in two world wars and then the Soviet Union during the Cold War), but from states that are too weak to control what happens inside their borders, with Pakistan as the most obvious and dangerous example.

As a result, the U.S. military is more likely to be called upon to counter insurgencies, intervene in civil strife and humanitarian crises, rebuild nations, and wage unconventional types of warfare than it is to fight mirror-image armed forces. We will not have the luxury of opting out of these missions because they do not conform to preferred notions of the American way of war. Insurgency against governments has existed as long as men have governed others; the United States was itself born in the crucible of insurgency. The final tragedy of Iraq and Afghanistan would occur if we again forget the many lessons we have learned about counterinsurgency over the past decade of war, and have to learn them yet again in some future war at the cost of many more American lives.

Both state and nonstate enemies will seek more asymmetric ways to challenge the United States and its allies. America's conventional military superiority, which remains substantial, will drive many of them to the same conclusion: when they fight America conventionally, they lose horribly in days or weeks. When they fight unconventionally, by employing guerrilla tactics, terrorism, and information operations, they have a better chance of success. It is unclear why even a powerful enemy would want to risk a costly head-to-head battlefield decision with the United States. As Gates has said, "Put simply, our enemies and potential adversaries—including nation states—have gone to school on us. They saw what America's technology and firepower did to Saddam's army in 1991 and again in 2003, and they've seen what [improvised explosive devices] are doing to the American military today."[2] When they decide to fight against us, they are much more likely to choose insurgency than to merely provide targets for our superior firepower by fighting conventionally.

The developing strategic environment will find state and nonstate adversaries devising innovative strategies to counter American military power by exploiting widely available technology and weapons and integrating tactics from across the spectrum of conflict.

The resulting conflicts will be protracted and will hinge on the affected populations' perceptions of truth and legitimacy rather than on the outcome of tactical engagements on the battlefield. This is the kind of war we have struggled to understand in Afghanistan, Yemen, Pakistan, Syria, and Egypt; it is the kind of war we are most likely to face in the future. The learning curve is not going to get any easier.

Counterinsurgency campaigns are messy and slow. I thought I understood that idea when I first read it in T. E. Lawrence's book in Oxford in 1996, but having the personal experience of fighting in a bitter counterinsurgency campaign in Iraq myself underlined just how grinding and exhausting they can be. The classic principles of counterinsurgency do work, but success in these wars is unsatisfying at best, and even then comes at a price higher than many would consider acceptable. The final calculation depends on how important are the national security objectives at stake. If they are vital, essential to the protection of the homeland or our national survival, then counterinsurgency may continue to be the least bad option available, and remembering the hard-earned lessons of counterinsurgency is a worthwhile insurance policy—like all insurance policies, one that we hope we will not have to call upon.

Long, hard, and slow as the wars in Iraq and Afghanistan have been, there is at least one silver lining among the clouds for the American people at large. In the wake of Vietnam, the United States began its grand experiment of an all-volunteer military. And it was most certainly an experiment: no one could have expected that the system would hold together in a major war, and for two generations young men have been required to register with the Selective Service in case general conflict erupted. But after two such grinding, protracted wars over the past decade, the all-volunteer force has come through these crucibles of blood and fire with enormous distinction.

Tempered by the Great Depression, the Greatest Generation of World War II fame helped defeat fascism on two continents and save civilization. As loudly as their contributions resound in history, two-thirds of them were drafted. This new greatest generation has fought longer if not harder than its grandparents did, and all have been volunteers.

My own tank task force lost twenty-two fine young men during the Second Iraq War and earned well over one hundred Purple Hearts. The nation owes its volunteer service members a debt of gratitude it can never fully repay. But it can begin by ensuring that we care for

Visiting Todd Bryant's grave at Arlington National Cemetery
with artist Jesse Small, April 25, 2009.

those who have borne the battle, and for their spouses and their orphans, to paraphrase America's greatest wartime president. The traumatic brain injury and post-traumatic stress disorder that are the signature wounds of these wars are invisible and hard to heal; as many as a fourth of those who fought in Iraq will suffer the ravages of these injuries for decades to come.

It would devalue the sacrifices of the many who have suffered if we were not to read these lessons written in blood, if our politicians did not approach future interventions with greater humility, if our military did not prepare for all possible wars rather than only for the ones that it wants to fight. We must hope that from such peril and toil, this great young generation, tempered by war and hardened by what its members have seen and done, will build a better future for a wiser and chastened America that may yet learn from her mistakes.

Epilogue
Good-bye to All That

I was happily working away in my office at the Center for a New American Security one day in the summer of 2011 when I received a call from a friend at the U.S. Naval Academy in Annapolis, Maryland. He told me that the Naval Academy's department of history was looking for its first Minerva professor and invited me to apply.

The Minerva program was begun by Secretary of Defense Gates to help the Department of Defense understand the importance of different cultures to U.S. national security policy. I was a big fan of the initiative, which had placed professors in a number of military establishments. It was now the Navy's turn, and I was intrigued by the offer to become a part of the Minerva program and the Naval Academy.

The Naval Academy had been my initial point of attraction into military service. My father, a product of the Naval Reserve Officer Training Corps at Marquette, in Milwaukee, Wisconsin, had been impressed by the Annapolis graduates he met in the Navy and recommended the Naval Academy to me when I began considering college options. I ended up turning down my appointment to Annapolis in favor of West Point, which sang to me in a deeply resonant way, but I had always wondered how my life would have turned out if I had attended the Navy's rather than the Army's service academy.

I knew Annapolis the least well of the three academies, having spent a semester at the Air Force Academy as a West Point junior. That had been a wonderful experience, as I had always wanted to attend a civilian college, and the notoriously unmilitary Air Force Academy (in the eyes of West Point and Annapolis students if not the nation at large) was the closest I'd gotten to a civilian college at that point. Still, even with the connection to my now-gone-a-decade father and my curiosity about a school I admired greatly but didn't know well, I told my friend at Navy that I was enjoying Washington and my leadership role at CNAS and wasn't going to apply for the Minerva chair.

When I went home late that night after yet another Washington dinner, not having seen Jack awake for yet another day, I told Susi about the call. She went straight to the point: "John, your son is growing up. He doesn't know you, and you don't know him. Why don't you call them back?"

Another fairly dramatic life intervention in a very few words. Susi is nothing if not consistent; she wanted me to make choices that had me spending more time with our little family. After some hard soul-searching about what really matters in life, I decided to apply for the Minerva professorship at Annapolis. Receiving the appointment meant that I would have to step down from the presidency at CNAS.

I began teaching in Navy's history department in January 2012, exactly three years after being asked to replace Michèle as president and five years after the founding of CNAS. I taught a course to juniors and seniors on the history of modern counterinsurgency, not dissimilar to the one I'd taught one semester at Georgetown to students earning a master's degree in strategic studies. (That was the same semester I was unexpectedly selected to become the president of CNAS; teaching a new course while learning how to run a think tank almost broke me.)

The course used as texts Mao's *On Guerrilla Warfare* (the best book on insurgency), David Galula's *Counterinsurgency Warfare* (the best book on counterinsurgency), and Daniel Marston and Carter Malkasian's wonderful *Counterinsurgency in Modern Warfare*, along with the *Army/Marine Corps Counterinsurgency Field Manual* and *Learning to Eat Soup with a Knife*.

I had expected teaching at Annapolis to be very similar to teaching at West Point and was surprised by how different the two institutions are. As I was pondering the comparison, a colleague pointed out the essential contrast. The Navy, he said, is a fundamentally conservative organization; its primary focus is keeping the water out of the ship. The Army is by comparison a bunch of liberals dedicated to social change; its purpose is to take land away from someone less deserving to give it to someone more deserving.

There was another difference, one I fully understood only after getting under way aboard a Virginia-class attack submarine a few months into my tenure at Navy. The Virginia-class boats are small, fast, quiet, and incredibly cramped; every cubic foot costs millions of dollars. This means not just that the crew sleeps among the torpedo racks, often hot bunking (sleeping in a rack that has recently held someone else who is now on shift), but that the crew is a little bit smaller than what is actually required to do all the work aboard ship. There is a lot of work to be done—monitoring the nuclear reactor, feeding the crew, piloting the boat, and fixing all the systems that make air and fresh water and that locate and target possible enemy ships. As a result, the small crew works *hard*, harder even on a peacetime training deployment than I have worked in the Army during all but the most intense periods of combat.

I was sleeping in a small officers' cabin with three bunk beds; the senior officer and guy with the best rack was the ship's engineer. When I fell asleep at one in the morning, he was awake, worrying about a trace element that was present in the boat's manufactured atmosphere; when I awoke four hours later, he was still working that problem. His diligence was appreciated, as he told me that a Chinese submarine had recently been lost because of a carbon monoxide leak, but he could have really used a backup so that he could sleep every once in a while.

The pressing demands of sea duty became clear to me during those forty-eight hours under way; in fact, they were part of the reason my father had encouraged me to go to West Point rather than Navy. "The Navy," he told me, "is on duty every day, around the world, whether we are at war or peace. The Army only works that hard when the country is at war. How often does that happen?" Only once in my first decade of Army service, as it turned out, but continuously in the decade that followed.

The difference in Army and Navy service responsibilities inevitably affect their service academies. Even when the nation was at war, the Army sent young officers like Dan Kaufman and David Petraeus to graduate school and then to teach at West Point. Young soldier-scholars like them, recently returned from active Army service, comprised the majority of the faculty. The Navy, which is always short of officers to man its ships at sea, relies instead primarily on a cadre of tenured civilian faculty members to teach its officer candidates.

There are advantages and disadvantages to both systems. There is no doubt that the tenured civilians at Navy, all with Ph.D.s, had more knowledge of their subject matter to share with their students than did the young officers with master's degrees doing most of the teaching at West Point. But the Army officers had an advantage as well; they were younger and better able to connect with their students. More important, they were full members of the military profession that their students aspired to join. In the classroom, West Point cadets may learn less history or math, but they learn more about being a serving military officer, and in many cases they are inspired by their officer teachers to follow similar career paths. I knew that I wanted to be an armored cavalryman because I so admired Dan Kaufman and Steve Daffron and Dave Clark; in them, I saw what I wanted to become. Few Naval Academy midshipmen want to grow up to be civilian professors, and in my eyes the mids lose something from the lack of young military role models in the classroom. The Navy also suffers because its most talented officers are too busy driving ships to spend time in graduate school and then teaching in the classroom themselves. Preparation for and then teaching Sosh was a formative influence in the careers of officers like Generals Petraeus and Peter Chiarelli, but too few Navy and Marine officers get the same opportunity to stretch themselves intellectually early in their careers, before their brains become less pliable in their forties.

Teaching again after being out of the classroom for a few years was a joy. The midshipmen were wonderful students and inspirational in their dedication to national service, my colleagues interesting intellectual companions, and my family quite unused to seeing me at breakfast and dinner. Although the long commute to Annapolis from Alexandria kept me from engaging as fully in the life of the Naval Academy as I would have liked to have done, I did work with the program to mentor Rhodes, Marshall, and Truman scholarship candidates at Annapolis, as I had at West Point, and became close to several of these immensely talented and driven young people. The Rhodes scholarship had enriched my life to an extraordinary degree and continued to serve as a bridge to fully engaged young people, several of whom sat in on my classes and elevated the level of discussion there.

I spent a lot of time talking with Navy scholarship candidates about their future plans and contemplated my own as well. I had always hoped to have three careers: one in the Army, one in Washington, and my last in academia, serving as a professor or perhaps as a college president. While at CNAS, someone had recommended me to an executive search firm as a candidate for an academic leadership job in Washington. I met with the recruiter, who told me that I wasn't the right person for that particular job but was an interesting candidate for some college leadership positions; she told me that she'd be in touch.

That call came just after my first semester at Navy, when she asked whether I was interested in applying for a college presidency. I agreed to apply, not expecting to do well in my first attempt, but got far enough in the process that I took Susi and Jack to the campus and community to take a look. As we were driving away, Susi made another fateful utterance: "Honey, I could do this for three years, but not for a decade." Since the college was seeking a long-term president, I called the recruiter to withdraw my name from consideration.

The recruiter was surprised. "John, tell me why."

"Not enough culture for my wife, not great schools for my son. This is a family move. Although I'd enjoy it, this move has to be one that is better for each of us, not just for me."

"Wow." There was a long pause. "I wouldn't have thought of you for this, but I have a highly ranked boys' school on Philadelphia's Main Line looking for a headmaster. That would be plenty of culture for your wife and a great school for your son. How would you feel about being a headmaster?"

I hadn't thought seriously about a boys' school since I had graduated from one twenty-eight years earlier, but I clicked on the Web site of this one and liked what I saw. We took another family trip. Wandering around unannounced on a weekend when the campus was empty, I tried to imagine myself at the Haverford School.

The first thing I saw was the main building—Wilson Hall, a freshly restored old stone structure, linked to a very modern glass and steel building. Peeking through the front doors, I saw Teddy Roosevelt's "Man in the Arena" quotation hanging in the front foyer, etched in glass:

It is not the critic who counts; not the man who points out how the strong man stumbles, or where the doer of deeds could have done them better. The credit belongs to the man who is actually in the arena, whose face is marred by dust and sweat and blood; who strives valiantly; who errs, who comes short again and again, because there is no effort without error and shortcoming; but who does actually strive to do the deeds; who knows great enthusiasms, the great devotions; who spends himself in a worthy cause; who at the best knows in the end the triumph of high achievement, and who at the worst, if he fails, at least fails while daring greatly, so that his place shall never be with those cold and timid souls who neither know victory nor defeat.

Pretty cool stuff. I walked farther around the thirty-acre campus, admiring the central quadrangle shaded by old oak trees. Over the gym was inscribed the words "A Sound Mind in a Sound Body"—in Latin. Respect for the past and a mission of inspiring muscular responsibility for oneself and for the world were values to which I could subscribe.

The last thing I found was a covered brick walkway inscribed with virtues—"Respect," "Courage," "Honesty,"—twenty-four in all. I later learned that on the first day of school every year, seniors walk hand in hand with kindergarten boys down the Walk of Virtues to opening-day ceremonies. Many parents have a fading photo of their son as a small boy, holding hands with a young man twelve years his senior, framed alongside a photo of their now-grown son holding the hand of another boy. That boy will in his turn grow to young manhood and lead a young boy along a path inscribed with manly virtues. This was a place I could see myself, helping boys grow into men. And I wanted Jack to be one of those boys, and to have a larger role myself in helping him grow than I had been able to have until that point in his life.

After returning to Washington with Jack and Susi, I soon took the train back to Philadelphia to meet with the selection committee—an impressive group of men and women who were spending a beautiful summer weekday cooped up in a conference room looking for the ninth headmaster of a school they loved. I first met with a panel of faculty that included a curmudgeonly art department chair and an intense football coach, then with the committee itself. Asked the best interview question there is—"Tell us why you're here"—I responded with a long answer. The interviewer summarized my response: "John, what I just heard you say is that you want your son to attend the Haverford School, and to make that happen, you're willing to become the headmaster. Is that correct?"

Assured that it was, he nodded sagely. I later learned that faculty children at the school are called "hostages"; the panel knew that if I took the job, they had me until Jack graduated, seven years thence. There were more questions, and a rollicking discussion about the characteristics of a solid liberal education and the values America needs in her young men, and then sooner than I wanted it to end, the interview was over.

I had been given the slot just before noon—a good sign, Susi had pointed out, because if they liked me, they could invite me to lunch. I thought that the interview had gone well, but there were no indications that a lunch invitation was forthcoming, so I packed up and departed. I was trying to figure out what I had done wrong and had already pushed the down button on the elevator when the board chair stuck his head into the hall and asked if I was free for lunch.

I was. After a delightful session with two of the selection committee members over a Philly cheesesteak, I headed back to D.C. The board sent Susi a dozen roses that night. After several more sessions in Philadelphia and Washington that included both Washington Nationals and Phillies games, foreshadowing some problems with competing loyalties I would soon face in the National League's East Division, I was appointed the ninth headmaster of the Haverford School on August 28, 2012, with the appointment effective July 1 of the following year.

Incoming headmasters usually make themselves scarce on campus between the date of their appointment and the day they begin work, but I was friendly with my predecessor, retired Army Colonel Joe Cox, who had been teaching in the English department at West Point when I was teaching Sosh. Because of Joe's hospitality, I was able to visit the campus several times over the course of the year that followed, often staying with him and his wife Kathy in the lovely old house adjoining the campus that came with the job. Joe pointed out that the good news was that I had a two-minute commute to work, and that the

Mark Nagl, Susi, Jack, and my mom, Judy, after the ceremony installing me as the ninth headmaster of The Haverford School, September 24, 2013.

bad news was that I had a two-minute commute to work.

After completing my too-short tenure at Annapolis, which was marked by Navy's best year in scholarship competition in recent memory—the school had two of its students selected as Marshall scholars and two as Rhodes, and I knew three of the winners well—Jack, Susi, and I packed up our house in Washington and headed to Philadelphia. We had been in our house on George Washington's River Farm for exactly five years, the longest residence in one place during our twenty years of marriage. Susi had in her car Jack, Maggie the black lab, and Sparky the Jack Russell terrier; I got stuck with Bunbun the rabbit, who did not mix well with Sparky.

Susi decorated the house and moved us in, Jack settled in to sixth grade at the Haverford School with the degree of discomfort I should

have expected from an adolescent who was now responding to "I love you, Jack," with a monosyllabic grunt, and I threw myself into the role of headmaster. I spent my time talking with students, planning a course on American foreign policy in the Middle East that I would team-teach in the second semester of the year with a Naval Academy graduate and Marine veteran of Al Anbar, and managing an enterprise with some two hundred faculty and staff, one thousand students, and thousands more parents and alums. It was challenging, rewarding, and exhausting—so full that I barely remembered an important anniversary during my first month of school.

It had been ten years before that Task Force 1-34 Armor arrived in Khalidiyah, Iraq. The date was marked for me by the arrival of a small package in my headmaster's office. Inside was an aluminum bracelet, inscribed with the names of soldiers from the task force who had died in that fight. I wear it now, in remembrance of their valor and sacrifice in a war that did not need to be fought, but that they fought well, good soldiers that they were.

Now, as I walk the halls of my school, I see their faces among the older boys laughing and jostling each other while complaining about chemistry exams. In the faces of the young boys playing tag or catch in the quad, I see the children they never had or left behind to face life without a father. And I hope to teach these boys that war is messy and slow and uncertain and horrible, unbelievably horrible, and I pray that they will learn of it only in books.

Acknowledgments

It's been almost twenty years since I started writing my first book, and there's a reason I waited so long to do it again. The process is painful but deeply worthwhile; I often think that you don't actually know how you feel about something until you've written it down. Writing this book both exorcised some demons and forced me to confront my few successes and many failings of the past two decades.

Scott Moyers was after me to write this book for years when he was an agent; I was fortunate that he had become an editor at Penguin when I finally took him up on the offer. Scott understood the book better than I did and earlier than I did. The title is his work, and the whole book is far better for all his efforts. Ann Godoff, the president of Penguin Press, has assembled a world-class team. Thanks to everyone at Penguin, including Akif Saifi and Janet Biehl, the copy editor, for cleaning up my messes.

Scott's previous employer was superagent Andrew Wylie. It was Mark Mazzetti, author of the excellent (and similarly titled) *Way of the Knife* who introduced me to Andrew, a relationship that I hope bears fruit again when I write my next book in another twenty years.

I have been fortunate to have been mentored by four men with doctorates in international relations and combat experience of one sort or another: Dan Kaufman, Bob O'Neill, Dave Petraeus, and Jim Miller. Thanks to each for their contributions to world security and for their patience with a slow but committed student.

I have also been privileged to teach at three universities and a prep school: West Point, Georgetown, Annapolis, and The Haverford School. Thanks to the faculty and especially the students at each institution of learning. Your questions made me think, and your dedication will keep America strong and safe.

The security studies community of which I have been a part for the past twenty-five or so years is full of people fascinated by the question of how force is employed to accomplish national interests. Many of its members are also practitioners, dedicated to learning from the past and making fewer and more original mistakes in the future. Although too many have helped me along the way to list all of them here, I would be remiss in not mentioning retired Army Colonel John Collins, Alexandria neighbor and mentor, who started his service in World War II and continues today to contribute to world security through his guidance of the WARLORD Loop that he created.

The two most important women in my life are my mother and my wife. Both are long suffering and have an obvious sense of humor. Mom never made it through my first book; I'm hopeful that she'll read this one. (It has fewer footnotes.) Susi has given me many gifts, the most important and best being the chance to be a father to Jack.

As a result of the mistakes described in this book, many men will never get the chance to be fathers themselves, and many children will grow up without knowing their parents. This book is dedicated to those who volunteer to go in harm's way, trusting in the wisdom of their elected and appointed leaders to make good decisions about the use of force in protecting the interests of America and her friends. My most sincere hope is that it leads to hard thinking before the next time the United States goes to war, helping ensure that American armed forces are ready to fight any kind of enemy, using any strategy. Being prepared for war while remaining conscious of its unbearable costs is the best way to increase the chances for peace.

Notes

Chapter 2: Learning to Eat Soup with a Knife

1. J. F. C. Fuller, *The Generalship of Alexander the Great*, p. 117, quoted in Robert Asprey, *War in the Shadows: The Guerrilla in History* (New York: William Morrow, 1994), p. 4.

2. Richard Clutterbuck, *The Long, Long War* (London: Cassell, 1966), pp. 51–52.

3. William Westmoreland, *A Soldier Reports* (New York: DaCapo, 1989), p. 164.

4. *The Pentagon Papers*, Senator Gravel Edition. (Boston: Beacon Press, 1971), p. 2:501.

5. *The Pentagon Papers*, p. 2:576.

6. Jack Keane, "Rumsfeld Defends Himself as Criticism from Retired Generals Mounts," *Jim Lehrer NewsHour*, April 18, 2006.

Chapter 3: Back to Iraq

1. Conrad Crane and W. Andrew Terrill, *Reconstructing Iraq: Insights, Challenges, and Missions for Military Forces in a Post-Conflict Scenario* (Carlisle, Pa.: U.S. Army War College Strategic Studies Institute, February 1, 2003).

2. Peter Maass, "Professor Nagl's War," *New York Times Magazine*, January 11, 2004.

Chapter 5: Clear, Hold, and Build

1. David Cloud and Greg Jaffe, *The Fourth Star: Four Generals and the Epic Struggle for the Future of the United States Army* (New York: Crown, 2009), p. 192. See also Bob Woodward, *The War Within: A Secret White House History, 2006–2008* (New York: Simon and Schuster, 2008).

2. John Nagl and Paul Yingling, "New Rules for New Enemies," *Armed Forces Journal* (October 2006).

Chapter 6: Proof of Concept

1. Stephen Biddle, Jeffrey A. Friedman, and Jacob N. Shapiro, "Testing the Surge: Why Did Violence Decline in Iraq in 2007?" *International Security* 37, no. 1 (Summer 2012), p. 39.

2. John A. Nagl, "Back in Baghdad: This Time, Things Are Looking Up," *Washington Post*, September 14, 2008.

Chapter 8: Counterinsurgency Revisited

1. Robert Gates, speech at National Defense University, Washington, D.C., September 29, 2008.

2. Robert Gates, remarks to the Association of the U.S. Army, Washington, D.C., October 10, 2007.

Further Reading

There are many great books on each of the subjects listed below. These are a few that have had the biggest impact on my thinking.

Strategy

    Carl von Clausewitz, *On War*

    Edward Luttwak, *The Grand Strategy of the Roman Empire*

    Peter Paret, *Makers of Modern Strategy*

U.S. Civil War

    Drew Gilpin Faust, *This Republic of Suffering*

    Ulysses S. Grant, *Personal Memoirs of U.S. Grant*

    James McPherson, *Tried by War*

First World War

    Paul Fussell, *The Great War and Modern Memory*

    Robert Graves, *Goodbye to All That*

    T. E. Lawrence, *Seven Pillars of Wisdom*

    Hew Strachan, *The Oxford Illustrated History of the First World War*

Second World War

    Rick Atkinson, *An Army at Dawn*

    Charles Macdonald, *Company Commander*

Williamson Murray and Allan R. Millett, *Military Innovation in the Interwar Period*

Anton Myrer, *The Last Convertible*

Evelyn Waugh, *Brideshead Revisited*

Korean War

T. R. Fehrenbach, *This Kind of War*

David Halberstam, *The Coldest Winter*

Vietnam

David Halberstam, *The Best and the Brightest*

Andrew Krepinevich, *The Army and Vietnam*

Karl Marlantes, *Matterhorn*

H. R. McMaster, *Dereliction of Duty*

Neil Sheehan, *A Bright Shining Lie*

Lewis Sorley, *A Better War*

Harry Summers, *On Strategy*

Afghanistan

Sarah Chayes, *The Punishment of Virtue*

George Crile, *Charlie Wilson's War*

Seth Jones, *In the Graveyard of Empires*

Carter Malkasian, *War Comes to Garmser*

Al Qaeda / The Long War

Peter Baker, *Days of Fire*

Peter Bergen, *The Longest War*

Steve Coll, *Ghost Wars*

Mark Mazzetti, *The Way of the Knife*

Stanley McChrystal, *My Share of the Task*

Eric Schmitt and Thom Shanker, *Counterstrike*

Lawrence Wright, *The Looming Tower*

Iraq

James Fallows, *Blind into Baghdad*

Nathaniel Fick, *One Bullet Away*

David Finkel, *The Good Soldiers*

Greg Jaffe and David Cloud, *The Fourth Star*

Peter Mansoor, *Surge*

George Packer, *The Assassins' Gate*

Tom Ricks, *Fiasco*

Insurgency and Counterinsurgency

Douglas Blaufarb, *The Counterinsurgency Era*

Alain Cohen, *Galula*

David Galula, *Counterinsurgency Warfare*

Fred Kaplan, *The Insurgents*

David Kilcullen, *The Accidental Guerrilla*

G. L. Lamborn, *Arms of Little Value*

Mao, *On Guerrilla Warfare*

Daniel Marston and Carter Malkasian, *Counterinsurgency in Modern Warfare*

David Ucko, *The New Counterinsurgency Era*

Future of War

John M. Collins, *Military Strategy*

Audrey Cronin, *How Terrorism Ends*

Robert Kaplan, *The Coming Anarchy*

David Kilcullen, *Out of the Mountains*

Steven Pinker, *The Better Angels of Our Nature*

Thomas Rid, *War 2.0*

Emile Simpson, *War from the Ground Up*

Peter Singer, *Wired for War*

Alvin Toffler, *Future Shock*

Service Academies: West Point and Annapolis

Rick Atkinson, *The Long Gray Line*

Craig Mullaney, *The Unforgiving Minute*

Robert Timberg, *The Nightingale's Song*

James Webb, *A Sense of Honor*

Veterans

David Finkel, *Thank You for Your Service*

Phil Klay, *Redeployment*

Karl Marlantes, *What It Is Like to Go to War*

James Wright, *Those Who Have Borne the Battle*

Prep Schools

Richard A. Hawley, *The Headmaster's Papers*

James Hilton, *Goodbye, Mr. Chips*

John McPhee, *The Headmaster*

Index

Page numbers in *italics* refer to illustrations.

Abizaid, John, 140, 157, 161
Abrams, Creighton, 36, 145, 213
Abu Abid, 168
Abu Ghraib, 76
Afghanistan, 2–3, 56, 58, 117, 122, 138, 152,
    158–60, 163, 171–73, 175, 177, 183, 185–210,
    213, 215–21, 226–29, 232, 234, 236, 238–40
    COIN Academy in, 188, 189, *189*, 192
    Counterinsurgency Field Manual and, 201,
        203, 205
    government in, 206–8, 218–19, 229–30
    increased troop strength in, 197–200, 204–5,
        217, 232
    map of, xii–xiii
    Pakistan and, 185–87, 193, 197, 199, 201, 206–7,
        210, 217, 219, 227–28
    rural nature of insurgency in, 186
    Soviet Union and, 185, 200, 208, 216, 225, 228
    withdrawal of troops from, 199–200, 204,
        217, 232
Afghan National Army, 198–99, 205
Afghan Police and Local Police, 198–99, 203, 205
AfPak hands, 191–92, 205
Africa, 221
agricultural-age warfare, 136
Air Force Academy, 244
AirSea Battle, 225
Al Anbar Awakening, 172, 176
Al Anbar Province, 66–106, 108, 113, 131, 143, 161,
    166, 168, 172–73, 177, 200, 203, 209, 230, 252
Alaska National Guard (Nanooks), 22–25, 28,
    46, 66
Al Askari Mosque, 138–39
Al Batin, 11, 12
Alexander the Great, 30
Algeria, 120, 132
All In: The Education of General David Petraeus
    (Broadwell), 161, 209

al-Maliki, Nouri, 169
Alpha Company (Ghostriders), 7, 15–16,
    21–22
Al Qaeda, 3, 52, 185, 186, 200, 207, 208, 210, 212,
    217–18, 227–28, 233, 235
Al Qaeda in Iraq (AQI), 89–91, 93–94, 104, 113,
    138–39, 167, 168, 173
Annapolis, 243–45, 247, 251
Apache Troop, 27–28
Arab Spring, 223–26, 231
Armed Forces Journal, 142, 146
Armitage, Rich, 110
Armor, 24, 27
Armor Officer Advanced Course, 24
Army, 245, 246
    increase in size of, 171
*Army/Marine Corps Counterinsurgency Field Manual,
    The, see U.S. Army/Marine Corps
    Counterinsurgency Field Manual, The*
Army War College, 143
Arnold, Benedict, 43
Assad, Bashar All, 223, 234–35
Assassin's Gate, The (Packer), 129
Assembly, 103
Atkinson, Rick, 60–61
Atlantic Monthly, 129, 137
August, Matt, 94–95
Augustine, Saint, 237
Ayers, Nick, 69

Ba'ath Party, 63, 112, 146
"Back in Baghdad: This Time, Things Are
    Looking Up" (Nagl), 177
Baghdad, 62, 64, 67, 77, 112, 113, 117, 121,
    134, 139, 144, 161, 166–69, 175, 176–77,
    198, 220
    T-walls in, 176, 186
Banana Wars, 213
Bangladesh, 226
Barno, Dave, 190–91

Basin Harbor conference, 116–18, 124, 129, 131, 140
Basra, 169
Belcher, Gary, 177
Ben Ali, Zine El Abidine, 232
Better Angels of Our Nature, The (Pinker), 224
Biddle, Steve, 170, 192, 194, 216–17
Biden, Joe, 194–95, 202
bin Laden, Osama, 185, 186, 206–7, 228
   killing of, 207, 217, 222–23, 235
Bismarck, Otto von, 212
Black Hawk Down, 91
Black Knights, 15, 16
Blackwater contractors, 95–96, 99, 100
Bohannan, Charles, 120
Booker, Cedric, 26
Bosnia, 27–28, 29–30, 44, 52, 61, 62, 224
Bouazizi, Mohamed, 232
Bremer, Paul, 63, 64, 77–78, 97, 112, 146
Brimley, Shawn, 175
British Malaya, 31–34, 37, 85, 176–77, 196
Broadwell, Paula, 161, 208–9
Bryant, Todd, 86–88, 90, 93, 105, *240*
Büdingen, 26–27
Buffy, 10
Burton, Brian, 182–83
Bush, George H. W., 11–13, 19
Bush, George W., 62, 86, 88, 109–11, 113, 118, 140–41, 148–49, 160–61, 172, 177, 190, 195–96, 214, 217, 231
   Iraq troop surge and, 161–63
   Rumsfeld fired by, 148–49, 214

Caldera, Louis, 108
Campbell, Kurt, 159–60, 180, 181
Camp Buckner, 48–49
Camp Funston, 154, *174*
Camp Habbaniyah, 72–74, 76, 83, 90, 91, 100, 101
Casey, George, 112–13, 117, 139–41, 156, 161, 162, 166, 187–88, 190
Center for a New American Security (CNAS), 159–60, 174–75, 177–83, *182*, 189, 191, 243, 244, 247
   Nagl selected as president of, 180, 192
Center for Naval Analysis, 158
Center for Strategic and International Studies, 159
Charlie Wilson's War (Criles), 185
Charlie Wilson's War (film), 208
Cheney, Dick, 118, 148–49
Chesterfield, Lord, 214–15
Chiarelli, Peter, 133–35, 148, 155, 158, 172, 247
China, 215, 224, 225, 235–36
Churchill, Winston, 214
CIA, 185
Civil War, 16, 136
Clark, Dave, 247
Claudio, Pablo, 5–8

climate change, 223, 226, 231
Clinton, Bill, 45, 144, 160, 209
Clinton, Hillary, 177, 231, 234
Clutterbuck, Richard, 32–33
Coalition Provisional Authority (CPA), 63, 64, 112
Cockerham, Gray, 12
Cody, Richard, 108, 112–13, 126, 151
Cohen, Eliot, 116, 120, 124, 126, 137
COIN Academy–Afghanistan, 188, 189, *189*, 192
Cold War, 19, 24, 46, 59, 110, 135–36, 213, 219, 225, 237–38
Cole, USS, 52
Coll, Steve, 175–76
Collins, John, *111*
Combined Action Platoon, 35
Command and General Staff College (CGSC), 51–52
Commander's Emergency Response Program (CERP), 82, 85
Communism, 215–16, 223
Communist Revolutionary Warfare: From the Vietminh to the Viet Cong (Tanham), 120
computing power, 222
Cooper, Walt, 45
Counter-Guerilla Operations: The Philippine Experience (Valeriano and Bohannan), 120
counterinsurgency, 2, 29–34, 45, 47, 50, 65, 69, 77–78, 81–82, 85, 88, 89, 92, 116–17, 123–28, 142–44, 153, 161
   barrier creation and, 176
   Basin Harbor conference on, 116–18, 124, 129, 131, 140
   books on, 120
   counterintuitive nature of, 127
   field manual on, *see U.S. Army/Marine Corps Counterinsurgency Field Manual, The*
   and learning from past mistakes, 211–41
Counterinsurgency Lessons from Malaya and Vietnam, see Learning to Eat Soup with a Knife
Counterinsurgency Warfare: Theory and Practice (Galula), 120, 132–33, 164–65, 245
Cox, Joe, 251
Cox, Kathy, 251
Crane, Conrad, 59–61, 126–27, 130, 137, 164, 230
Criles, George, 185
Cuban Missile Crisis, 224
Cucolo, Tony, 165–66
Cunningham, Sergeant First Class, 15–16
Custer Hill, 154
Cutchall, Christopher, 75, 88

Daffron, Steve, 41, 43, 247
Daily Show with Jon Stewart, The, 165–66
Dammam, 6, 12
Davidson, Janine, *115*, 129, 144, 209
Davis, Jud, 8–9, *9*

Defense Department, 110, 145, 153, 213–14
  Directive 30000.05 of, 144–45
  Minerva program of, 243, 244
  Strategic Guidance of, 221
Defense Science Board, 144
DeGroat, Art, 156n
Democratic Peace Theorem, 195
democratization, 195–96, 206
Deputy Assistant Secretary of Defense
  (DASD), 144
*Dereliction of Duty: Lyndon Johnson, Robert
  McNamara, the Joint Chiefs of Staff, and the Lies
  That Led to Vietnam* (McMaster), 92, 141
Dien Bien Phu, 34, 224
Downie, Richard, 37, 131
Dunwoody, Ann, 172

Egypt, 196, 223, 227, 232, 233, 239
Eisenhower, Dwight D., 34, 42, 224
England, Gordon, 144–45
Euphrates River, 72, 74, 76, 80, 93, 94
explosive ordnance detachment (EOD), 75–76
Exum, Andrew, 192

"Failure in Generalship, A" (Yingling and Nagl),
  146–48
Fallon, William "Fox," 157
Fallows, James, 129, 137
Fallujah, 68, 72, 95–96, 98–101, 113–14
Fiasco: The American Military Adventure in Iraq
  (Ricks), 149
Fields, Craig, 144
Feith, Doug, 64
Fick, Nate, 174–75, 180–81, 190, 192
Filkins, Dexter, 201
First Cavalry Division, 6–19, 30, 99–100
First Infantry Division, 17, 28, 55
Flournoy, Michèle, 159–60, 180, 181, 190, 244
Floyd, Price, 182
Fort Hood, 5–6, 19, 24, 71
Fort Irwin, 21–22
Fort Knox, 5, 24
Fort Riley, 53, 55–56, 58–60, 65, 67, 86–87,
  104–5, 107, 108, 119, 151–55, 159, 171, 173,
  186–88, 198
Franks, Tommy, 112
Friedman, Jeffrey, 170
Frist, Bill, 162
Fuller, J. F. C., 30–31
Future Combat System, 30
Future Shock (Toffler), 136

Galula, David, 117, 120–21, 132, 134, 155, 164–65,
  205, 245
Galvin, Jack, 42, 45–46
Garner, Jay, 63, 112
Gates, Robert, 70, 149, 155–56, 156, 158, 160–61,

171, 172, 182, 191, 200, 214, 217, 221, 237,
  238, 243
Gentile, Gian, 220
George C. Marshall Award, 52–53
Geren, Peter, 142–43, 171–72
Germany, 63, 237
Ghostriders (Alpha Company), 7, 15–16, 21–22
Ghostrider Six, 10
Ghost Wars (Coll), 175
Gingrich, Newt, 92–93, 113, 118, 119
globalization, 223, 237
global warming, 223, 226, 231
Golby, Jim, 45
Grafenwöhr, 27
Graham, Jeff, 103, 216
Graham, Kevin, 103
Graham, Mark, 103
Green Revolution, 223
guerrilla warfare, 30–31, 33, 238
Gulag Archipelago, The (Solzenitsyn), 223

Haas, Richard, 227
Habbaniyah, 72–74, 76, 83, 90, 91, 100, 101
Ham, Carter, 166
Hammes, T. X., 116, 124
Harrison, Sergeant, 7–8
Hastings, Michael, 202
Haverford School, 248–53, 251
Helmer, Dan, 188, 189, 189
Helmick, Frank, 58, 108–9, 121–22, 125–26,
  151, 191
"Here Bullet" (Turner), xi
History of Counterinsurgency Warfare (Marston and
  Malkasian), 245
Ho Chi Minh, 215
Hoffman, Frank, 131
Hoffman, James, 94–95
Homa, Matt, 86, 87
Horvath, Jan, 123, 127, 137
Howard, Michael, 37–38, 213
Hufstedler, Doyle, 103–4, 104
Hussein, Major, 98, 101–2

IEDs, 75–76, 82, 86, 88, 95, 100, 102–4, 143
In a Time of War (Murphy), 88
Indermuehle, Dave, 70–72
industrial-age warfare, 136
information revolution, 136–37, 222–24, 226
Ingram, Jeff, 60, 64, 75, 77, 174
"Institutionalizing Adaptation: It's Time for a
  Permanent Army Advisor Corps" (Nagl),
  158–60
International Security, 170
International Security Assistance Force
  (ISAF), 198
Internet, 223, 237
In the Company of Soldiers (Atkinson), 60–61

Iran, 223, 227
Iraq, 2–3, 5–19, 58–106, 139–49, 185–91, 195, 196, 198, 201, 204, 211–21, 226–27, 230–31, 233, 235, 236, 238–41
  Al Anbar Province, 66–106, 108, 113, 131, 143, 161, 166, 168, 172–73, 177, 200, 203, 209, 230, 252
  Al Qaeda in, 89–91, 93–94, 104, 113, 138–39, 167, 168, 173
  costs of second war in, 211–12
  Khalidiyah, 67–68, 72, 73, 78–80, 82, 84, 92, 949, 95, 97, 101–3, 105, 121, 173, 176–77, 203, 252
  Operation Desert Shield, 6, 9, 11, 25
  Operation Desert Storm, 19, 21, 24, 25, 30, 40, 44, 46, 51–52, 55, 57, 63, 65, 68, 71, 72, 75, 85, 92, 99, 177, 211–12, 224, 225, 230
  reduction in violence in, 169–70, 177, 178–79
  surge troops sent to, 161–63, 166–67, 169, 192, 204, 217
  "sweep and clear" strategy in, 143
  in 2007–2008, 151–83
  Washington fight and, 107–28
Iraqi Air Force, 73
Iraqi Army, 63–65, 77, 96–97, 97, 98, 101–2, 112, 121, 139, 146, 169, 176, 198, 214
Iraqi Civil Defense Corps (ICDC), 96–99, 101, 105
Iraqi Police (IP), 78–81, 84, 89–90, 99–100, 103, 139, 176
Ishmael, Brigadier General, 99–101
Islamic extremism, 135, 193
Israel, 231, 233

Jaffe, Greg, 92, 129
Japan, 63
Johnson, Harold K., 35–36
Johnson, Lyndon B., 215, 224
Johnson, Pete "Blue One," 10, 20, 20

Kabul, 198, 207, 210, 218, 219, 228–29
  COIN Academy in, 188, 189, 189, 192
Kagan, Fred, 192
Kahl, Colin, 144, 175
Kandahar, 197
Kaplan, Fred, 142
Karzai, Hamid, 195, 196, 229
Kaufman, Daniel, 39–41, 40, 42–43, 246, 247
Kaufman, Kathryn, 40
Keane, Jack, 46–47, 162, 183, 204
Kebble, Jim, 8, 12
Kennedy, Chris, 74
Kennedy, John F., 34–35, 215, 224
Khalidiyah, 67–68, 72, 73, 78–80, 82, 84, 92, 949, 95, 97, 101–3, 105, 121, 173, 176–77, 203, 252
Kilcullen, David, 114–16, 115, 117, 120, 123, 124, 129, 139, 163, 208–9
Kilcullen, Harry, 115
Korea, 105, 196, 233

Korean War, 224
Kuehl, Dale, 168, 169
Kuwait, 5–6, 13, 16, 71–72, 230

Lacquement, Rich, 124, 127, 144
Lawrence, T. E., 31, 34, 47, 172, 215, 235, 239
Learning from Conflict: The U.S. Military in Vietnam, El Salvador, and the Drug War (Downie), 37
Learning to Eat Soup with a Knife: Counterinsurgency Lessons from Malaya and Vietnam (Nagl), 31, 52, 56, 78, 89, 92–93, 113–15, 118–20, 140, 142, 163, 191, 245
Lebanon, 224
Lehrer, Jim, 46–47
Leners, Marty, 57, 69, 72
Libya, 196, 212, 221, 223, 227, 232–34, 236
Lieberman, Joe, 180
Ling, Roger, 103, 216
Long Gray Line, The (Atkinson), 60
Lord, Kristin, 181–82
Lute, Doug, 159

M1 Abrams tank, 13
M1A1 tank, 13–14, 17, 23, 57–58
Maass, Peter, 88–89, 91–92, 108, 116
MacArthur, Douglas, 42, 224
MacFarland, Sean, 172–73
Maddow, Rachel, 199
Malaya, 31–35, 37, 85, 145, 176–77, 196
Malayan Emergency, 140, 213
Malaysia, 32
Malkasian, Carter, 158, 245
Manning, Bradley, 222
Mao Zedong, 101, 245
Marine Corps Small Wars Manual, 164, 213
Marjah, 200–201
Marlantes, Karl, 16
Marston, Daniel, 245
Martins, Mark, 204
Mattis, Jim, 95–96, 99, 128, 130–31, 166
Mauldin, Bill, 146
McAllister, John "Mac," 9, 9
McCain, John, 160, 177, 180
McCary, John, 83, 84, 92
McChrystal, Stanley, 172, 191–94, 197, 200–202
McKiernan, David, 189–91
McMaster, H. R., 92, 129, 141–43, 163, 170–72, 203, 206
Mearsheimer, John, 230–31
Meese, Mike, 122
Meigs, Montgomery, 28
Metz, Steve, 114–15
Michaelis, Patrick, 133–35, 155
Military Operations Other Than War (MOOTW), 27
Military Review, 117, 123, 127, 133–34, 137, 140, 158–59

Miller, Ben, 67, 75–76, 78–79, 90, 91
Miller, Jim, 49, 59, 159, 160, 174, 180, 181
Minerva program, 243, 244
Modern Warfare: A French View of Counterinsurgency (Trinquier), 120
Moore's Law, 222
Mubarak, Hosni, 223, 233
Mullaney, Craig, 45, 190
Mullen, Michael, 187, 191, 200
Multi-National Security Assistance Command–Iraq (MNSTC-1), 121
multiple-launch rocket system (MLRS), 18, 19
Murphy, Bill, Jr., 88
Muslim Brotherhood, 235

Nadaner, Jeb, 144
Nagl, Emily, 50
Nagl, Jack Frederick, 71, 107, 115, 157, 244, 248–52, 251
  birth of, 56
Nagl, John A.:
  selected as CNAS president, 180, 192
  father of, 50–51, 153, 243, 244, 246
  as Haverford School headmaster, 248–53, 251
  marriage of, 25–26, 26, 71
  mother of, 51, 53, 153, 157, 251
  move to Alexandria, 174
  move to Philadelphia, 251
  retirement from Army, 20, 173–74, 180
  talks given by, 115–16, 124, 126, 143, 157–58, 163
  as teacher at Naval Academy, 244–45, 247, 251
Nagl, Mark, 251
Napoleon I, Emperor, 81, 136, 167
Nasrawi, Frank, 83–84
National Public Radio (NPR), 157, 163
National Training Center (NTC), 21–25, 28, 41, 46, 65–66, 159
NATO, 205, 218, 228
Naval Academy, 243–44, 247, 251
Navy, 245, 246
New American Foundation, 175
Newbold, Greg, 61, 146, 147
"New Rules for New Enemies" (Nagl and Yingling), 142
Newsweek, 122
New Yorker, 129, 175, 176
New York Times, 75, 88–89, 91–92, 108, 116, 142, 165, 201, 202
North Korea, 105, 224, 233
nuclear weapons, 223, 224–25
Nunn, Sam, 177

Obama, Barack, 144, 160, 177–80, 189–90, 195–97, 204, 205, 209–10, 217–18, 221, 231–35
O'Connor, Sean, 109
Odierno, Ray, 103, 117–18, 143, 167

Odierno, Tony, 103
Office for Reconstruction and Humanitarian Assistance (ORHA), 63
O'Hanlon, Mike, 192, 193
oil markets, 216, 217, 218, 230
One Bullet Away: The Making of a Marine Officer (Fick), 181
O'Neill, Robert, 38–39, 39, 158
On Guerrilla Warfare (Mao), 245
On Strategy (Summers), 136, 219
Operation Desert Shield, 6, 9, 11, 25
Operation Desert Storm, 19, 21, 24, 25, 30, 40, 44, 46, 51–52, 55, 57, 63, 65, 68, 71, 72, 75, 85, 92, 99, 177, 211–12, 224, 225, 230
Operation Enduring Freedom, 224
Operation Iraqi Freedom, 224
Operation Knight Strike, 16
Operation Netscape, 75
organizational learning chart, 38
Oxford University, 5, 26, 28, 29, 38, 40, 41, 49, 50, 53, 69, 79, 81, 158
Oxford University Strategic Studies Group (OUSSG), 39

Pace, Peter, 118, 162, 187
Packer, George, 129, 183
Pakistan, 3, 138, 185–87, 193, 197, 199, 201, 206–7, 210, 217, 219, 221, 226–29, 235, 238, 239
Pakistani Army, 206
Pakistani Taliban, 206, 228
Palin, Sarah, 180
Panetta, Leon, 221, 234
Paris Peace Talks, 136
Parker, Jay, 41, 43
Parks, Sheldon, 65, 72
Patriquin, Travis, 172
Patton, George, 42
Petraeus, David, 41–43, 53, 60–61, 64, 118, 121–26, 121, 156, 163, 166–70, 172–73, 176, 177, 182, 183, 198, 200–205, 209–10, 214–15, 217, 220, 246, 247
  Bremer and, 77
  Broadwell and, 161, 208–9
  counterinsurgency manual and, 128, 129–32, 137, 156, 157
  Keane and, 162
  son of, 103
  Syria and, 234
  Yingling and, 148
Petraeus, Holly, 203
Pfaff, Tony, 47
Philippines, 213, 221
Pinker, Stephen, 224
Places in Between, The (Stewart), 194
population growth, 223, 226, 232
Powell, Colin, 45–46, 59, 62, 109–10
Powell-Weinberger Doctrine, 46, 53

Power, Samantha, 165
Praeger Press, 52, 92, 120, 132
Program for the Pacification and Long-Term Development of South Vietnam (PROVN), 36

Qaddafi, Muammar, 223, 233–34

Raddatz, Martha, 175
Ramadi, 67–68, 72, 76, 168
Rayburn, Joel, 176
Red Aces, 6–7
Reidel, Bruce, 190, 192
Republican Guard, 17
Revolutionary War, 42, 43
revolution in military affairs (RMA), 29–30
Rice, Condoleezza, 109, 143–44
Rickover, Hyman, 50
Ricks, Thomas, 149
Riggs, Scott "Turtle," 10, 21
Robinson, Linda, 61
Rolling Stone, 202
Romans, 81–82, 237
Romeo and Juliet (Shakespeare), 88
Roosevelt, Theodore, 248–49
Rumsfeld, Donald, 61–63, 67, 73, 109–13, 118, 122, 130, 142, 144–46, 148–49, 156, 160–62
   firing of, 148–49, 214

Saddam Hussein, 3, 5–6, 11, 13, 14, 16, 19, 59, 61, 62, 64, 111, 122, 139, 145, 211, 212, 214, 216, 230, 231, 238
   capture of, 89, 91
Sadr City, 169
Saigon, 208, 229
Sanchez, Ricardo, 112, 113, 117, 139
Santoriello, Neil, 104–5
Saudi Arabia, 13, 14, 228, 233
Scales, Robert, 147
Schlesinger, Arthur, Jr., 2, 220–21
Schoomaker, Peter, 113, 119, 122
Schwarzkopf, H. Norman, 19
SCUD missiles, 11–12
Security Forces (SECFOR), 152
Senate Foreign Relations Committee, 193–94, 216–17
Sepp, Kalev "Gunnar," 116–17, 120, 124, 127, 140
September 11 attacks, 55–56, 111, 117, 159, 218, 221, 227, 229
Seven Pillars of Wisdom: A Triumph (Lawrence), 31, 239
Sewall, Sarah, 123–24, 126, 129, 144, 164, 165
Shakespeare, William, 88
Shapiro, Jacob, 170
Sheehan, Michael, 120
Shias, 73, 77, 96, 139, 149, 162, 168, 176, 217
Shi'ites, 169

Shinseki, Ric, 61–62, 108
Shoemaker, Ted "Shoe," 8–9, 9, 11, 17–19, 57, 154
Simpson, Erin, 115
Singh, Vikram, 144
Skelton, Ike, 61, 148
Small, Jesse, 240
Small Wars Manual (U.S. Marine Corps), 164, 213
Smith, Brian, 104
Smith, Jim, 49
Snider, Don, 47
Snowden, Edward, 222
social media, 223, 237
Solzenitsyn, Alexander, 223
Somalia, 52, 91, 138, 217, 224
Sons of Iraq, 172, 176
Sorley, Bob, 145
South Korea, 105, 196
Soviet Union, 3, 135, 212, 223–25, 235
   Afghanistan and, 185, 200, 208, 216, 225, 228
   Cold War, 19, 24, 46, 59, 110, 135–36, 213, 219, 225, 237–38
Srebrenica, 27
Stavridis, Jim, 174
Stewart, Jon, 165–66
Stewart, Rory, 193–94
Strongest Tribe, The (West), 175
Suleiman, Lieutenant Colonel, 96, 98–99, 101, 113
Summers, Harry, 136, 219
Sunflower Press, 164
Sunni Awakening, 167, 173, 214
Sunnis, 64, 65, 66, 73, 96, 139, 149, 162, 168–69, 173, 217
Supreme Headquarters of the Allied Powers Europe (SHAPE), 42, 60
Sustaining U.S. Global Leadership: Priorities for 21st Century Defense, 221
Swat Valley, 228
Swisher, Jeff, 66, 67, 69, 71, 72, 84, 88, 91, 104–5
Syria, 196, 212, 221, 223, 227, 231, 234–36, 239

Taiwan, 196, 225
Taji, 140
Tal Afar, 141, 142, 170
"Tale of Two Battles, A" (Nagl), 24
Taliban, 3, 56, 58, 117, 157, 185–87, 194–95, 197–98, 200, 201, 204–8, 210, 216–17, 219, 227–29
   Pakistani, 206, 228
Tanham, George, 120
Taqquadam Airfield (TQ), 73, 105
Teamey, Kyle, 124–25, 127
Tell Me How This Ends: General David Petraeus and the Search for a Way Out of Iraq (Robinson), 61
Templer, Gerald, 34, 117, 145, 196
Terrill, W. Andrew, 59–60
Thomas, Jim, 114
Tiananmen Square, 236
Tibbets, Nate, 180

Time, 61, 146
Toffler, Alvin, 136
Tora Bora Mountains, 186
Traugott, Chris, 107
Treaty of Westphalia, 222
Trinquier, Roger, 120
Truman, Harry, 215, 224
Tryneski, John, 163–64
Tunisia, 232–33
Turner, Brian, xi
Turquoise Mountains, 194
Twain, Mark, 62
Twitter, 223

University of Chicago Press, 163–65
UN Security Council, 233, 236
urbanization, 223, 226, 237
U.S. Army/Marine Corps Counterinsurgency
   Field Manual, The (Sewall, Nagl, Petraeus,
   and Amos), 124–28, 151, 155–57, 161,
   163–67, 245
   Afghanistan and, 201, 203, 205
   campaign design in, 131–32, *131,* 138
   Chiarelli/Michaelis diagram in, 133–35, *133*
   civilian casualties and, 201
   "clear, hold, and build" technique in, 141, 170
   competitions in learning in, 130
   Daily Show and, 165–66
   on executing counterinsurgency operations,
      132–34
   influence of, 138
   information operations not included in, 135
   McChrystal and, 201, 203
   on nonmilitary tasks, 134–35
   review conference on, 128, 129
   on top priority in counterinsurgency, 130
   University of Chicago edition of, 163–65
U.S. Information Agency (USIA), 135–36
U.S. military superiority, 223, 225

Valeriano, Napoleon, 120
Vann, John Paul, 201

Varga, Susanne "Susi," 6, 20–21, 24, 26, 28, 29, 31,
   39, 43, 45, 48, *48,* 55, 71, 107, 157–58, 173,
   244, 248–50, *251*
   Jack's birth and, 56
   marriage of, 25–26, *26,* 71
   move to Alexandria, 174
   move to Philadelphia, 251
Vietnam War, 3, 13, 15, 16, 19–22, 27, 34–40,
   45–47, 52, 55, 61, 69, 85, 86, 92, 101, 103, 113,
   120, 136, 143, 145, 162, 177, 201, 211–19, 224,
   231–32, 239
   British campaign in Malaya compared with, 31,
      32, 34, 37
   Dien Bien Phu, 34, 224
   fall of Saigon, 208, 229
   information technology and, 136–37, 223
   Tet Offensive, 36

Wadi Al Batin, *9,* 11, 14, 16
Waghelstein, John, 116
Wall Street Journal, 92, 129
Walt, Stephen, 230–31
Washington, George, 42, 43, 60
Washington Post, 175, 177
West, Bing, 175, 176
Westmoreland, William, 35, 36, 145, 213
West Point, 29, 39–45, 47–50, 86, 88, 103, 107, 122,
   169, 198, 199, 243–47, 251
What It Is Like to Go to War (Marlantes), 16
Wilson, Doug, 181–82
Wolfowitz, Paul, 61–62, 108–11, *111,* 114, 119,
   121–22, 125–26, 142
"Won't Get Fooled Again" (Newbold), 61, 146
World Affairs, 47
World War I, 31, 55, 136, 154, 224, 237
World War II, 3, 32, 55, 63, 136, 154, 222, 224,
   237, 240

Yemen, 138, 217, 232, 235, 239
Yingling, Paul, 44–45, *44,* 51, 94, 142, 146–48, *148,*
   158, 209
Young, Liz, 45